Contemporary

Russian

Poetry

Contemporary

A Bilingual

Russian

Anthology

Poetry

Selected, with

an Introduction,

Translations, and Notes

*by **Gerald S. Smith***

Indiana University Press | Bloomington & Indianapolis

The paper used in this publication meets the minimum requirements of
American National Standard for Information Sciences—Permanence of
Paper for Printed Library Materials, ANSI Z39.48-1984.

Manufactured in the United States of America

Library of Congress Cataloging-in-Publication Data

Contemporary Russian poetry : a bilingual anthology / selected, with
   an introduction, translations, and notes by Gerald S. Smith.
      p.   cm.
   Includes bibliographical references and index.
      ISBN 0-253-35333-5 (cloth : alk paper). — ISBN 0-253-20769-X
(pbk. : alk. paper)
      1. Russian poetry—20th century—Translations into English.
I. Gerald Stanton Smith.
PG3237.E5C55   1993
891.71'4408—dc20   92-17482

1 2 3 4 5 97 96 95 94 93

For Dimitri Obolensky

CONTENTS

Bulat Okudzhava

Vladimir Kornilov

German Plisetsky

Evgenii Rein

Dmitrii Bobyshev

Natalya Gorbanevskaya

Aleksandr Kushner

Bella Akhmadulina

Yunna Morits

Lev Loseff

Dmitrii Prigov

Yurii Kublanovsky

Aleksei Tsvetkov

Elena Shvarts

Ivan Zhdanov

Olga Sedakova

Bakhyt Kenzheev

Aleksandr Eremenko

Aleksei Parshchikov

ACKNOWLEDGMENTS

I am deeply grateful to the poets represented here for their permission to include their works in this anthology.

I would like also to thank the students who have participated in the lectures and seminars out of which this anthology has taken shape over the years, especially the graduate students at Berkeley, Indiana, and Oxford universities. David Howells and Grigorii Kruzhkov have given me a good deal of assistance with Russian sources. For patient and tactful help with translations and notes I am indebted to Dmitrii Bobyshev, Lev Loseff, Olga Sedakova and Igor Shaitanov, to Vitalii and Tatyana Shentalinsky, and especially to Barbara Heldt, Catriona Kelly, Andrew Reynolds, and N. S. Thompson.

Final responsibility for the selections, translations, and notes and for the opinions in the introductory matter remains my own.

PREFACE

I have compiled this anthology mainly for anglophone students of Russian litera-
ture. It was undertaken because in the course of teaching I came to feel that these
students are relatively uninformed about what has been going on in Russian poetry
during recent years. There are various reasons for this state of affairs. Academic
scholars and teachers share with the general public a preference for prose above
poetry; prose is felt to be more accessible, more teachable, more "relevant." Poetry
is thought to be written by poets for each other or for an initiated and dedicated
minority. And understandably, there is a reluctance among those scholars in the
field who are interested in poetry to allow that the recent period may have produced
work of outstanding value. This is mainly because of the numinous authority pos-
sessed by the modernist period of Russian poetry; after Akhmatova, Mandelstam,
Pasternak, and Tsvetaeva, none of whom has yet been adequately published and
studied, what time and effort can reasonably be spared for the pygmies of our own
time? And almost as forbidding is the deterrent effect of information overload. In
the West, there is simply too much for any single person to keep track of, let alone
digest and assess—a bewildering array of newspapers, journals, and books
(although the full range of these publications is only available to those fortunate
enough to have access to a major Slavic library). And there are many factions and
lobbyists, each urging the claims of their own particular individual or aspect of
recent work.

These are serious factors, but they do not excuse neglect or throwing in the
towel. The most constructive way to improve the situation, it seemed to me, would
be to provide a single source in which a good proportion of the most important
Russian poets of about the last twenty years could be sampled. This anthology does
not aim to be comprehensive, nor could it hope to be. The selection of poets and
poems will seem arbitrary and capricious to many informed observers. The contents
inevitably reflect the "old thinking" of a foreigner whose taste in Russian poetry
was formed in the 1960s. Not surprisingly, there is very little in common between
the list of poets here and the established roster of Soviet poets as reflected in pre-
glasnost metropolitan histories of literature. At the time this anthology was being
prepared (it was put into final shape late in 1990), that roster was starting to under-
go radical revision as Soviet intellectual life passed through the first stages of score-
settling polemic that may eventually calm down and make way for reasonably

objective literary criticism and history—insofar as such a thing is possible and even desirable. But it will be a long time before the dissident and émigré streams of Russian poetry are thoroughly assimilated by readers and critics in Russia. At the present stage of the history of Russian poetry, and of Russian literature as a whole, the canon of texts (and the very idea of a canon) has become unusually problematical. At the outset of the 1990s it is even more difficult than at most times to choose texts with confidence in their durability and value as a representative selection. And so the primary aim here has been to select work that stands up as strong and interesting poetry, wherever it was originally written or published.

In general, the poems included in this anthology were written during the late 1970s and the 1980s. But there are some exceptions: I have included some older work only recently published or collected for the first time in Russia, in the majority of cases after previously being published obscurely at home, or published abroad. The selections from Okudzhava, Akhmadulina, and Morits provide several examples; it would have been possible to add many more from Chichibabin, Rein, Chukhontsev, and Prigov. The hardest poet to anthologize in this respect is Slutsky, who stopped writing in 1977, but whose work is anyway notoriously difficult to date. But some other kinds of "new old" poetry have been excluded. There are several eminent Russian poets, above all Aleksandr Galich (1919–1977) and Vladimir Vysotsky (1938–1980), whose work, while being widely available through clandestine recordings, only became legitimately available in the USSR in recent years and could reasonably have been included in this anthology. The work of several other important older poets has been held back; they include, for example, Daniil Andreev (1906–1959), whose oeuvre has only become generally accessible a quarter-century after his death. From the point of view of the average Soviet reader, the most important "recent" work in the sense of publication may well be poetry written seventy to eighty years ago by poets long dead who were substantially published for the first time in the USSR between 1986 and 1991; they include such giants as Gumilev, Khodasevich, and Georgii Ivanov.

In making my selection I was concerned that the poems should interact with each other thematically. In particular, many poems here are about the nature and function of poetry itself; recent developments in Russian and Soviet history and the relationship of those developments to the country's past; reactions to their new environment on the part of émigré poets, continuing the old debate on Russia versus the West; men defining women and women defining men—the former category still far outweighing the latter in persistence and self-confidence; and the characteristic Russian genre of the "confessional" philosophical lyric, in which a poet defines his or her place as a member of a particular generation ("fathers and sons"). There is constant anxiety about the nature of freedom. And in evidence throughout the anthology are the obsessive heartsearchings of the Russian intelligentsia: Who is to blame? What to do? We may also observe, however, an effort on the part of the poets born after 1945 to avoid these sanctified themes in their effort to write "just poetry," as if the social command had never existed.

This anthology is personal; it contains poems that have spoken to me. My concentration on "strict form" poets reflects my own taste, but it does seem also to be the majority taste among serious students of Russian poetry. Dozens of Russians have published memorable poems during the last twenty years, but I have preferred to offer larger selections from a smaller number of poets rather than the other way round. This decision has inevitably led to the exclusion of many figures who arguably rank with some of the poets represented here. It is invidious even to mention the names of individuals, but it has been particularly hard to exclude Naum Korzhavin (b. 1929), Genrikh Sapgir (b. 1929), Gennadii Aigi (b. 1934), Vsevolod Nekrasov (b. 1934), Viktor Sosnora (b. 1936), Vladimir Uflyand (b. 1936), Aleksandr Velichanskii (1940–1990), and Viktor Krivulin (b. 1945), to say nothing of a number of younger poets whose work has not yet been substantially published. Furthermore, I have excluded some important poets who were publishing mature work before 1970 and did not seem to me to have continued to evolve since that date; the most unfortunate victims of this policy are the émigré masters Igor' Chinnov (b. 1914), Ivan Elagin (1917–1986), Nikolai Morshen (b. 1917), and Valerii Pereleshin (b. 1915). In general I have excluded poems, and indeed the entire work of some poets, that are already well known to the anglophone readership through existing anthologies and individual collections. Finally, this is in principle an anthology of shorter poems. The exclusion of longer poems means that certain poets who favor extended statement are represented in a one-sided way.

INTRODUCTION:

RECENT RUSSIAN POETRY

This anthology brings together the work of twenty-three poets writing in Russian during the 1970s and 1980s, a period that will probably prove to be no more self-contained than any other in the convoluted continuum of the history of literature. These twenty years may be viewed preliminarily as the second half of a phase that began in the USSR in 1956, when there was a politically led release of creative energies that had been held down since the rise of Stalin's system of totalitarian control in the early 1930s. In 1956 Nikita Khrushchev made his "Secret Speech" at the XX Congress of the Communist Party of the Soviet Union, with its negative remarks about Stalin; at about the same time a large number of prisoners were released from the Gulag; foreign visitors began to appear in the USSR, and a few selected Soviets to go abroad; in 1961 Yurii Gagarin led the world into space; and in the same year, in connection with the XXII Congress of the Party, its confident new Programme was published, confirming the post-Stalinist message of 1956. These and other events fostered a climate of optimism, and the creative intelligentsia sensed that greater freedom of expression was to be tolerated. They responded with great enthusiasm, apparently preferring to repress certain omens such as the invasion of Hungary in 1956 and the vicious campaign against Pasternak in 1958.

But this enthusiasm was relatively short-lived. Under pressure from the diehards in the Party, Khrushchev soon began retrenchment, cracking down on Soviet writers particularly hard in 1963, but it was too late, and he was toppled in 1964. Conformity proved hard to impose and maintain, however, and the 1960s saw a pitched battle between some brave individuals and groups and the forces of Party and State. The physical triumph of the latter now seems to have been inevitable, given that there had been no relaxation of the State's Party-decreed monopoly of the means of production or the Party's self-arrogated monopoly in ideology, no reduction in the effectiveness of the Union of Writers and the KGB as enforcers, and a continuing willingness among people to collaborate with them, perhaps now through greed or inertia rather than through fear or conviction. Joseph Brodsky was arrested in 1964. Sinyavsky and Daniel were arrested in 1965, tried and sentenced in 1966. Through the second half of the 1960s Solzhenitsyn waged his titanic struggle against the authorities and was expelled from Soviet literature and eventually from the country. In August 1968 the USSR led the Warsaw Pact invasion of Czechoslovakia, an event that put an end to any optimism that lingered among Soviet intellectuals. The cynical, corrupt stagnation of the Brezhnev years began, lasting until the death of the old leader in 1982 and, more fitfully, those of his two successors before 1985. This anthology is mainly concerned with the work of poets who defined themselves during the Brezhnev period. It was characterized by disillusion. Consistent with that disillusion was the Party-State policy of silencing nonconformists by exclusion and exile rather than by physical extermination. All but one of the poets represented here (Slutsky) have lived to see the end of the system under which they matured.

When Mikhail Gorbachev came to power in 1985, a series of unprecedentedly radical reforms of the system began to be attempted, taking effect in the media and the arts earlier than anywhere else. The liberal survivors of the Khrushchev period (the "sixties people," *shestidesyatniki*) were the principal initiators of the new developments, with all the assumptions and prejudices that followed from their own experience. An increased openness to external influences marked the Gorbachev Spring as it did the Khrushchev Thaw, but this factor was not fundamental to internal developments. Nor did the period between 1985 and 1991 see a considerable number of new individual talents emerge in the arts. The last five years of the Soviet system were marked mainly by an attempt to recapture the hitherto repressed Russian culture of the past rather than by the emergence and promotion of new talent, the opposite of the situation during the Khrushchev years. This recapturing of the past has no real equivalent in earlier periods of Russian literary history; Stalin's totalitarianism and the philistinism of Brezhnev's apparatus had defined the cultural canon with unheard-of effectiveness.

But there had been some slow progress before 1985. Two poets in particular were returned to the Soviet readership in the 1960s and 1970s: Osip Mandelstam (1891–1938) and Marina Tsvetaeva (1892–1941). The importance of their renewed presence for Russian poets born in the 1930s and 1940s cannot be overestimated. As has often been the case in Russia, they were esteemed as much for their lives as for what they wrote. They went against the literary and political establishments of their time and pursued their own destinies in a way that led to persecution, dreadful suffering, and premature death. Two other great poets of Russian modernism, Boris Pasternak and Anna Akhmatova, chose less drastic courses and managed to survive into the lifetime of the poets represented in this anthology. Again, the importance of their presence cannot be overestimated. They embodied the noble autonomous culture of pre-Revolutionary times that had been anathematized for later generations. Pasternak was the idol of the younger Moscow poets, Akhmatova that of the younger Leningraders. For many Russian intellectuals, their passing marked the end of Russian culture worthy of the name; the juggernaut of the Soviet cultural system, with its fearful suppression of spiritual values, its chauvinism, its promotion of servile mediocrity and persecution of talent, its death-grip on the media and the education system, had broken the great tradition. The words of Bella Akhmadulina about the deaths of Pasternak and Akhmatova sum up this attitude:

> By the compulsion of these two deaths
> the future of the word is so exhausted.
> Neither lips nor reasons remain
> for us to undertake it anew.

And in his Nobel Prize address, Joseph Brodsky coupled the names of Mandelstam, Tsvetaeva, and Akhmatova with those of Robert Frost and W. H. Auden and declared:

> ... it is impossible to be better than them on paper; it is impossible to be better than them in life, and it is precisely their lives, no matter how tragic and bitter they were, that make me often—evidently, more often than I ought—regret the passage of time.

And to these hallowed names should be added that of another long-dead poet, Velemir Khlebnikov (1886–1922), the guru of those Russian intellectuals who reject even Akhmatova and Pasternak as compromisers and seek to be a perpetual avant-garde that spurns both politics and the marketplace. There is no equivalent in the West (except among symbiotic Slavists) for the adulation in which the Russian intelligentsia holds these hero-martyrs of high culture. For the poets who have come after them there is a heavy sense of living in an age of bronze, or even of lead.

To refer to the Brezhnev years as "the period of stagnation" became an official cliché in the Gorbachev years. Olga Sedakova has referred to those years more vividly as "the gray terror." But it is too easy now to forget certain processes, such as the return to the Soviet readership of the poets just mentioned and of several others, that continued, however sluggishly, throughout the period. And under Brezhnev, as at every stage since the Revolution—even during the worst years of Stalinism—there was a succession of poets who attempted to create in a way that either consciously opposes the demands placed upon literature by the Party and the State or has nothing to do with them. The way their lives were lived should be seen not in terms of the West, where to be a professional poet is well-nigh impossible (which is right and proper, most people would think), but in terms of the old Soviet system, within which poets who did the right thing—accept the Party's mandate, to put it crudely—could not only survive on their earnings but also become highly privileged and even wealthy. This system is one of the few enclaves of the classic Soviet economy that led to manifest overproduction. Not all the poets who operated within it have been bad, any more than those who operated outside it have been good. Some professional poets published one kind of poem while writing others for the future; since 1986 it has been confirmed that this was the case with almost every prominent officially acknowledged poet, and work of this kind by Slutsky, Okudzhava, and Morits is included in the present anthology. Yet others survived by doing the various kinds of literary day labor which the Soviet system provided in good sufficiency: translation (especially into Russian from the languages of the various minorities of the USSR), children's literature, editing, film scripts, running creative-writing workshops, refereeing manuscripts, ghost writing. Such were the options of Plisetsky, Rein, and Chukhontsev, three major poets who hardly published a line of their original work in the USSR between 1965 and 1983, while being members of the Union of Writers and part of the metropolitan literary scene. Other poets were never allowed even onto the sidelines of professional literature, or did not choose to seek access. Such were Shvarts and Sedakova, and many more; one member of this "lost generation" born between 1945 and 1960 has said that "they kept us like a cat in a sack, and when they let us out, nobody needed us." Other underground poets included Bobyshev, Kublanovsky, Tsvetkov, and Kenzheev; they lived and worked outside the official literary system during the 1970s, emigrating around the end of the decade when the desire for freedom of creation and publication (and in Kublanovsky's case, the threat of physical reprisals) proved paramount.

For many poets who were not officially recognized, publication in a form more substantial than typescripts passed from hand to hand was too important to do without; and securing it enmeshed them in the political process. They produced *samizdat* journals and formed a network of unofficial groups. They published abroad, with admirable fearlessness and despite continued threats and harrassment. These measures were backed up by legal sanctions when the USSR signed the International Copyright Convention in 1973 and set up the All-Union Association of Authors' Rights (VAAP) to supervise international publishing relations; that proved to be the last mechanism of literary control to be established in the USSR. Starting in the 1960s, the existence of the tape recorder in private hands provided a new means of clandestine "publication" and circulation, known as *magnitizdat*, that was independent of the public media and their attendant controls. Out of this resource was born the performance genre of "guitar poetry," the most distinctive innovation in Russian poetry of the period since 1956; it brought immense popularity to Okudzhava, Vysotsky, and Galich. But increasingly, poets left the country, voluntarily or otherwise: the possibility of getting out was the most important nonliterary factor for Russian poets in the Brezhnev period. They were led by Brodsky, and after him came Gorbanevskaya, Loseff, Bobyshev, Tsvetkov, Kublanovsky, Kenzheev, and many others.

Brodsky maintains that he was forced to leave the USSR against his will, but he has been harshly categorical about his options: "It is better to be a total failure in democracy than a martyr or *la crème de la crème* in tyranny." There is some friction between those poets who left and those who stayed behind; the latter tend to regard themselves as more worthy, because they did not "surrender," as some of them put it, but continued the struggle in the place where their efforts really mattered, and where persecution was both the result and a guarantee of this importance. Aleksandr Kushner has one particularly explicit poem here on this subject. And there is animosity between those who stayed and prospered and those who stayed and did not make brilliant careers; the latter can now boast of their former sub-rosa status, as do Morits, Kornilov, and Chichibabin in poems in this anthology. But those who stayed also have found reasons to lament the new freedom, when, as Kornilov observes, "the lyre has fewer/ Watchmen posted around it"; they have lost the situation that gave them a strong sense of civic mission, and the conspiratorial solidarity that bonded them in dissidence. On this subject Kornilov, again, has been particularly eloquent. And Yunna Morits has some cutting remarks about the younger generation's failure to understand what their forebears had to face. But in its turn, the younger generation reacts with understandable cynicism to the publication of work by older poets (who now control the major journals) "from out of the drawer," arguing that precedence should be given to genuinely new work, and complaining that they are just as frustrated as they were under Brezhnev. Nonconformist poets in the emigration, incidentally, make similar complaints about editorial gatekeeping.

The poetry in this anthology reflects a paramount concern with the cruel history of Russia and the USSR, and its general tone is appropriately grim. (Significantly, this tone gets lighter as the dates of birth get later.) This inward-looking sense of involvement and commitment is sometimes seen as one of Russian poetry's greatest strengths, giving it a seriousness, authenticity, and centrality compared to which other national literary traditions may seem superficial and escapist. The dignified, old-fashioned quality that is often sensed in Russian poetry by its foreign observers also derives from its linguistic and versificatory form. On the whole, its language and themes do not contravene what are for the Western world long-obsolete standards of propriety; it is astonishing to the uninitiated, for example, to learn that Elena Shvarts's poetry has for years been regarded as unacceptably "physiological" by the arbiters of Soviet taste. Though we may detect something of a general inclination toward the colloquial end of the stylistic spectrum, a middle register is prevalent; the extremes of the stylistic spectrum are avoided as impediments to communication. (We may find a little folksy coloring, as in Chichibabin, Kornilov, and Gorbanevskaya; or a tendency toward archaism, as in Bobyshev and Kublanovsky.) This stylistic restraint goes hand in hand with a similar tendency in subject matter and intellectual level. Russian poets can still address the conventional permanent themes: love, death, the seasons, and—in a suspiciously incestuous way—poetry itself. More than that: they can discuss these subjects head-on, without self-consciousness or saving irony, in terms of their souls, their spirits, and their hearts. For most Russian poets, the aim is immediate, effective communication with the emotional world of the reader.

Difficulty is still rare, in all the four senses of the word defined in George Steiner's classic essay of 1978. Broadly speaking, difficulty appears in modern Russian poetry in the early Pasternak and in Mandelstam (early and late), in Khlebnikov and the absurdist poets of the 1920s, and is then in suspense until it begins to appear in a different form in the work of Brodsky, and then, different yet again, in the work of Aleksei Tsvetkov in the early 1970s. At about the same time, and again led by Brodsky (perhaps taking a cue from Rein), irony begins to make inroads, bringing a new complexity and ambiguity. With the appearance of Sedakova, Zhdanov, and Parshchikov, the language and conceptual level of Russian poetry in Russia have again begun to exhibit richness and complexity. But plain, straightforward, sentimentally tinged poetry continues to be viable. The desire to challenge the reader at the level of comprehension rather than of the emotions, in terms of aesthetics rather than ethics, is unusual. Figurative language and particularly metaphor, the essential device of other poetic traditions, tends to be used sparingly by most poets, and sometimes not at all. Slutsky and Kushner exemplify this stripped classic style; Zhdanov and Parshchikov are part of a recent minority trying to write against it. Meanwhile, the unfortunately labeled "conceptualists," represented here by Dmitrii Prigov, attempt to make poetry out of the language and notions of nonintelligentsia Soviet life, materials even more unpretentious and unliterary than have been the norm in Russian poetry since the 1920s. The perceived simplicity of Russian poetry tends to invalidate much of it for foreign readers faced with translations that delete its all-important music and its linguistic overtones. Translations also alienate the text from its author's speaking voice, the only medium through which—many people think—Russian poetry attains its full significance. It is true that appearances can be deceptive: the apparent naivete of Okudzhava, for example, so direct in its emotional appeal, in fact masks a tantalizingly evasive worldview. And Loseff's polished surface hides some profound depths.

But the most individual poetic voice of the last thirty years has been Brodsky's, challenging the mainstream with a persistent and indisputably powerful alternative. His mature poetry presents formidable conceptual difficulties. He is capable of occasional captivating simplicity, especially in his love poetry, but much more characteristic is a mode of discourse that makes few concessions to the common reader. The broad Russian audience has only recently been exposed to this style, and although some gallant attempts have been made at interpretation by Western commentators, there is as yet no consensus about the way in which Brodsky's work might best be approached. There is, however, an increasingly general agreement that Brodsky's poetry is the most important and original contribution of the last thirty years. The scale of his achievement, his insistence on the aesthetic imperative, and—inevitably—the fated aura of his life, call into question the assumptions of practically all his contemporaries.

As regards versification, the poets of recent years still find generally adequate the traditional syllabo-tonic repertoire that has been developed and refined over two and a half centuries. In one poem in this anthology Bella Akhmadulina refers to her "armament": "Iamb, trochee, anapaest, amphibrach, and dactyl with them." Imagining their loss, she asks: "What is there left?" In a moment of exasperation, Lev Loseff's poet fumes with sarcastic rage about the seeming inevitability of "our empty iambs... and our rotten trochees." And the continuing commitment of Russian poets to rhyme is celebrated here by Vladimir Kornilov in his poem on the subject. Syntax obediently goes hand in hand with this high degree of patterning (except in Brodsky, who consistently plays syntax against meter). The result of such formal conservatism is poetry that to the non-Russian reader has the feel of light verse: excessively well made, sing-song, juvenile, boxed into endless alternatingly rhymed quatrains. To most Russians, however, this well-wrought formal articulation is essential if the poem is to merit serious attention. To skilled native speakers the restricted and shared devices that the non-Russian reader perceives as monotonous possess a richly individualized variety. Through the subtleties of rhythmical variation, each poet's iambic pentameter, say, is as personal as a fingerprint. And each poet's use of rhyme represents the same kind of individuality within convention.

Besides personalizing their texts through verse rhythm, Russian poets communalize them by retaining the traditional system of meters. They can set up delicate cross-references within the tradition. Perhaps the most obvious example of this procedure in the present anthology is Kushner's poem "Light flows...." Here, the use of trochaic pentameter in quatrains with alternating masculine and feminine rhyme immediately summons up a paradigm of poems in this meter eventually going back to Lermontov's famous "Alone I go out onto the road," and evoking what has been called the "semantic aura" of this paradigm. In this case Kushner comes to the verge of overkill by actually quoting Lermontov's poem in his text; usually, such intertextuality is not made so explicit. And the overall preferences in selecting formal resources mean that each poet has a metrical repertoire as distinctive as his or her face. The metrical inventiveness belied by the apparent naivete of Okudzhava's forms, and Loseff's assured use of the entire range of traditional structures—to take but two examples from the material here—all testify to an abundant and sufficient variety within what the reader used to Anglo-American poetry perceives as monotonous conventionality. But this is not to say that there has been no experimentation. Brodsky, in this as in other respects, is on his own. Beginning at about the time of his emigration, Brodsky has developed the long-line free *dolnik* with liberal enjambment as his personal formal signature. But Brodsky still rhymes, and with seemingly inexhaustible inventiveness.

It was suggested earlier that a very important characteristic of the last twenty years has been the existence of a major tradition outside the metropolitan territory. Russian poetry before the Revolution was made by relatively small and sociologically homogeneous groups who worked and lived in close communication with each other in Moscow and St. Petersburg, for the most part able to go abroad and return at will. However, a significant number of the major modernist poets emigrated after the Revolution and in some ways took the legacy of that age with them. The last of them was Georgii Ivanov (1894-1958), arguably the most important Russian poet in the world during the last twenty years of his life. The émigrés of Ivanov's generation were joined by a smaller and on the whole culturally less well favored group of émigrés after World War II. There was very little interplay between the poetry of the internal and that of the external streams; and the external stream seemed incapable of real innovation. In the 1970s the center of gravity shifted. The departure of Joseph Brodsky in 1972 heralded this change. The poets of the "Third Wave," as the emigration of the 1970s is commonly called, formed a much more active and creative contingent than their predecessors.

For most of the period reflected in this anthology, the official stream and the émigré stream flowed separately, as they had since the Revolution. It was only in 1987-88 that Russian poetry originally published abroad by living émigré poets began to appear in the Soviet press. The turning point was the appearance of a selection of Brodsky's poems in the December 1987 issue of *Novyi mir*. The publication of texts by émigré poets has been accompanied by a flood of biographical and historical materials (so much so that, again, younger indigenous poets have complained of being crowded out). One publication in particular deserves mention: issue number 49 of *Ogonek* for 1988 carried the transcript of Brodsky's trial for "parasitism" in 1964, including the now legendary exchange that exposes the gulf between the mentalities of the poet and the bureaucrat:

> *Judge:* And who said you were a poet? Who numbered you among the poets?
> *Brodsky:* Nobody. (Without being asked:) And who numbered me among the human race?
> *Judge:* But did you study it?
> *Brodsky:* What?
> *Judge:* To be a poet? Didn't you try and graduate from college, where they prepare... where they teach....
> *Brodsky:* I didn't think... I didn't think you got it through education.
> *Judge:* So how do you then?
> *Brodsky:* I thought that it... (perplexed) came from God.

Of course, the divide that existed between the Soviet and the émigré streams was bridged in many ways. To begin with, the blockage was one-way: Soviet-published poetry was always readily available in the West in the original publications to those who cared to read it, while the average Soviet reader could not easily get hold of Russian poetry published abroad. Chance and good fortune got some émigré poets through, but it will be a long time before the émigré legacy is fully available to the indigenous population. This situation obtains not just with the émigré legacy: the return to the Soviet reader of older poets such as those mentioned earlier, Mandelstam and Tsvetaeva, had always been qualified and selective. The fullest editions of them and literally dozens of other modern Russian poets, and the most adequate interpretations of their work, have been published by Western and émigré scholars and are not easily available in Russia.

The Soviet literary elite, however, was not deeply affected by the division into internal and external streams, at least in its private knowledge. Its members had reasonably reliable access to émigré publications. Beginning in the early 1960s, Soviet poets in good standing had been traveling outside the USSR. The pioneers were Evtushenko and Voznesensky, and they continued to go abroad except when their occasional brushes with the authorities held them up (never for very long, however). They also found good Western translators for their work, and have reached beyond their native audience to an extent not matched by earlier Russian poets during their own lifetimes. But their credibility on the outside has been severely undermined by the arrival of the Third Wave émigrés, who regard them in the same way as do most Russian intellectuals born after 1935, as bright innovators of the early 1960s who soon degenerated into little more than opportunists and hacks. And in terms of reaching the non-Russian audience they have been definitively left behind by Brodsky; his personal charisma and the translations of his poetry into English and other languages, usually carried out with the poet's own participation, have secured him a special niche and a unique authority in the modern literary world.

The current situation is that five or six major Russian poets are living outside their native country. None of them has been silenced by this displacement. All of them began to be published in the USSR before it collapsed; it has become quite common for new work to be published simultaneously in an émigré and a home-based journal. Several of them have made visits to Russia. So far, no poet has chosen to go back on a permanent basis. But there is a more extensive and serious public dialogue between the internal and the external streams than there has ever been before.

Needless to say, there is considerable ferment among poets living in Russia as they adjust to the new conditions. The end of the Party's ideological control over the Soviet press has given them substantial freedom of expression. It is legally possible, though still very difficult practically, to publish privately. Poets can publish abroad with impunity, and travel is restricted by material rather than ideological factors. The erosion of state economic control may eventually bring about a free market in publishing and revolutionize the conditions under which Soviet Russian poets lived and worked. It is unlikely that poets in Russia will be able to exist for much longer as full-time professionals in their metropolitan hothouses, supported by an ideologically manipulated and subsidized publishing system and by the Union of Writers, that dinosaur of a men's club and welfare organization. Russian poetry has embarked on what Aleksandr Eremenko in one poem here calls "the long journey out of the dead forest." As it begins, Russian poets face the same marginalization as do poets in most other contemporary cultures; their historic role and killing burden as the conscience of the nation may well become superfluous in a liberated civil society. Poets may simply be drowned out by the newly unleashed electronic mass media, or upstaged by a liberated and commercialized entertainment industry. But on the other hand, as The Poet fades away, the poems themselves may have a better chance.

NOTE ON THE TEXTS, TRANSLATIONS, AND ANNOTATION

The poets in this anthology appear in chronological order of birth. Within the work of each poet, the texts have been arranged roughly in order of composition. Dates of composition are given only when the poets themselves have cared to supply them. Data concerning previous publications are given under "Sources of the Texts" at the end of the volume; these data have been made as comprehensive as possible in order to illustrate the chronological and geographical complexities in the textual history of these poems.

The orthographical conventions of the original texts have been retained, which leads to inconsistency: some poets, for example Kushner, capitalize every line-initial letter, while others, for example Gorbanevskaya, capitalize only those which are also sentence-initial. The recently loosened Soviet convention of using lower-case initials for the name of God and pronouns referring to this concept has been replaced in the translations with capitalization.

The translations into English in this anthology make no claim to any literary merit or to elegance. They are provided here, obviously, to make the anthology at least in part accessible to students of poetry without Russian. But they are mainly intended to provide a way into the original texts for anglophone students of Russian poetry whose grasp of the language is not secure enough for them to proceed with these texts on their own.

An effort has been made, sometimes at the expense of English idiom, to retain the same word order as in the original, the same parts of speech, and the same weight of words to the line. But Russian conventions in punctuation have not been followed, because in many cases they obscure meaning if transferred exactly into English. The author is painfully aware that in many instances the translations give at best a brutally foreshortened impression of the allusiveness of the originals.

Annotation has been kept to an absolute minimum and restricted to the English translations, where annotated words and phrases are marked by asterisks; no attempt has been made to explicate the difficulties in the Russian texts. Also, nothing has been annotated that can be found in readily available reference works in English.

Contemporary

Russian

Poetry

Борис Слуцкий

1

Любое начало—начало конца.
Поэтому мы начинаем с яйца,
кончаем же битою скорлупою
и этим венчаем начало любое.

5 Но нас обучили, но нас накачали
не думать о горьком исходе вначале,
не думать, не знать, не стараться узнать,
а—раз мы решили начать—начинать.

Начнем. Поиграем жестокой судьбой,
10 затеем сражение, ввяжемся в бой.

2

Плохие времена тем хороши,
что выявленью качества души
способствуют и казни, и война,
и глад, и мор—плохие времена.

5 Пока ты цел, пока ты сыт, здоров,
не зван в суды, не вызвал докторов,
неведомы твой потолок и цель,
параметры—темны, пока ты цел.

Когда ты бит, когда тебя трясут,
10 и заедает вошь, и мучит суд,

Boris Slutsky

1

Any beginning is the beginning of the end.
That's why we begin with an egg,
but end up with a smashed shell,
and this is the way we crown any beginning.

5 But we've been taught, but we've been drilled
not to think about the bitter outcome in the beginning,
not to think, not to know, not to try and find out,
but—once we've decided to begin—to make a beginning.

Let's begin. Let's play with cruel fate,
10 let's start the conflict, let's plunge into the fray.

2

Bad times are good because
they help the qualities of the soul to show themselves,
—executions, war,
famine, pestilence, bad times.

5 While you're still in one piece, while you're fed and healthy,
haven't been summoned to the courts, haven't called the doctors,
your ceiling and purpose are unknown,
your parameters are unclear while you're still in one piece.

When you've been hit, when you're being shaken up,
10 lice eating at you, court tormenting you,

ты бытию предпочитаешь быт.
Все выясняется, когда ты бит.

Но иногда все существо твое
предпочитает все же
бытие
15 и власть теряет над людьми беда
когда бывает это иногда.

3

Философской лирики замах—рублевый,
а удар—грошовый, небольшой.
Может, обойтись пустой и плевой—
как ее фамилия—душой?

5 Пусть уж философствуют философы.
Пусть они изыскивают способы
мир уговорить еще терпеть.
Нам бы только песенку попеть.

В песенке же все: объект, субъект,
10 бытие с сознанием, конечно.
Кто ее от цели от конечной
отклонит, с пути собьет?

И пока громоздкая земля
пробирается средь пыли звездной,
15 мировое труляля
торжествует над всемирной бездной.

4 Прощение

Грехи прощают за стихи.
Грехи большие—
за стихи большие.
Прощают даже смертные грехи,
5 когда стихи пишу от всей души я.

А ежели при жизни не простят,
потом забвение с меня скостят.

you would rather have everyday life than higher being.
It all becomes clear when you've been hit.

But sometimes your entire being
nonetheless prefers higher being
15 and disaster loses its power over people
when this happens, sometimes.

3

The cocked-arm gesture of the philosophical lyric is worth a ruble,
its punch is worth a penny, it's small.
Perhaps we should make do with the empty and contemptible
—what's its name?—soul?

5 Let the philosophers do their philosophizing.
Let them look for ways
to persuade the world to go on putting up with things.
We should just sing a little song.

In a song there is everything: object, subject,
10 existence and consciousness, of course.
Who could divert it from its ultimate aim,
knock it off its path?

And while the clumsy earth
makes its way through starry dust
15 the world's tra-la-la
triumphs over the world-wide abyss.

4 Forgiveness[*]

Sins are forgiven for poetry.
Great sins
for great poetry.
Even mortal sins are forgiven
5 when I write poetry with my whole soul.

But if people don't forgive me while I'm still alive
Later they'll smite oblivion from me.

Пусть даже лихо деют—
вспоминают
10 пускай добром,
не чем-нибудь.
Прошу того, кто ведает и знает:
ударь, но не забудь.
Убей, но не забудь.

5

У людей—дети. У нас—только кактусы
стоят, безмолвны и холодны.
Интеллигенция, куда она катится?
Ученые люди,

где ваши сыны?

5 Я жил в среде, в которой племянниц
намного меньше, чем теть и дядéй.
И ни один художник-фламандец
ей не примажет больших грудей.

За что? За то, что детские сопли
10 однажды побрезговала стереть,
сосцы у нее навсегда пересохли,
глаза и щеки пошли стареть.

Чем больше книг, тем меньше деток,
чем больше идей, тем меньше детей.
15 Чем больше жен, со вкусом одетых,
тем в светлых квартирах пустей и пустей.

6 Семейная ссора

Ненависть! Особый привкус в супе.
Суп—как суп. Простой бульон по сути,
но с щепоткой соли или перцу—
даром ненавидящего сердца.

5 Ненависть кровати застилает,
ненависть тетради проверяет,
подметает пол и пыль стирает:
из виду никак вас не теряет.

Even though they're evil-doers
let them remember [me]
10 for something good
not just for any old thing.
I ask the person who has knowledge and knows:
strike, but do not forget.
Kill, but do not forget.

5

Real people have children. We only have cacti
standing there speechless and cold.
The intelligentsia, where is it rolling away to?
Learned people, where are your sons?

5 I have lived in an environment where there are many fewer
nieces than aunts and uncles.
And not a single Flemish painter
would daub on big breasts if he painted her.

What for? Because there came a time when she
10 got finicky about wiping away infant dribblings
her nipples have dried up forever,
her eyes and cheeks have started getting old.

The more books, the fewer kids,
the more ideas, the fewer children.
15 The more wives, tastefully dressed,
the emptier it gets in these well-lit apartments.

6 Family Quarrel

Hatred! A special added taste to the soup.
The soup's just soup. Simple stock really,
but with a pinch of salt or pepper
from the heart that hates in vain.

5 Hatred makes the bed,
hatred corrects the notebook,
sweeps the floor and wipes away the dust:
and never lets you out of its sight.

Ничего не видя. Ненавидя.
10 Ничего не слыша. Ненавидя.
Вздрагивает ненависть при виде
вашем. Хвалите или язвите.

А потом она тихонько плачет,
и глаза от вас поспешно прячет,
15 и лежит в постели с вами рядом,
в потолок уставясь долгим взглядом.

7

Мужья со своими делами, нервами,
чувством долга, чувством вины
должны умирать первыми, первыми,
вторыми они умирать не должны.

5 Жены должны стареть понемногу,
хоть до столетних дойдя рубежей,
изредка, впрочем, снова и снова
вспоминая своих мужей.

Ты не должна была делать так,
10 как ты сделала. Ты не должна была.
С доброй улыбкою на устах
жить ты должна была,
долго должна была.

Жить до старости, до седины
15 жены обязаны и должны,
делая в доме свои дела,
чьи-нибудь сердца разбивая
или даже—была не была—
чарку—в память мужей—распивая.

Seeing nothing. Hating.
10 Hearing nothing. Hating.
Hatred trembles when it sees
you. You can praise it or curse it.

And then it weeps on the quiet,
and hurriedly hides its eyes from you,
15 and lies in the bed beside you,
fixing a long gaze on the ceiling.

7

Husbands with their doings and nerves,
sense of duty and sense of guilt,
ought to die first, first,
they ought not die second.*

5 Wives ought to grow old little by little
reaching even hundred-year limits,
on rare occasions, but over and over again
remembering their husbands.

You should not have done it the way
10 you did. You should not.
With a kind smile on your lips
you should have lived,
you should have lived a long time.

To live to old age, to gray hairs
15 is what wives are obliged and ought to do,
Getting on with your things at home,
breaking certain men's hearts
or even—well, why not?—
drinking a toast in memory of your husbands.

8

На похоронах не смеются,
разве только в душе.
Покуда раздаются
речи, мерно дыши.

5 И замеряй на правдивость
слезы или хвалу,
зная, что справедливость
тихо ждет в углу.

8

People don't laugh at funerals,
except maybe in their hearts.
For as long as the speeches are ringing out,
breathe evenly.

5 And measure against veracity
the tears or the praise,
knowing that justice
is quietly waiting in the corner.

Борис Чичибабин

9 Признание

Зима шуршит снежком по золотым аллейкам,
надежно хороня земную черноту,
и по тому снежку идет Шолом Алейхем
с усмешечкой в очах, с оскоминкой во рту.

5 В провидческой тоске, сорочьих сборищ мимо
в последний раз идет по родине своей—
а мне на той земле до мук необъяснимо,
откуда я пришел, зачем живу на ней.

Смущаясь и таясь, как будто я обманщик,
10 у холода и тьмы о солнышке молю,
и все мне снится сон, что я еврейский мальчик,
и в этом русском сне я прожил жизнь мою.

Мосты мои висят беспомощны и шатки,
уйти бы от греха, забыться бы на миг...
15 Отрушиваю снег с невыносимой шапки—
и попадаю в круг друзей глухонемых.

В душе моей поют сиротские соборы
и белый снег метет меж сосен и берез,
но те, кого люблю, на приговоры скоры
20 и грозный суд вершат не в шутку, а всерьез.

О, нам хотя б на грош смиренья и печали,
безгневной тишины, безревностной любви!
Мы смыслом изошли, мы духом обнищали,
и жизнь у нас на лжи, а храмы на крови.

Boris Chichibabin

9 Confession

Winter rustles in snow along golden avenues,
reliably burying the earth's blackness,
and through that snow walks Sholom Aleikhem*
with a sarcastic grin on his glasses, an acid taste in his mouth.

5 In prophetic anguish past the starlings' musterings
for the last time he walks through his native land—
but for me on this earth it's so inexplicable it's torture,
from whence I came and why I live in it.

Embarrassed and hiding, as if I were a deceiver,
10 I plead with cold and dark for sun,
and I keep having a dream that I'm a Jewish boy,
and in this Russian dream I've lived my life.

My bridges hang helpless and rickety,
if only I could leave sin behind, find oblivion for an instant...
15 I sweep the snow from my unbearable fur hat
and enter the circle of deaf-and-dumb friends.

In my soul sing orphan cathedrals
and the white snow sweeps between pines and birches,
but those I love are quick to sentence
20 and carry out a dread judgment not in jest, but seriously.

O, if only we had a pennyworth of humility and sadness,
quietness without anger, love without jealousy!
We've lost all our sense, we're beggared in spirit,
our lives are built on lies, and our churches on blood.

25 Мы рушим на века—и лишь на годы строим,
 мы давимся в гробах, а Божий свет широк.
 Игра не стоит свеч, и грустно быть героем,
 ни Богу, не себе не в радость и не впрок.

 А я один из тех, кто ведает, и мямлит,
30 и напрягает слух пред мировым концом.
 Пока я вижу сны, еще я добрый Гамлет,
 но шпагу обнажу—и стану мертвецом.

 Я на ветру продрог, я в оттепели вымок,
 заплутавшись в лесу, почуявши дымок,
35 в кругу моих друзей, меж близких и любимых,
 о как я одинок! О как я одинок!

 За прожитую жизнь у всех прошу прощенья,
 и улыбаюсь всем, и плачу обо всех—
 но как боится стих небратского прочтенья,
40 как страшен для него ошибочный успех...

 Уйдет вода из рек, и птиц не станет певчих,
 и окаянной тьмой затмится белый свет.
 Но попусту звенит дурацкий мой бубенчик
 о нищете мирской, о суете сует.

45 Уйдет вода из рек, и льды вернутся снова,
 и станет плотью тень, и оборвется нить.
 О как нас Бог зовет! А мы не слышим зова.
 И в мире ничего нельзя переменить.

 Когда за мной придут, мы снова будем квиты.
50 Ведь на земле никто ни в чем не виноват.
 А все ж мы все на ней одной виной повиты
 и всем нам суждена одна дорога в ад.

10

Не верю в то, что русы
любили и дерзали:
одни врали и трусы
живут в моей державе.

25 We destroy for centuries—and build only for years,
we're crushed into coffins, but God's world is wide.
The game's not worth the candle, and it's sad to be a hero,
neither to God nor to oneself bringing joy and use.

But I am one of those who know and mutter,
30 and strain to hear in the face of the world's end.
Thus far I have dreams, I'm still the good Hamlet,
but I'll bare my rapier—and become a dead man...

I've shivered in the wind and got wet through in the thaw,
losing my way in the forest but sensing smoke,
35 among my friends, my near ones and dear ones,
O how lonely I am! O how lonely I am!

I ask forgiveness for the life I've lived,
I both smile at everyone and weep about everyone,—
but how my verse fears being read by someone not a brother,
40 how fearful for it is false success...

The water will leave the rivers, there'll be no songbirds,
an accursed dark will eclipse the wide world.
But my foolish little bell rings out in vain
about the world's poverty, about vanity of vanities.

45 The water will leave the rivers, the ice will come again,
shadow will be made flesh, the thread will snap.
O how God is calling us! But we don't hear the call.
And nothing can be changed in this world.

When they come for me, we'll be quits once more.
50 No one on earth's to blame for anything, after all.
But all the same we all on it are wound in a single guilt
and to all of us is fated a single road to hell.

10

I don't believe that the Russians
used to love and to dare:
there's only liars and cowards
in this state of mine.

5 В ней от рожденья каждый
железной ложью мечен,
а кто измучен жаждой,
тому напиться нечем.

Вот и моя жаровней
10 рассыпалась по рощам,
бесплодно и черно в ней,
как в городе полнощном.

Юродливый, горбатенький,
стучусь по белу свету,
15 зову народ свой батенькой,
а мне ответа нету.

От вашей лжи и люти
до смерти не избавлен,
не вспоминайте, люди,
20 что был я Чичибабин.

Уже не быть мне Борькой,
не целоваться с Лилькой,
Опохмеляюсь горькой,
закусываю килькой.

11

Сними с меня усталость, матерь Смерть.
Я не прошу награды за работу,
но ниспошли остуду и дремоту
на мое тело, длинное как жердь.

5 Я так устал. Мне стало все равно.
Ко мне всего на три часа из суток
приходит сон, томителен и чуток,
и в сон желанье смерти вселено.

Мне книгу зла читать невмоготу,
10 а книга блага вся перелисталась.
О матерь Смерть, сними с меня усталость,
покрой рядном худую наготу.

5 In it from birth every man
is marked by iron falsehood,
if anyone is tormented by thirst
there's nothing for him to drink.

Mine too like a brazier
10 has been scattered through the bushes,
no people, blackness,
like in a city at midnight.

A holy fool, hunchbacked,
I knock around the wide world,
15 I call my people my daddy,
but get no reply.

Of your lies and savagery
I'll not be rid until I die,
don't remember, folks,
20 that I was Chichibabin.

Too late for me to be Boris,
or cuddle up with Lilya,
I take bitter vodka for my hangover
with sprats to help it down.

11

Take this tiredness from me, mother Death.
I do not ask for reward for my work,
but send down coolness and drowsiness
to my body, long as a stake.

5 I am so tired. I don't care about anything now.
To me for only three hours in every twenty-four
comes sleep, anxious and highly strung,
and into this sleep the desire for death is planted.

I haven't the strength to read the book of evil,
10 and the book of bliss has been read right through.
O mother Death, take this tiredness from me,
cover with thy garment my miserable nakedness.

На лоб и грудь дохни своим ледком,
дай отдохнуть светло и беспробудно.

15 Я так устал. Мне сроду было трудно,
что всем другим привычно и легко.

Я верил в дух, неистов и упрям,
я Бога звал—а видел ад воочью,
И рвется тело в судорогах ночью,

20 и кровь из носу хлещет по утрам.

Одним стихам вовек не потускнеть,
да сколько их останется, однако.
Я так устал. Как раб или собака.
Сними с меня усталость, матерь Смерть.

1968

12

Тебе, моя Русь, не Богу, не зверю—
молиться—молюсь, а верить—не верю.

Я сын твой, я сон твоего бездорожья,
я сызмала Разину струги смолил.

5 Россия русалочья, Русь скоромошья,
почто не добра еси к чадам своим?

От плахи до плахи по бунтам, по гульбам
задор пропивала, порядок кляла—
и кто из достойных тобой не погублен,

10 о гулкие кручи ломая крыла.

Нет меры жестокости ни бескорыстью,
и зря о твоем же добре лепетал
дождем и ветвями, губами и кистью
влюбленно и злыдно еврей Левитан.

15 Скучая трудом, лютовала во блуде,
шептала арапу: кровцой полечи.
Уж как тебя славили добрые люди—
бахвалы, опричники и палачи.

Into my brow and breast breathe thy chill,
let me rest, brightly and with no awakening.
15 I am so tired. Things have been hard for me, ever since I was born,
that for all others are customary and easy.

I believed in the spirit, being furious and stubborn,
I called upon God, but saw hell with my own eyes.
And my body shudders in spasms at night,
20 and the blood gushes from my nose in the mornings.

It is only poetry that will never grow dim.
But there again, how much of it will remain…
I am so tired. Like a slave or a dog.
Take this tiredness from me, mother Death.

1968

12

To thee, my Russia, not to God nor to the wild beast
if I should pray, I pray, but if I should believe, I do not believe.

I am thy son, I am the dream of thy pathlessness,
since I was little I've tarred Razin's* boats.
5 Water-nymph Russia, jester Russia,
why art thou not kind to thy offspring?

From one execution block to another through revolts and riot
thou hast given drink to passion and cursed good order,
and who of the worthy has not been brought to destruction by thee,
10 made to break their wings against resonant steeps.

There is no measure for the cruelty nor the selflessness,
and in vain about thy goodness prattled
in his rain and boughs, his lips and brush
lovingly and churlishly the Jew Levitan.*

15 Growing bored with industry, thou grew savage in lechery,
and whispered to the alien: cure us by bloodletting.
And how much good people have praised thee—
braggarts, *oprichniki** and executioners.

А я тебя славить не буду вовеки,
20 под горло подступит—и то не смогу.
Мне кровь заливает морозные веки.
Я Пушкина вижу на жженом снегу.

Наточен топор, и наставлена плаха.
Не мой ли, не мой ли приходит черед?
25 Но нет во мне грусти и нет во мне страха.
Прими, моя Русь, от сыновних щедрот.

Я вмерз в твою шкуру дыханьем и сердцем,
и мне в этой жизни не будет защит,
и я не уйду в заграницы, как Герцен,
30 судьба Аввакумова в лоб мой стучит.

13

Дай вам Бог с корней до крон
без беды в отрыв собраться.
Уходящему—поклон.
Остающемуся—братство.

5 Вспоминайте наш снежок
посреди чужого жара.
Уходящему—рожок.
Остающемуся—кара.

Всяка доля по уму:
10 и хорошая, и злая.
Уходящего—пойму.
Остающегося—знаю.

Край души, больная Русь—
перезвонность, первозданность
15 (с уходящим—помирюсь,
с остающимся—останусь)—

дай нам, вьюжен и ледов,
безрассуден и непомнящ,
уходящему—любовь,
20 остающемуся—помощь.

But I shall never ever praise thee,
20 even if [a knife] is at my throat I could not.
The blood fills my frosty eyelids.
I see Pushkin on the burned snow.

The ax is sharpened and the execution block set out.
Is it not my turn that is coming?
25 But there is no sadness in me and no fear.
Accept, my Russia, from filial bounty.

I have frozen into thy pelt with my breath and heart,
there will be no defenses for me in this life,
and I shall not leave for foreign parts like Herzen,*
30 the fate of Avvakum* hammers at my brow.

13

May God grant you from roots to crown
to prepare without disaster for the break.
To him who is departing, a bow.
To him who is remaining, brotherhood.

5 Remember from time to time our snow
amid your alien heat.
To him who is departing, a shepherd's horn.
To him who is remaining, retribution.

Every lot is according to [the person's] mind,
10 both the good and the evil one.
Him who is departing, I will understand.
Him who is remaining, I know.

Land of the soul, sick Russia—
so filled with bells, primordiality
15 (with him who is departing, I will make my peace,
with him who is remaining, I will remain)—

grant us, you snowstormy and icy,
mindless and short of memory,
to him who is departing, love,
20 to him who is remaining, aid.

Тот, кто слаб, и тот, кто крут,
выбирает каждый между:
уходящий—меч и труд,
остающийся—надежду.

25 Но в конце пути сияй
по заветам Саваофа,
уходящему—Синай,
остающимся—Голгофа...

Я устал судить сплеча,
30 мерить временным безмерность.
Уходящему—печаль.
Остающемуся—верность.

14 Битва

В ночном, горячем, спутанном лесу,
где хмурый хмель, смола и паутина,
вбирая в ноздри беглую красу,
летят самцы на брачный поединок.

5 И вот, чертя смертельные круги,
хрипя и пенясь чувственною бурей,
рога в рога ударятся враги,
и дрогнет мир, обрызган кровью бурой.

И будет битва, яростью равна,
10 шатать стволы, гореть в огромных ранах,
и будет ждать покорная она,
дрожа душой за одного из равных...

В поэзии, как в свадебном лесу,
но только тех, кто цельностью означен,
15 земные страсти весело несут
в большую жизнь—к паденьям и удачам.

Ну, вот и я сквозь заросли искусств
несусь по строфам шумным и росистым
на милый зов, на роковой искус—
20 с великолепным недругом сразиться.

He who is weak, and he who is short-tempered,
every one has to choose between:
he who is departing, sword and labor,
he who is remaining, hope.

25 But at the end of the road shine forth
according to the testaments of Sabaoth,
to him who is departing, Siniai,
to him who is remaining, Golgotha.

I'm tired of making sweeping judgments,
30 measuring immensity by the temporal.
To him who is departing, sadness.
To him who is remaining, faithfulness.

14 The Battle

In the nocturnal, burning, tangled forest,
where there is the gloomy hop, resin and spiderwebs,
inhaling into their nostrils this transient beauty,
the males rush to their nuptial duel.

5 And now, describing fatal circles,
snorting and foaming in the storm of their feelings,
the enemies strike horn to horn,
and the world trembles, sprinkled with dark-brown blood.

And the battle, equal-sided in fury, will
10 make tree trunks stagger and will burn in the enormous wounds,
and the female will wait humbly,
her soul trembling for one of the equals…

In poetry, as in the nuptial forest,
but only affecting those who are marked by wholeness,
15 earthly passions merrily transport
into a big life, toward fallings and successes.

Well, and I too through the thickets of the arts
rush through sonorous and dewy stanzas
toward that sweet call, that fatal ordeal—
20 to do battle with the magnificent foe.

15

Цветы лежали на снегу,
твое лицо тускнело рядом—
и лишь дыханием и взглядом
я простонать про то смогу.

5 Был воздух зимний и лесной,
как дар за годы зла и мрака,
была могила Пастернака
и профиль с каменной слезой.

О счастье, что ни с кем другим
10 не шел ни разу без тебя я,
на строчки бережно ступая,
по тем заснежьям дорогим.

Как после неуместен был
обед в полупарадном стиле,
15 когда еще мы не остыли
от пастернаковской судьбы...

Звучи, поэзия, звучи,
как Маяковский на Таганке!
О три сосны, как три цыганки,
20 как три языческих свечи...

Когда нам станет тяжело,
ты приходи сюда погреться,
где человеческое сердце
и под землей не зажило.

25 Чужую пыль с надгробья смой,
приникни ртом к опальной ране,
где я под вещими ветрами
шумлю четвертою сосной.

15

Flowers lay on the snow,
your face showed dimly next to them,
and only through breathing and glancing
will I be able to make my groan about it.

5 The air was wintery and foresty,
like a gift for the years of evil and gloom,
there was the grave of Pasternak*
and his profile with a stone tear.

O happiness, that with nobody else
10 did I ever go without thee,
stepping carefully on the lines of verse,
through those precious snow-covered places.

Afterward, how inappropriate was
lunch in a semiformal style,
15 when we had not yet cooled down
from Pasternak's fate…

Sound out, poetry, sound out,
like Mayakovsky at the Taganka!*
About the three pine trees, like three gypsy women,
20 like three pagan candles…

When things get hard for us,
come here to get warm,
where the human heart
has not closed up even under the soil.

25 Wash the alien dust from the headstones,
bend down and press your lips to the disgraced wound,
where I, touched by the prescient winds,
rustle like a fourth pine tree.

Булат Окуджава

16

Все глуше музыка души,
все звонче музыка атаки.
Но ты об этом не спеши:
не обмануться бы во мраке,
5 что звонче музыка атаки,
что глуше музыка души.

Чем громче музыка атак,
тем слаще мед огней домашних.
И это было только так
10 в моих скитаниях вчерашних:
тем слаще мед огней домашних,
чем громче музыка атак.

Из глубины ушедших лет
еще вернее, чем когда-то—
15 чем звонче музыка побед,
тем горше каждая утрата,
еще вернее, чем когда-то,
из глубины прошедших лет.

И это все у нас в крови,
20 хоть этому не обучили:
чем выше музыка любви,
тем громче музыка печали,
чем громче музыка печали,
тем чище музыка любви.

Bulat Okudzhava

16

The music of the soul is ever fainter,
the music of the attack is ever more resonant.
But don't hasten [to comment] on that:
so as not to be deceived in the darkness,
5 that the music of the attack is more resonant,
and the music of the soul ever fainter.

the louder is the music of the attacks,
the sweeter is the honey of the lights of home.
And this was only that way
10 in my yesterday's wanderings:
the sweeter the honey of the lights of home,
the louder the music of the attacks.

From out of the depths of years gone by
more sure than ever before,
15 the more resonant the music of victories,
the more bitter is every loss,
the surer than ever before,
from the depths of years gone by.

And this is all in our blood,
20 even though we were not taught it:
the more sublime the music of love,
the louder is the music of grief,
the louder is the music of grief,
the more pure is the music of love.

17

Как наш двор ни обижали—он в классической поре.
С ним теперь уже не справиться, хоть он и безоружен.
Там Володя во дворе,
его струны в серебре,
5 его пальцы—золотые, голос его нужен.

Как с гитарой ни боролись—распалялся струнный звон.
Как вино стихов ни портили—все крепче становилось.
Кто сначала вышел вон,
кто потом украл вагон—
10 все теперь перемешалось, все объединилось.

Может, кто и нынче тоже хрипоте его не рад,
Может, кто намеревается подлить в стихи елея...
А эти песни не горят,
они в воздухе парят,
15 чем им делают больнее—тем они сильнее.

Что ж печалиться напрасно: нынче слезы лей—не лей,
но запомним хорошенечко и повод, и причину...
Ведь мы воспели королей
от Таганки до Филей,
20 пусть они теперь поэту воздают по чину.

18

Римская империя времени упадка
сохраняла видимость твердого порядка.
Главный был на месте, соратники рядом,
жизнь была прекрасна, судя по докладам.

5 А критики скажут, что слово соратник—не римская деталь,
что эта ошибка всю песенку смысла лишает.
Может быть, может быть, может и не римская, не жаль,
мне это совсем не мешает,
и даже меня возвышает.

17

No matter how they insulted our courtyard, it's in a classic period.
No way of coping with it now even though it's been disarmed.
There's Volodya* in the courtyard
with his silver strings,
5 his golden fingers, his voice is needed.

No matter how they fought against the guitar, the peal of strings kept getting
      hotter.
No matter how they watered the wine of verse, it kept getting stronger.
Who was the first to leave,
who then stole the wagon,*
10 it's all mixed up now, all rolled into one.

Maybe someone even now isn't happy about his hoarse voice again.
Maybe someone intends to slip some unction into the poems...
But after all, songs do not burn,
They hover in the air,
15 The more painful it's made for them, the stronger they get.

Why be sad for no good reason: these days, weep or not,
We'll remember very well the cause and the reason...
For after all, we sang the praises of kings
from the Taganka* to Fili,*
20 may they now pay tribute to the poet according to his rank.

18

The Roman empire in its period of decline
retained the appearance of firm order.
The chief was in place, his comrades-in-arms by his side,
life was fine, judging by the reports.

5 But critics will say that the word "comrades-in-arms" isn't a Roman item,
that this mistake deprives the whole song of sense.
Perhaps, perhaps, perhaps it isn't Roman, I'm not sorry,
this doesn't hinder me at all,
and even lifts me up.

10 Юношам империи времени упадка
снились постоянно то скатка, то схватка.
То они в атаке, то они в окопе,
то вдруг на Памире, а то вдруг в Европе.

А критики скажут, что скатка, представьте, не римская деталь,
15 что эта ошибка всю песенку смысла лишает.
Может быть, может быть, может и не римская, не жаль,
мне это совсем не мешает,
и даже меня возвышает.

Мужики империи времени упадка
20 ели, что достанут, напивались гадко.
А с похмелья каждый на рассол был падок—
видимо, не знали, что у них упадок.

А критики скажут, что слово рассол, мол, не римская деталь,
что эта ошибка всю песенку смысла лишает.
25 Может быть, может быть, может и не римская, не жаль,
мне это совсем не мешает,
и даже меня возвышает.

Женщинам империи времени упадка—
только им, красавицам, доставалось сладко.
30 Все пути открыты перед ихнем взором,
хочешь—на работу, а хочешь—на форум.

А критики хором: ах, форум, ах, форум, вот римская деталь!
Одно лишь словечко, а песенку как украшает!
Может быть, может быть, может быть и римская, а жаль,
35 мне это немного мешает,
и замысел мой разрушает.

19

У поэта соперников нету
ни на улице и ни в судьбе.
И когда он кричит всему свету,
это он не о вас—о себе.

5 Руки тонкие к небу возносит,
жизнь и силы по капле губя.

10 The youths of the empire in its period of decline
   dreamed constantly of rolled-up capes and combat.
   First they'd be on the attack, then in the trenches,
   Now in the Pamirs, and then suddenly in Europe.

   But critics will say that the word "capes," imagine, isn't a Roman item,
15 that this mistake deprives the whole song of sense.
   Perhaps, perhaps, perhaps it isn't Roman, I'm not sorry,
   this doesn't hinder me at all,
   and even lifts me up.

   The peasants of the empire in its period of decline
20 ate what they could get hold of, and got vilely drunk.
   And as a cure for their hangovers each one was partial to *rassol**—
   they evidently didn't know there was a decline.

   But critics will say that the word "*rassol*" isn't a Roman item,
   that this mistake deprives the whole song of sense.
25 Perhaps, perhaps, perhaps it isn't Roman, I'm not sorry,
   this doesn't hinder me at all,
   and even lifts me up.

   The women of the empire in its period of decline,
   they were the only ones, those beauties, whose lot was sweet.
30 All paths were open before their gaze,
   if they wanted they went to work, if they didn't they went to the forum.

   And the critics in chorus: Oh, the forum, oh, the forum, there's a Roman
      item!
   Just one little word, but how it improves the song!
   Perhaps, perhaps, perhaps it's Roman, but I'm sorry,
35 it hinders me a bit
   and destroys my idea.

19

   The poet has no rivals
   either on the street or in his destiny.
   And when he cries out to the whole world,
   it's not about you, but about himself.

5 He raises his delicate hands up to heaven,
   expending his life and powers drop by drop.

Догорает, прощения просит:
это он не за вас—за себя.

Но когда достигает предела
10   и душа отлетает во тьму...
Поле пройдено. Сделано дело.
Вам решать: для чего и кому.

То ли мед, то ли горькая чаша,
то ли адский огонь, то ли храм...
15   Все, что было его—нынче ваше.
Всё для вас. Посвящается вам.

20

Давайте придумаем деспота,
чтоб в душах царил он один
от возраста самого детского
и до благородных седин.

5   Усы ему вырастим пышные
и хищные вставим глаза,
сапожки натянем неслышные,
и проголосуем все—за.

Давайте придумаем деспота,
10   придумаем, как захотим.
Потом будет спрашивать не с кого,
коль вместе его создадим.

И пусть он над нами куражится
и пальцем грозится из тьмы,
15   пока наконец не окажется,
что *сами* им созданы мы.

Burning out, he asks for forgiveness,
not for you, but for himself.

But when he reaches the limit
10 and his soul flies off into darkness...
The field's been crossed.* The deed is done.
It's for you to decide for what and for whom.

Whether honey, or a bitter cup,
or the fires of hell, or a temple...
15 Everything that was his now is yours.
All for you. Dedicated to you.

20

Let's dream up a despot,
who will rule alone in our hearts
from the most childish age
right down to noble gray hairs.

5 Let's have him grow a luxuriant moustache
and let's put in rapacious eyes,
pull on jackboots that make no noise,
and let's all vote yes.

Let's dream up a despot,
10 dream one up the way we want him.
Later there will be no one to ask,
if we create him together.

And let's have him posture over us
and threaten from the darkness with a finger,
15 until at last it turns out
that we ourselves were created by him.

21 Примета

А. Жигулину

Если ворон в вышине,
дело, стало быть, к войне.

Чтобы не было войны,
надо ворона убить.
5 Чтобы ворона убить,
надо ружья зарядить.

А как станем заряжать,
всем захочется стрелять.
Ну а как стрельба пойдет,
10 пуля дырочку найдет.

Ей не жалко никого,
ей попасть бы хоть в кого,
хоть в чужого, хоть в свово...
Во и боле ничего.

15 Во и боле ничего.
Во и боле никого.
Кроме ворона того:
стрельнуть некому в него.

22 Письмо к маме

Ты сидишь на нарах посреди Москвы.
Голова кружится от слепой тоски.
На окне—намордник, воля—за стеной,
ниточка порвалась меж тобой и мной.
5 За железной дверью топчется солдат...
Прости его, мама: он не виноват,
он себе на душу греха не берет—
он не за себя ведь—он за весь народ.

Следователь юный машет кулаком.
10 Ему так привычно звать тебя врагом.

21 The Omen

To A. Zhigulin*

If there is a raven up above
It means things are moving toward war.

So there shouldn't be a war,
The raven has to be killed.
5 To kill the raven
A gun has to be loaded.

But when we start loading it
Everyone will want to shoot.
And as soon as the shooting starts
10 The bullet will find a hole.

The bullet pities nobody,
Wants to hit just anybody,
One of theirs, one of ours...
That's it, there's nothing more.

15 That's it, there's nothing more.
That's it, there's nobody left.
Except for that raven,
And now there's nobody to shoot it.

22 Letter to My Mom

You're sitting on your wooden planks in the middle of Moscow.
Your head's spinning from blind anguish.
On the window is a muzzle, freedom's the other side of the wall,
the thread between you and me is broken.
5 Behind the iron door struts a soldier...
Forgive him, mom, he's not to blame,
he doesn't take any sin onto his soul,
he's not doing it for himself, after all, he's doing it for the whole people.

The youthful investigator waves his fist.
10 It's so normal for him to call you an enemy.

За свою работу рад он попотеть...
Или ему тоже в камере сидеть?
В голове убогой—трехэтажный мат...
Прости его, мама: он не виноват,
15 он себе на душу греха не берет—
он не за себя ведь—он за весь народ.

Чуть за Красноярском—твой лесоповал.
Конвоир на фронте сроду не бывал.
Он тебя прикладом, он тебя пинком,
20 чтоб тебе не думать больше ни о ком.
Тулуп на нем жарок, да холоден взгляд...
Прости его, мама: он не виноват,
он себе на душу греха не берет—
он не за себя ведь—он за весь народ.

25 Вождь укрылся в башне у Москвы-реки.
У него от страха паралич руки.
Он не доверяет больше никому,
словно сам построил для себя тюрьму.
Всё ему подвластно, да опять не рад...
30 Прости его, мама: он не виноват,
он себе на душу греха не берет—
он не за себя ведь—он за весь народ.

23

Памяти А. Д. Сахарова

Когда начинается речь, что пропала духовность,
что людям отныне дорога сквозь темень лежит,
в глазах удивленных и в душах святая готовность
пойти и погибнуть, как новое пламя дрожит.

5 И это не есть обольщение или ошибка,
а это, действительно гордое, пламя костра,
и в пламени праведном этом надежды улыбка
на бледных губах проступает, и совесть остра.

Полночные их силуэты пугают загадкой.
10 С фортуны не спросишь—она свои тайны хранит.
И рано еще упиваться победою сладкой,
еще до рассвета далече... И сердце щемит.

He's glad to sweat at his work...
Or should he too be sitting in a cell?
In his pathetic head are three-storey curses...
Forgive him, mom, he's not to blame,
15 he doesn't take any sin onto his soul,
he's not doing it for himself, after all, he's doing it for the whole people.

A bit further than Krasnoyarsk is your logging camp.
The guard has never been at the front.
He'll [hit] you with his rifle butt, give you a kick,
20 so you'll never think anymore about anyone.
His fur coat's hot, but his glance is cold...
Forgive him, mom, he's not to blame,
he doesn't take any sin onto his soul,
he's not doing it for himself, after all, he's doing it for the whole people.

25 The leader's hidden himself in the tower by the Moscow River.
From fear he has paralysis of one arm.
He doesn't trust anyone anymore,
as if he'd built a prison for himself.
Everything's in his power, but he's still not happy...
30 Forgive him, mom, he's not to blame,
he doesn't take any sin onto his soul,
he's not doing it for himself, after all, he's doing it for the whole people.

23

To the memory of A. D. Sakharov[*]

When a speech begins, saying that spirituality has been lost,
that the way for people from now on lies through darkness,
in their astounded eyes and in their souls a holy readiness
to go forth and perish trembles like a new flame.

5 And this is not delusion or error,
it is the genuinely proud flame of a bonfire,
and in this just flame a smile of hope
comes over pale lips, and conscience is keen.

Their midnight silhouettes scare one with their enigma.
10 Of fortune you musn't ask; she keeps her secrets.
And it's too early yet to relish sweet victory,
it's still a long way to dawn... And my heart aches.

24

Что-то сыночек мой уединением стал тяготиться.
Разве прекрасное в шумной компании может родиться?
Там и мыслишки, внезапно явившейся, не уберечь:
в уши разверстые только напрасная проситься речь.

5 Папочка твой не случайно сработал надежный свой кокон.
Он состоит из дубовых дверей и зашторенных окон.
Он состоит из надменных замков и щеколд золотых...
Лица незваные с благоговением смотрят на них.

Чем же твой папочка в коконе этом прокуренном занят?
10 Верит ли в то, что перо не продаст, что строка не обманет?
Верит ли вновь, как всю жизнь, в обольщения вечных химер:
в гибель зловещего Зла и в победу Добра, например?

Шумные гости, не то чтобы циники—дети стихии,
ищут себе вдохновенья и радости в годы лихие,
15 не замечая, как вновь во все стороны щепки летят,
черного Зла не боятся, да вот и Добра не хотят.

Все справедливо. Там новые звуки рождаются глухо.
Это мелодия. К ней и повернуто папочки ухо.
Но неуверенно как-то склоняется вниз голова:
20 музыка нравится, но непонятные льются слова.

Папочка делает вид, что и нынче он истиной правит.
То ли и впрямь не устал обольщаться, а то ли лукавит,
что, мол, гармония с верою будут в одно сведены...
Только никто не дает за нее даже малой цены.

25 Все справедливо. И пусть он лелеет и холит свой кокон.
Вы же ликуйте и иронизируйте шумно и скопом,
но погрустите хотя бы, увидев, как сходит на нет
серый, чужой, старомодный, сутулый его силуэт.

24

My son seems to be finding seclusion hard to take.
But the beautiful can't be born in noisy company, can it?
There, you can't keep a hold on a little thought that suddenly appears:
into ears wide open only pointless speech asks to enter.

5 Your daddy has deliberately constructed his reliable cocoon.
It consists of oaken doors and shuttered windows.
It consists of haughty locks and golden latches...
Uninvited persons look at them with reverence.

What is your daddy busy with in this smoke-filled cocoon?
10 Does he believe that his pen won't betray him, his verse line won't deceive?
Does he believe once again, as he has all his life, in the eternal chimeras of
     enchantment:
the downfall of malevolent Evil, the victory of Good, for example?

The noisy guests aren't really cynics, they're children of their habitat,
searching for inspiration and joy in these difficult years,
15 not noticing that once again the chips are flying in all directions,
they're not scared of black Evil, neither do they want Good.

Everything's fair. New sounds are obscurely being born there.
It's a melody. Daddy's ear too is bent to it.
But somehow his head hangs down, unsure,
20 the music's nice, but incomprehensible words pour out.

Daddy pretends that nowadays he still controls the truth.
Could be he really isn't tired of enchantment, or perhaps he's being cunning,
saying that harmony and faith will be brought into one...
Only, nobody gives even a small price for it.

25 Everything's fair. Let him cherish and tend his cocoon.
As for you, you can rejoice and make fun noisily in a bunch,
but be sad, at least, when you see fading to nothing
his gray, alien, old-fashioned, hunched silhouette.

Владимир Корнилов

25 Музыка для себя

Словно бы в перекличке
Банджо и контрабас—
За полночь в электричке
За город мчался джаз.

5 Скопом на барабане,
Струнах и на трубе,
Что-то свое лабали
Лабухи о себе.

Видно, нет счастья слаще,
10 Чувства растеребя,
Мчать по равнине спящей
С музыкой для себя!

...Музыка в электричке,
Смысла в тебе—ничуть,
15 И потому-то трижды
Благословенна будь!

Кто ты ни есть—искусство,
Почва или судьба—
Нету в тебе паскудства,
20 Музыка для себя!

Только восторг свободы
Да разворот души—
И никакой заботы,
Проповеди и лжи!

Vladimir Kornilov

25 Music for Oneself

As if doing roll call,
Banjo and double bass;
After midnight in an electric train
A jazz band swept out of town.

5 The whole bunch, on drums,
Strings and trumpet,
These jazzers were pounding out
Something of their own about themselves.

There's no sweeter happiness, it seems,
10 Than, plucking at your feelings,
To sweep through the sleeping plain
With music for yourself!

…Music in an electric train,
There's no sense in you at all,
15 And that's why thrice-
Blessed be!

Whoever you are: art,
Soil, or fate—*
There's no filthiness in you,
20 Music for oneself!

There's only the rapture of freedom
And the soul turning inside out,
And no anxiety at all,
No preaching, no lying!

25 ...Сильно меня задела,
Ужасом осеня,
Исповедь без предела,
Музыка для себя!

1980

26 Сорок лет спустя

Подкидыш никудышных муз
И прочей нуди,
Я скукой день-деньской томлюсь
В Литинституте.

5 И замыслов невпроворот,
И строчек вздорных...
А за окном асфальт метет
Упорный дворник.

Сутулый, тощий, испитой,
10 Угрюм он, болен.
Но шут с ним и с его бедой—
Я дурью полон.

...Когда бы знать, что он лишен
Других доходов,
15 Что от журналов отлучен
Отцом народов,

С того и проза тех времен
Вдруг стала тусклой...
Зато просторный двор метен
20 Литинститутский.

...Всю жизнь гляделся я в себя,
А в ближних—мало,
И все равно его судьба
Меня достала.

25 Такой или сякой поэт,
Я кроме смеха
На склоне века, склоне лет—
Уборщик снега.

25 …It touched me powerfully,
Making terror come over me,
Confession without limit,
Music for oneself!

1980

26 Forty Years On

Foundling of aimless muses
And other stuff like that,
I'm in an agony of boredom day in, day out
In the Literary Institute.*

5 Stacks of schemes,
And rubbishy lines…
But through the window the asphalt is being swept
By a dogged yardman.

Bent, scraggy, hollow-cheeked,
10 He's morose and sick.
But never mind him and his problems—
I'm full of stupidity.

…If I'd have known that he had been deprived
Of other income,
15 That he'd been excommunicated from the journals
By the father of the peoples,

On account of which the prose of those times
Suddenly lost its luster…
The spacious yard was swept, though,
20 Of the Literary Institute.

…All my life I'd looked into myself,
Into my neighbors, but little.
And all the same his fate
Came to me.

25 This kind or that kind of poet,
I, joking aside,
At the age's decline, in my declining years
Am a snow sweeper.

Кого от нашего житья
30 Возьмут завидки?
Он от чахотки сник, а я—
От щитовидки.

...Тащу отверженность, не гнусь,
Не бью поклонов,
35 Но перед вами повинюсь,
Андрей Платонов!

И сорок лет спустя молю:
В своем зените
Простите молодость мою,
40 За все простите—

За спесь, и черствость, и сполна
Еще за скуку,
С какой глядел я из окна
На вашу муку.

январь 1985

27 Русский рай

Стать могла бы русским раем
Ярославская земля,
Но распята тракторами
Тут любая колея.

5 И каким был край чудесным,
И как много растерял,
Сразу понимаешь, если
Ездишь по монастырям.

Все величие России
10 И разор ее земли
Все соборы отразили,
Все обители несли.

Здесь и прежде жили туго,
Знали горе и нужду,

Who of our way of life
30 Would feel jealous?
He was brought down by consumption, but I
By thyroid.

...I bear my outcast lot, I don't bend,
I don't bow down,
35 But I ask absolution of you,
Andrei Platonov!*

And forty years on I pray:
At your zenith
Forgive my youth,
40 Forgive me everything—

Arrogance, callousness, and in full
The boredom as well
With which I looked through the window
At your torment.

January 1985

27 A Russian Paradise

It could have become a Russian paradise,
The Yaroslavl' region,*
But by tractors has been crucified
Every single rut here.

5 What a marvelous area it used to be,
And how much it has lost,
You understand straightaway, if
You travel around the monasteries.

All the grandeur of Russia
10 And the ruin of its land
All the cathedrals reflected,
All the monks' cells bore.

Life used to be hard here too,
They knew grief and need,

15 Но однако над округой
   Возносили красоту.

   А теперь в провалах стены
   И в прорехах купола,
   И такое запустенье,
20 Будто тут Орда была.

   Будто каменные были—
   Церкви и монастыри—
   Страстотерпцы возводили,
   А хранили дикари.

   1986

28 Безбожие

   Стали истины ложны—
   Что же делать старью?
   Я последний безбожник
   И на этом стою.

5 Если челюсти стисну,
   Сбить меня не пустяк:
   Черный хмель атеизма
   И в крови, и в костях,

   Чести-совести ради
10 Думал жить, не греша—
   Все равно с благодатью
   Разминулась душа.

   Но стиха ни в какую
   Не сменю на псалом
15 И свое докукую
   На пределе земном.

   ...От основ непреложных
   Отошли времена.
   Я последний безбожник,
20 Не жалейте меня.

   1986

15 But nevertheless over the neighborhood
They raised up beauty.

But now the walls are breached,
And the cupolas have rents in them,
And there is such desolation
20 As if the Horde* had been here.

It's as if these true stories in stone—
Churches and monasteries—
Had been erected by martyrs
But maintained by savages.

1986

28 Godlessness

Truths have become false—
What can old things do?
I am the last godless one,
And on that I stand.

5 If I tense my jaw,
It's not easy to knock me down:
The black intoxication of atheism
Is in my blood, in my bones,

For the sake of honor and conscience
10 I thought to live, without sinning,
All the same with grace
My soul has failed to meet.

But my verse no way
Will I exchange for a psalm,
15 And my own thing I'll cuckoo
At the earth's limit.

...From the indisputable fundamentals
The times have moved away.
I'm the last godless one,
20 Don't be sorry for me.

1986

29 Свобода

Не готов я к свободе,
По своей ли вине?
Ведь свободы в заводе
Не бывало при мне.

5 Никакой мой прапрадед
И ни прадед, ни дед
Не молил Христа ради:
«Дай, подай!»
Видел: нет.

10 Что такое свобода?
Это кладезь утех?
Или это забота
О себе после всех?

Неподъемное счастье,
15 Сбросив зависть и спесь,
Распахнуть душу настежь,
А в чужую не лезть.

Океаны здесь пота,
Гималаи труда!
20 Да она несвободы
Тяжелее куда.

Я ведь ждал ее тоже
Столько долгих годов,
Ждал до боли, до дрожи,
25 А пришла—не готов.

1987

30 Молодая поэзия

Поэзия молодая,
Тебя еще нет почти,
Но славу тебе воздали,
Не медля, твои вожди.

29 Freedom

I'm not ready for freedom,
Is it my fault?
After all, freedom's never been the custom
In my time.

5 No great-great-grandfather of mine,
Nor great-grandfather, nor grandfather
Ever prayed for the sake of Christ:
"Give it, give!"
He saw [the answer was] no.

10 What is freedom?
Is it a well of pleasures?
Or is it being concerned
About yourself after everyone else?

It's happiness beyond reckoning—
15 Having cast off envy and conceit,
To open wide your own soul
And not poke into other people's.*

Oceans of sweat here,
Himalayas of labor!
20 And it's far more difficult
Than unfreedom.

I was waiting for it too, you know,
So many long years,
Waiting so long, I felt pain and trembling;
25 Now it's come, I'm not ready.

1987

30 Young Poetry*

Young poetry,
You hardly exist yet,
But you've been glorified
Without delay, by your leaders.

5 И те, лет кому семнадцать,
Кому восемнадцать зим,
Уверены: все—эрзацы,
И надо дерзать самим.

И надо смахнуть с насеста
10 Заевшихся стариков,
Преемственность и наследство,
И прочую смерть стихов.

Тут сразу без сиволдая
Закружится голова.
15 Поэзия молодая,
Наверное, ты права.

Но нынче поменьше к лире
Приставлено сторожей,
И ей одиноко в мире,
20 Свободнее и страшней.

И душу ободрить сиру
Пред волею и бедой
Навряд ли сейчас под силу
Поэзии молодой.

1987

31 Рифма

Не владею белым стихом
Для себя, для своей работы.
Белый стих пополам с грехом
Истребляю на переводы.

5 Белый стих меня не берет
Ни в балладах, ни даже в песнях,
Не познал я его высот,
Не гулял в его тайных безднах.

Помню, в молодости с тоской,
10 Ошалелый и оробелый,

5 And people aged about seventeen
Or who've eighteen winters behind them
Are convinced: everything's ersatz,
And one has to dare oneself.

And one must sweep off their perches
10 The old men spoiled with good food,
Continuity and inheritance,
And other such death to verse.

At this point straightaway without hooch
Your head starts to spin.
15 Young poetry,
You're probably right.

But these days the lyre has fewer
Watchmen posted around it,
And the lyre feels alone in the world,
20 Freer, and more scared.

And to cheer up the desolate soul
In the face of liberty and misfortune
Is hardly likely to be within the power
Of young poetry.

1987

31 Rhyme

I can't manage blank verse
For myself, for my work.
Blank verse I force myself
to do to death on translations.

5 Blank verse doesn't get me
Either in ballads or even in songs,
I've not discovered its heights
Nor wandered in its secret depths.

I remember that in my youth, with anguish
10 Going crazy and made shy,

Я глядел, как наставник мой
Километры гнал пены белой.

Этих тысяч двенадцать строк,
А быть может, еще поболе,
15 Я без рифмы жевать не мог,
Как жевать не могу без соли.

...Рифма, ты ерунда, пустяк,
Ты из малостей—микромалость,
Но стиха без тебя никак,
20 Хоть зубри, не запоминалось.

Рифма, ты и соблазн и сглаз,
Ты соблазном и сглазом сразу
Отравляешь лирикой нас,
И несем ее, как заразу.

25 Рифма, нет на тебе креста,
Ты придумана сатаною,
Но и жизнь без тебя пуста,
Хоть намучаешься с тобою.

32 Два жанра

О. Е.

Отчего отстает поэзия?
От чего отстает она?
Да и что ее бесполезнее
В переломные времена?

5 Получается, будто истина
От стиха, как жена ушла,
А талантлива публицистика
И воинственно-весела!

Это радостно! Это правильно!
10 Вот кто нашу спасет страну!
А поэзия неприкаянно
Прозевала свою страду.

I watched my tutor
Crank out kilometers of white foam.*

These twelve thousand or so lines,
And perhaps even more,
15 I couldn't chew without rhyme,
Just as I can't chew without salt.

…Rhyme, you're nonsense, an empty thing,
A microtrifle of trifles,
But verse without you no way,
20 Though you can study hard, will be remembered.

Rhyme, you're temptation and the evil eye,
With temptation and the evil eye straight off
You poison us with lyricism,
And we carry it like an infection.

25 Rhyme, you don't wear the cross,*
You were devised by Satan,
But life itself is empty without you,
Though one tortures oneself sick with you.

32 Two Genres

To O. E.

Why has poetry fallen behind?
Behind what has it fallen?
Anyway, what's more useless than it
At a turning point in time?

5 It turns out that it's as if truth
Has left poetry, like a wife leaves,
And writing on current affairs is talented
And militantly joyful!

This is cheering! This is correct!
10 Here's who will save our country!
But poetry like a lost soul
Has missed its harvest time.

Публицистика рушит надолбы,
Настилает по топям гать,
15 А поэзии думать надобно,
Как от вечности не отстать.

1988

33 Спор

В спор не надобно кидаться,
Без него поймешь:
Родина и государство—
Не одно и то ж.

5 Присягнув гербу и флагу,
Не затянешь гимн,
И в атаку, и на плаху
Не пойдешь с таким.

Родина—любовь и память,
10 Проза, стих и песнь...
Много мог еще добавить,
Места нету здесь.

А еще—овраг и поле,
Роща и река,
15 А еще—тоска и воля,
Воля да тоска.

Только больше неохота
Зря словами трясть.
Родина—всегда свобода,
20 Государство—власть.

1988

Current affairs writing breaks down obstacles,
Lays a log road over the swamps,
15 But poetry ought to be thinking
How not to fall behind eternity.

1988

33 An Argument

No need to rush into an argument,
You can understand without one:
Motherland and state
Are not the same thing.

5 When you take the oath to arms and flag
You don't start singing the anthem.
Neither into the attack, nor onto the scaffold
Would you go with a thing like that.

The Motherland is love and memory,
10 Prose, verse, and song...
Much more could be added,
There's no space here.

It's ravine and field too,
Grove and river,
15 It's longing and liberty too,
Liberty and longing.

Only I've no further desire
To spin words for nothing.
Motherland is always freedom,
20 State is authority.

1988

34

Оттого, что дела никакого
Нету никому ни до кого,
Стало тускло, холодно и голо,
Как в кино, где кончилось кино.

5 Где подруги, добрые, как феи,
На звонок спешащие друзья?
Всем уже до лампочки, до фени,
Даже и поплакаться нельзя.

Жизнь осиротела, оскудела,
10 Вымерзла, как сельское кино,
Оттого, что никакого дела
Нету никому ни до кого.

1990

34

Because nobody cares
About anybody,
It's got dull, cold, and bare
Like in a movie house where the movie's over.

5 Where are the girlfriends, kind as fairies,
The friends who come in a hurry when you call?
None of them gives a hoot or a cuss,
You can't even weep.

Life's been orphaned and grown thin,
10 Frozen to death like the village movie house;
Because nobody cares
About anybody.

1990

Герман Плисецкий

35 Кустари

Им истина светила до зари
в сыром углу, в чахоточном подвале.
Шли на толкучку утром кустари
и за бесценок душу продавали.

5 У перекупщиков был острый глаз.
Был спрос на легковесных и проворных.
Бездарный, но могущественный класс
желал иметь талантливых придворных.

И тот, кто половчей, и тот, кто мог—
10 тот вскоре ездил в золотой карете.
И, опускаясь, дохли у дорог
к подделкам не способные калеки.

О, сколько мыслей их потом взошло,
наивных мыслей, орошенных кровью!
15 Но это все потом произошло,
уже за рамками средневековья.

36

Приснился мне город, открытый весне,
и ты подошла к телефону во сне.

Звонил я, как прежде, из будки с угла,
но ты ничего разобрать не могла.

German Plisetsky

35 The Handicraftsmen

Truth shone for them before dawn
in damp corners, in tubercular basements.
Then the handicraftsmen went off to the fleamarket
and sold their souls for a song.

5 The second-hand dealers had a sharp eye.
There was a demand for those who were lightweight and adroit.
The ungifted but mighty class
wished to have talented courtiers.

And he who was more smart, and he who was able
10 were soon riding in golden carriages.
And, losing heart, there died by the roadsides
the cripples who were incapable of making fakes.

Oh, how many of their thoughts later rose up,
naive thoughts bathed in blood!
15 But all that happened later on,
beyond the borders of the middle ages.

36

I dreamed of a city open to the springtime,
and you came to the phone in my dream.

I was calling like I used to from the box on the corner,
but you couldn't make out anything.

5 Твой голос, ослабленный дальностью лет,
«Нажмите на кнопку!»—давал мне совет.

А я все кричал, задыхаясь: «Прости!»,
над сломанной трубкой сосулькою стыл.

И с крыш, и с ресниц на подушку текло,
10 и звонкой монетой стучали в стекло.

Меня торопили, и не было сил
припомнить: за что ж я прощенья просил...

37 Филармония

Одинокие женщины ходят в концерты,
как в соборы ходили—молиться.
Эти белые лица в партере—как в церкви,
как в минуту любви—обнаженные лица.

5 И еще туда ходят рыцари долга,
в гардеробе снимают доспехи,
и ничтожными кажутся ненадолго
деловые дневные успехи.

Среди буйных голов, на ладони упавших,
10 среди душ, превратившихся в уши,
узнаю Прометеев, от службы уставших,
и Джульетт, обращенных в старушек.

Это музыка—опытный реставратор—
прожитое снимает пластами,
15 открывает героев, какими когда-то
стать могли и какими не стали.

Здесь не надо затверженного мажора,
здесь высокой трагедии мера.
Поддержите, крылатые дирижеры,
20 эту взлетную тягу партера!

5 Your voice, made weak by the far distance of years,
kept advising me: "Press the button!"

But I kept on yelling, short of breath, "Forgive me!"
Growing stiff as an icicle over the broken receiver.

It was pouring from roofs and eyelashes onto the pillow,
10 while people knocked on the glass with ringing coins.

I was being hurried, and I hadn't the strength
to remember what I was asking forgiveness for...

37 The Philharmonic

Lonely women go to concerts
like they used to go to cathedrals, to pray.
These white faces in the stalls are—like in church,
like in the moment of love—naked faces.

5 And also go there the knights of duty,
they take off their armor in the vestibule,
and for a short while seem not to matter
their successes of the day in business.

Among the luxuriant heads dropped into palms,
10 among the souls which have turned into ears,
I recognize Prometheuses tired from their work,
and Juliets converted into old women.

It's music—that expert restorer—
that removes in layers what's been lived through,
15 and uncovers the heroes that once upon a time
we could have become, but didn't.

Here no well-rehearsed major key is needed,
here we have the measure of high tragedy.
Winged conductors, uphold
20 this thrust to ascend that's in the stalls!

38 Мертвый час

Больничных корпусов каре.
На окнах шторы выгорают.
На солнцепеке во дворе
две девочки в пинг-понг играют.

5 Дрожит за окнами жара,
все в мареве—как будто снится.
Мелькают посреди двора
два лоскута цветного ситца.

Спит населенье мертвым сном.
10 В живых—одни девчонки эти.
Их шарик, точно метроном,
стучит на вымершей планете.

39

Ты не ревнуй меня к словам,
к магическим «тогда» и «там»,
которых не застала.
Ложится в строфы хорошо
5 лишь то, что навсегда прошло,
прошло—и словом стало.

Какой внутриутробный срок
у тех или у этих строк—
родители не знают.
10 Слова, которые болят,
поставить точку не велят
и в строчку не влезают.

Прости меня, что я молчу.
Я просто слышать ночь хочу
15 сквозь толщину бетона.
Я не отсутствую, я весь
впервые без остатка здесь,
впервые в жизни—дома.

38 Quiet Hour

A square inside hospital blocks.
On the windows the shutters are burning up.
In the sun's heat in the yard
two girls are playing ping-pong.

5 The heat trembles outside the windows,
everything's in heat haze, as if you were dreaming it.
A glimpse in the middle of the square
of two pieces of colored cotton cloth.

The inhabitants sleep the sleep of the dead.
10 Alive are only these little girls.
Their ball, like a metronome,
clicks on the extinct planet.

39

Don't be jealous of my words,
the magic "then" and "there"
that you missed.
Into stanzas lies down well
5 only that which has gone forever,
gone—and become a word.

What is the term inside the womb
of these lines or those—
the parents don't know.
10 Words that are still painful
forbid you to put a full stop
and they won't fit into the line.

Forgive me for being silent.
I just want to hear the night
15 through the thickness of concrete.
I'm not somewhere else, I'm completely
for the first time here without anything left over,
for the first time in my life at home.

Прости меня. Я просто так.
20 Я просто слушаю собак,
бездомных, полуночных.
Я просто слушаю прибой,
шумящий вокруг нас с тобой
в кварталах крупноблочных...

40

Уснули мы, обняв друг друга.
Устав любить, уснули мы
внутри магического круга,
в дремучих зарослях зимы.

5 Я спал—и ты меня касалась,
но остывал угольев жар.
Одна зола в душе осталась.
Остался лишь вороний кар.

Как будто черные старухи:
10 «Прощай! Прощай! Прощай!»—кричат
среди войны, среди разрухи,
где остовы печей торчат...

41

Разбудил меня грохот на крыше:
лист железа от ветра гремел.
Между шкафом и полками, в нише
ужас прятался белый, как мел.

5 Будто кто-то родной помирает
в темной комнате рядом с тобой.
Будто хрупкую жизнь попирает
великан многотонной стопой.

И мерещилось мне, что планета—
10 мертвый мир, позабытый людьми,
что не будет теперь ни рассвета,
ни зеленой листвы, ни любви.

Forgive me. It's nothing special.
20 I'm just listening to the dogs,
homeless, of the midnight.
I'm just listening to the tide
that sounds around you and me
in the big-towered blocks...

40

We fell asleep, embracing each other.
Tired with loving, we fell asleep
inside a magic circle,
in the dense thickets of winter.

5 I was sleeping, and you were touching me,
but the heat of the coals had died down.
Only ashes remained in my soul.
Only the crow's croak remained.

As if black old women were calling
10 "Goodbye! Goodbye! Goodbye!"
amidst war, amidst devastation,
where the shells of stoves stick out...

41

I was awoken by thundering noise on the roof:
a sheet of iron was rattling in the wind.
Between the wardrobe and the shelves, in the niche
hid a horror white as chalk.

5 As if someone close to you were dying
in the dark room next to you.
As if frail life were being trampled
by a giant with feet weighing many tons.

And I imagined that the planet
10 was a dead world, forgotten by people,
that now there would be no dawn,
no green leaves, no love.

Что сомкнуть пересохшие очи
мне не даст ни сегодня, ни впредь
15 металлический грохот средь ночи,
равномерный и твердый, как смерть.

42 Натюрморт

О, рыбные прилавки давних лет!
Нежнейшей семги декадентский цвет,
копченой осетрины дух, и спины
лоснящейся, атласной лососины...

5 Что говорить о поколенье новом
с его тоскою о филе тресковом?
Пенсионеров детская игра:
какая сколько стоила икра?

А запахи в селедочном отделе!
10 Залом, дебелый, словно баба в теле,
аристократка—керченская сельдь:
разок отведать—а потом на смерть!

О крабах в банках говорить не стану.
Но повторять до смерти не устану
15 слова, что в ранней юности постиг:
форель, стерлядка, нельма, омуль, сиг!

Те рыбы, как и раки-раскоряки,
остались лишь, как знаки в Зодиаке.

Я вспоминаю, а не протестую.
20 Селедочницу, уж давно пустую,
своей рукой убрал я со стола...
Все миновалось. Молодость прошла.

To close my dried-up eyes
would not allow me, today or henceforth,
15 this metallic thundering in the night,
even-paced and steadfast as death.

42 Still Life

Oh, the fish counters of years long gone by!
The decadent color of the most tender salmon,
the scent of smoked sturgeon, the backs
of glistening, satin salmon flesh...

5 What to say about the new generation
with its nostalgia for cod fillets?
The childish game of pensioners:
how much did which kind of caviar cost?

And the smells in the sardine department!
10 The plump Caspian herring, like a buxom woman,
that aristocrat, the Kerch herring:
taste it once, and die!

About tinned crab I won't say anything.
But I'll never tire of repeating until I die
15 words that I grasped in my youth:
trout, sterlet, char, omul,* whitefish!

These fish, just like the bowlegged crab,
only remain as signs of the zodiac.

I'm remembering, not protesting.
20 The herring dish, long now empty,
with my own hand I cleared from the table...
Everything's past. Youth has gone by.*

43

Стоять с утра в хвосте за *Огоньком*,
потом стоять в хвосте за коньяком,
перекрывая стойкости рекорды,
а выстояв, отгадывать кроссворды:
5 по вертикали—Чехова рассказ,
река в Европе—по горизонтали...
Едва ль годится «Человек в футляре».
Но Стикс подземный подойдет как раз.

Ты, летописец временных годов,
10 послушный с детства кличу «Будь готов!»—
всегда готов стоять в строю по росту.
Но вот вопрос: готов ли ты к сиротству?
Готов ли ты к утратам, как Иов?

44 Сонет

Б. Слуцкому

Когда русская муза ушла в перевод
(кто—на Запад, а кто—на Восток),
не заметил утраты российский народ,
но заметил всевидящий Бог.

5 Да и то: на колхозных полях недород—
это отнятый хлеба кусок.
А на ниве поэзии—наоборот:
Данте, он и по-русски высок.

Ну и что, коль чужбина иссушит мозги?
10 Ведь и дома не видно ни зги
(между нами, бродягами, говоря)!

А вообще-то, как ни крути,
под тосканское вечное небо уйти
предпочтительней, чем в лагеря.

43

To stand in line from early morning for *Ogonek*,*
then stand in line for cognac,
breaking endurance records,
and then to try and solve the crossword:
5 down: a story by Chekhov,
across: a river in Europe…
"The Man in the Box" will hardly do.
But the subterranean Styx is just right.

You, chronicler of times that were,*
10 obedient from childhood to the watchword "Be Prepared,"*
are always prepared to stand in formation by height.
But here's the question: are you prepared for orphanhood?
Are you prepared for losses, like Job?

44 Sonnet

To B. Slutsky*

When the Russian muse went off into translation
(some went West, and some went East),
the Russian people didn't notice the loss,
but all-seeing God did notice.

5 That's just it: harvest failure in the kolkhoz fields
is a crust of bread taken away.
But on the cornfield of poetry, it's the opposite:
Dante is the tops in Russian as well.

So what, if abroad dries up their brains?
10 After all, here at home you can't see a thing
(between us, us bums, be it said)!

But all in all, no matter which way you look at it,
to go off to beneath the eternal Tuscan sky
is preferable to going off to the camps.

Евгений Рейн

45 Монастырь

Как Волги вал белоголовый
Доходит целый к берегам!
                    Н. Языков

За станцией «Сокольники», где магазин мясной
И кладбище раскольников, был монастырь мужской.
Руина и твердыня, развалина, гнилье—
В двадцатые пустили строенье под жилье.
5 Такую коммуналку теперь уж не сыскать.
Зачем я переехал, не стану объяснять.
Я, загнанный, опальный, у жизни на краю
Сменял там отпевальню на комнату свою...
Шел коридор верстою, и сорок человек,
10 Как улицей Тверскою, ходили целый день.
Там газовые плиты стояли у дверей.
Я был во всей квартире единственный еврей.
Там жили инвалиды, ночные сторожа,
И было от пол-литра так близко до ножа.
15 И все-таки при этом, когда она могла,
С участьем и приветом там наша жизнь текла.
Там зазывали в гости, делилися рублем,
Там были сплетни, козни, как в обществе любом.
Но было состраданье, не холили обид...
20 Напротив жил Адамов, хитрющий инвалид.
Стучал он рано утром мне в стенку костылем,
Входил, обрубком шарил под письменным столом,
Где я держал посуду кефира и вина—
Бутылку на анализ просил он у меня.
25 И я давал бутылки и мелочь иногда,
И уходил Адамов. А рядом занята
Рассортировкой семги, надкушенных котлет,

Evgenii Rein

45 The Monastery

> ...as the white-headed Volga wave
> Comes in entire to its shores!
>> N. Yazykov

Behind Sokolniki metro station, where there's a meat shop
And an Old Believer cemetery, there was a monastery for men.
A ruin and a fortress, a wreck, decayed,
In the 1920s it was made into accommodation.
5 You couldn't find a communal dwelling like that these days.
Why I moved in there I won't start to explain.
Oppressed, in disfavor, on the edge of life
I made the funeral chapel my room...
The corridor was one verst long, and forty people
10 Walked along it every day, like along Tverskaya Street.
Gas stoves stood by the doors,
I was the only Jew in the whole building.
Invalids lived there, and night watchmen,
And it was not far from half a bottle of vodka to a knife fight.
15 And all the same, whenever it could
Our life flowed along with people to listen and make you welcome.
There, guests were invited in, a ruble shared,
There, there was gossip, practical jokes, like in any group of people.
There was compassion, no one nurtured offense...
20 Opposite me lived Adamov, an incredibly sly cripple.
Early in the morning he would knock on my wall with his crutch,
Come in, rummage around with his stump under the writing table,
Where I kept containers for kefir and drink—
He would ask me for a bottle to take for analysis.
25 And I would give him a bottle and sometimes some small change,
And Adamov would leave. And next door would be busy—with
Sorting out salmon, cutlets with bites out of them,

Закусок и ватрушек, в неполных двадцать лет
Официантка Зоя, мать темных близнецов.
30 За нею жил расстрига Георгий Одинцов.
Служил он в гардеробе издательства Гослит
И был в литературе изрядно знаменит.
Он Шолохова видел, он Пастернака знал,
Он с нобелевских премий на водку получал,
35 Он Юрию Олеше галоши подавал,
Но я-то знал: он тайно крестил и отпевал.
Но дело не в соседях, типаж тут не при чем—
Кто эту жизнь отведал, тот знает, что - почем.
Почем бутылка водки и чистенький гальюн.
40 А то, что люди волки, сказал латинский лгун.
Они не волки. Что же? Я не пойму, Бог весть.
Но я бы мог такие свидетельства привесть,
Что обломал бы зубы и лучший богослов.
И все-таки спасибо за все, за хлеб и кров
45 Тому, кто назначает нам пайку и судьбу,
Тому, кто обучает бесстыдству и стыду,
Кто учит нас терпенью и душу каменит,
Кто учит просто пенью и пенью аонид,
Тому, кто посылает нам дом или развал
50 И дальше посылает белоголовый вал.

46 Сосед Григорьев

Нас двое в пустынной квартире,
Затерянной в третьем дворе.
Пока я бряцаю на лире,
Он роется в календаре
5 Где все еще свежие краски
И чьи-то пометки видны,
Но это касается русско-
японской забытой войны.
Ему уже за девяносто.
10 Куда его жизнь занесла!
Придворного орденоносца
И крестик его «Станислав».
Придворным он был ювелиром
Низложен он был в Октябре.
15 Нас двое, а наша квартира
Затеряна в третьем дворе.

Snacks and cheese pasties—not twenty years old
Waitress Zoya, the mother of dusky twins.
30 Beyond her lived the unfrocked priest Georgii Odintsov.
He worked in the cloakroom of the Goslit* publisher
And was exceedingly well known in literature.
He had seen Sholokhov, known Pasternak,
Had been given vodka money that came from Nobel Prizes,
35 He'd handed Yurii Olesha* his galoshes.
But *I* knew that in secret he baptized and buried people.
But it's not a matter of neighbors, this range of characters doesn't count—
Anyone who has tasted this life knows what's what.
What price a bottle of vodka and a nice clean john.
40 And some Latin liar said that people are wolves.
They aren't wolves. What? I don't get it, God knows.
But I could give such testimony
That even the best theologian would break his teeth.
And all the same, thank you for everything—for bread and a roof over my
    head
45 To the one who gives us our rations and fate,
The one who instructs us in shamelessness and shame,
Who teaches us tolerance and hardens our souls,
Who teaches ordinary singing and the song of the Aonides,
The one who sends us our house or our ruin
50 And sends on its way the white-headed wave.

46 My Neighbor Grigoriev

There were two of us in this derelict apartment,
Forsaken on the third courtyard [from the street].
While I twang my lyre,
He rummages in a calendar
5 Where there are still fresh colors
And someone's annotations to be seen,
But this is to do with the Russo-
Japanese forgotten war.
He's past ninety.
10 Where has life brought him to!
This courtier with his decoration
and his "Stanislav" cross.
He used to be the court jeweler,
He was deposed in October.
15 There's two of us, and our apartment
is forsaken on the third courtyard.

А он еще помнит заказы
К светлейшему дню именин,
Он помнит большие алмазы
20 И руки великих княгинь.
Он тайные помнит подарки,
Эмаль и лазурь на гербах,
И странные помнит помарки
На девятизначных счетах.
25 Когда он, глухой, неопрятный,
Идет, спотыкаясь, в сортир,
Из гроба встает император,
А с ним и его ювелир.
И тяжко ему. Но полегче
30 Вздыхает забытый сосед,
Когда нам приносят повестки
На выборы в суд и Совет.

Я славлю Тебя, Государство!
Твой счет без утрат и прикрас,
35 Твое золотое упрямство,
С которым ты помнишь о нас.

47 Кот на причале гавани в Ленинграде

Швед «Королевский Одиссей»[1]
прилип к заливу,
на что ленивый котофей
глядит брезгливо.
5 Он вылез нынче из таких
глухих подвалов,
что шведский флаг поник и стих,
как в девять баллов.
Выходят леди, буржуа,
10 посол Гвинеи.
Кот жаждет только барыша,
да поскорее.
Ему ни «Мальборо», ни джин,
ни героинчик,
15 и больше не смягчает сплин,
увы, графинчик.
Кусок заморской колбасы
иль отбивную
у пограничной полосы

But he can still remember orders placed
For the most august name day,
He can remember big diamonds
20 And the hands of the Grand Princesses.
He can remember secret gifts,
Enamel and azure on the coats of arms
And he can remember the strange markings
On accounts in nine figures.
25 When he, deaf and unkempt
Goes stumbling to the john,
From his coffin rises the emperor*
And with him his jeweler.
It's hard for him. But easier
30 Sighs my forgotten neighbor
When they bring us the papers
For elections to law court and Soviet.

I sing Thy praises, O State!
Thy counting without losses and embellishments,
35 Thy golden obstinacy,
With which Thou remembers us.

47 The Tomcat by the Quay in Leningrad Harbor

The Swede "Royal Odysseus"[1]
stuck close to the gulf
and at it this lazy puss
looks fastidiously.
5 He's just come up from such
far distant cellars
that the Swedish flag drooped and grew still
as in a force 9 wind.
A lady emerges, a bourgeois,
10 and the ambassador of Guinea.
The tomcat only wants some loot
and fast.
He doesn't want Marlboros, nor gin,
nor heroin,
15 and the decanter, alas,
no longer softens his spleen.
A piece of overseas sausage
or a chop
by the borderline

20 стоит, взыскуя.
За что нам котю укорить
среди хворобы,
теперь его должна кормить
рука Европы.
25 Глядит на бело-голубой
всесветный лайнер,
кивает умной головой
на трап, на мрамор.
Потом опять во тьму, в подвал,
30 мышам на горе.
Он так доволен—побывал
в открытом море.

1. Шведский лайнер в ленинградской гавани

48 На полях книги В. Ходасевича

> И мне давно являться начал
> совсем другой автомобиль.
> В. Х.

Москвы ночная панорама,
высотки красные огни
все мне мерещится упрямо
в больничные пустые дни.
5 Еще вчера, еще сегодня
глядел на пестрый семафор,
но быстрая сманила сводня—
загнала в этот коридор.
Мое окно висит над моргом,
10 и, приглядевшись, узнаю
в расположенье полумертвом
Психею грязную мою.
Она лежит, и кепка сбита,
и достает сержант планшет.
15 Была на ощупь дверь открыта,
упала, не вошла, о нет.
Еще ей здесь по грубым лавкам,
еще ей здесь по площадям
шататься под закатом плавким,
20 гнить с требухою пополам.
Она поднимется в подтеках
мазутной лужи городской.

20 he stands searching for.
Why should we reproach this tomcat
among this sickness,
for now he should be fed
by the hand of Europe.
25 He looks at the white and sky-blue
radiant liner,
and nods his wise head
at the gangway and the marble.
Then once more into the darkness, the cellar,
30 grief to the mice.
He's so content; he's spent some time
on the open sea.

1. A Swedish liner in Leningrad Harbor.

48 In the Margins of a Book by V. Khodasevich*

> Long since there began to appear to me
> A car of quite a different sort.
> > V. Kh.

The nocturnal panorama of Moscow,
the red lights of a tall building
still stubbornly I seem to see
during these empty hospital days.
5 Just yesterday, just today
I was still looking at those multicolored lights,
but a deft procuress tempted me
and chased me into this corridor.
My window hangs above the morgue,
10 and as my eyes become accustomed I recognize
in the half-dead arrangement of things
my dirty Psyche.
She lies there, her cap knocked off,
and the police sergeant reaches for his notebook.
15 The door was open to the touch,
but she fell down, didn't come in, oh no.
She will still among these coarse shops,
she will still among these squares
have to stagger along beneath the liquid sunset,
20 to rot along with the offal.
She will rise stained
by an oily urban puddle.

Она наплачется в упреках,
заноет с болью и тоской.
25 Пока она не проглядела
безумного грузовика
и Владиславу не успела
сказать, к чему была близка.

49 Посвящается станциям метро Кировская-Радиальная и Парк культуры-Кольцевая

Апреля сиротская глина
Обмажет подошвы твои.
Рассыпься, моя дисциплина!
Не мучь, не мути, не дави!

5 Под хладный кирпич пятилеток
Спускаюсь в могилу метро.
Как хочется, чтоб напоследок
Мне стало светло и тепло.

О, сколько же выпало дальней
10 И бедной судьбы кочевой
До смерти моей радиальной,
По жизни моей кольцевой.

Хватило на долгие годы
Всего, чтобы мне ошалеть.
15 И не было только свободы.
О ней и не стоит жалеть.

Не стоит рыдать и браниться,
Бросать грязноватый кулак.
Свобода—свободная птица,
20 Ее не прокормишь никак.

Тем более в комнатах наших
Замучены сном и трудом,
Мы ей надавали пятнашек
И руки умыли потом.

She will weep her reproaches
and moan with pain and anxiety.
25 Until she has made out the shape
of that insane truck,
and managed to tell Vladislav
what she was intimate with.

49 Dedicated to the Metro Stations
Kirovskaya (Radial Line) and
Park of Culture and Rest (Circle Line)

The orphan clay of April
Will coat your soles.
Fall apart, my discipline!
Don't torture me, confuse me, oppress me!

5 Beneath the cold brick of the Five-Year Plans
I go down into the tomb of the Metro.
How much I want things as a result
to get bright and warm for me.

Oh, how long and how poor a vagabond fate
10 has come my way
Before my radial line death
During my circle line life.

There's been enough for many long years
Of everything, enough to drive me crazy.
15 The only thing there hasn't been is freedom.
It's not worth regretting it.

It's not worth sobbing and cursing,
Brandishing a grubby fist.
Freedom is a free bird,
20 And there's no way to teach it to feed.

All the more so that in our rooms
Tormented by dream and toil,
We've played enough games of tag with it
And then washed our hands.

25 И вот, от размокшей землицы
    Спасаясь в московском метро,
    Глядите, глядите на лица:
    Все кончено, ясно, мертво.

50 «Ночной дозор»

    У «Ночного дозора» я стоял три минуты,
    и сигнал загудел, изгоняя туристов.
    Я бежал, я споткнулся о чекан Бенвенуто,
    растолкал итальянок в голландских батистах.
5 Что-то мне показалось, что-то мне показалось,
    что все это за мной, и мой ордер подписан,
    и рука трибунала виска мне касалась,
    и мой труп увозили в пакгаузы к крысам.
    Этот вот капитан—это Феликс Дзержинский,
10 этот в черном камзоле, это—Генрих Ягода.
    Я безумен? О нет. Даже не одержимый,
    я задержанный только с тридцать пятого года.
    Кто дитя в кринолине? Это дочка Ежова?
    А семит на коленях? Это Блюмкин злочастный?
15 Подведите меня к этой стенке, и снова
    я увижу ее и кирпичной и красной.
    Заводите везде грузовые моторы,
    пусть наганы гремят от Гааги до Рима,
    это вы виноваты, ваши переговоры
20 словно пули в «десятку»—«молоко» или мимо.
    И когда в Бенилюксе запотевшее пиво
    проливается в остром креветочном хламе,
    засыпайте в ячменном отпаде глумливо.
    Ничего. ВЧК наблюдает за вами.
25 Вас разбудят приклады «Ночного дозора»,
    эти дьяволы выйдут однажды из рамы.
    Это было вчера и сегодня и скоро...
    И тогда мы откроем углы пентаграммы.

51 Под гербами

    Все сбывается: тент и стакан «Хайнекена»,
    и хмельная ухмылка того манекена,
    что глядит на меня из соседнего «шопа»,

25 And so, as from the sodden soil
　You seek refuge in the Moscow Metro,
　Look, look at the faces:
　Everythings's finished, clear, dead.

50 "The Night Watch"

　I had been standing by "The Night Watch"* three minutes
　when the buzzer went to chase the tourists away.
　I ran, bumping against Benvenuto's armor,
　pushing aside Italian women in Dutch batiste.
5 Somehow it seemed to me, somehow it seemed to me
　that all this was after me, and the order for my arrest had been signed,
　the tribunal's hand was touching my temple,
　and my corpse was being carted out to the rats in the warehouses.
　That captain there is Feliks Dzerzhinsky,*
10 That one in the black surcoat is Genrikh Yagoda.*
　Am I out of my mind? O no. I'm not even possessed,
　I've been detained only since 1935.
　Who is the child in the crinoline? Is it Yezhov's* daughter?
　And the Semite on his knees? Is it Blyumkin* of evil memory?
15 Lead me up to this wall, and once more
　I'll see it brick and bloody.
　Start up everywhere the motors of the trucks,
　let the pistols thunder from The Hague to Rome.
　You are to blame, your negotiations
20 are like bullets aimed at the bull's-eye but going into the white or past.
　And when in the Benelux countries the sweating beer
　is poured out among the pungent remains of prawns,
　go to sleep mockingly in the barleycorn fallout.
　Don't worry. The VChK* is looking after you.
25 You'll be woken up by the rifle butts of "The Night Watch,"
　these devils one day will come out of their frame.
　It happened yesterday, and today, and soon...
　And then we will open the corners of the pentagram.

51 Beneath the Coats of Arms

　Everything's coming true: awning, glass of Heineken,
　and the boozy grin on that tailor's dummy
　that's looking at me from the shop next door,

невезуха, разруха, Россия, Европа...
5 Вот на ратуше блещут гербы Роттердама,
отчего ж я теперь повторяю упрямо:
«Ничего не хочу, не умею, не надо».
Невезуха, разруха, блокада, досада.
Все верните, проклятые демоны суток,
10 обновите мне плоть, обманите рассудок,
пусть покроются коркой рубцы и стигматы.
Боже, Боже, ты видишь, мы не виноваты!
Дайте мне ленинградскую вонь продувную,
отведите меня на Фонтанку в пивную,
15 пусть усядутся Дима, и Толя, и Ося.
И тогда я скажу: «Удалось, удалося!»
Будь ты проклята, девка, тоска и отрава,
моя вечность налево, твоя вечность направо.
Так подскажем друг другу кое-что по секрету,
20 поглядим на прощанье за Мойку, за Лету,
за толпу серафимов, Магомета и Будду.
Ты меня не забудешь, я тебя не забуду.
Там, за временем вечным, за эйнштейновым мраком,
всякий снова хорош и нескладен и лаком
25 на последнее слово, что молвить негоже,
на движок первопутка, что проходит по коже.

52 Перед Пасхой

Пасмурный день над кудрявым морем.
Отдохнем. Отменяются все затеи.
Перед обедом руки умоем
вслед за прокуратором Иудеи.
5 Понимаю, что это пошлая шутка,
но в пошлой шутке—пошлая правда,
и она свежее, чем дохлая утка,
на газетном листе провонявшая безотрадно.
Глядя на серенькую мерлушку,
10 трудно вообразить величие Посейдона,
легче представить средненькую постирушку,
где рубахи над тазом капают учащенно.
И под эти слезы и мелкий ветер
как не вспомнить симпатичного идеалиста—
15 человек на треть или даже на четверть,
значит, это дата братоубийства.
И, конечно, самоубийства тоже,

bad luck, ruin, Russia, Europe...
5 There on the town hall gleam the arms of Rotterdam,
which is why I stubbornly say again and again:
"I want nothing, know nothing, stop it."
Bad luck, ruin, blockade, annoyance.
Give me everything back, accursed demons of the day,
10 renew my flesh, deceive my reason,
may my scars and stigmata crust over.
O God, O God, you can see that we're not to blame!
Give me that sly Leningrad stink,
take me back to that beer bar on the Fontanka,
15 let Dima,* and Tolya,* and Osya* take their seats.
And then I will say: "Success, success!"
Curse you, wench, longing and poison,
my eternity's on the left, yours on the right.
So let's whisper each other something in secret,
20 take a farewell look beyond the Moika, beyond Lethe,
beyond the crowd of seraphim, Mahomet and Buddha.
You won't forget me, I won't forget you.
There, beyond eternal time, beyond Einstein's gloom,
every man once more is good-looking, and awkward, and partial
25 to having the last word—that it's useless to utter—
and to the runner on the first snow, that passes over your skin.

52 Just before Easter

Overcast day over curly-headed sea.
Let's have a rest. All schemes canceled.
Before lunch we'll wash our hands
following the procurator of Judaea.
5 I realize that's a vulgar joke,
but in a vulgar joke is vulgar truth,
and it's fresher than the dead duck*
stinking joylessly on a sheet of newspaper.
Looking at the gray lambskin,
10 it's hard to imagine the greatness of Poseidon,
easier to imagine the average washday,
where shirts over a basin drip frequently.
And to these tears and the little breeze
how not to remember the pleasant idealist,
15 one-third a man or even one-quarter one,
that means it's the day of fratricide.
And, of course, of suicide too,

не считая расправы с отцом и духом.
И сидеть под навесом сейчас негоже,
20 хоть не сложно по гальке проехаться брюхом.
Он ведь тоже по берегу шел и видел
хлябь и твердь, парусину над серой лодкой,
значит, и он неслучайный ревнитель
вечного подвига жизни такой короткой.
25 Значит, он понял, что дальше случится—
чем замутится сияние это—
смутность и пасмурность всякой водицы
после слепящего Генисарета.

not counting reprisal against the father and spirit.
And sitting under an awning now is no good,
20 although it's not hard to ride the pebbles on your belly.
After all, he too walked along the shore and saw
the ripples and the main, canvas over a gray boat,
that means he too is no accidental amateur
of the eternal exploit of life, which is so short.
25 That means he understood what happens further on—
what was going to dull this radiance—
the dim, overcast quality of any water
after blinding Gennesaret.*

Дмитрий Бобышев

53

Мама, пишет тебе твой сын,
глядя на родину окном ночлега,
не от родины ли уплыв один
с борта Таврического ковчега.

5 У меня бесхлебная всюду хлябь,
и пируют за столом буруны.
Твой же корабль смастерен на-ять,
яблоками набиты трюмы.

Ежели не в книгу—в прибрежный гнейс
10 не строкой—собою мне впечататься завтра;
в сыне твоем, вероятно, есть
что-то от человекозавра.

Ящера выбраковал Господь.
Ты же—я верую—поймешь, дорогая,
15 что пусть отломленный я ломоть,
но—от доброго каравая!

54 Полнота всего

Вечерние чужие города,
сравнимые с пульсирующим мозгом,
который вскрыт без боли и стыда
(а кровь размыта в зареве заморском)—
5 внушают глазу выморгнуть туда,

Dmitrii Bobyshev

53

Mommy, this is your son writing to you,*
looking at his homeland through the window of his place for the night,
is not the only outflow from the homeland
from on board the Tauride ark?

5 I have a breadless ripple everywhere,
and the bow waves celebrate at the table.
But your boat is crafted down to the last detail,
its holds packed tight with apples.

If not into a book, then into the gneiss of the shoreline
10 if not with a verse line, then with myself I must imprint tomorrow;
in your son, probably, there is
something of the manosaur.

That salamander was junked by the Lord.
You, though—I believe—will understand, my dear,
15 that even though I may be a broken-off piece,
I'm still off a good loaf!

54 The Fullness of Everything

Eventide alien cities,
comparable with a pulsating brain,
that has been dissected without fear or shame
(but the blood wiped across in the overseas afterglow),
5 impel the eye to look over there,

в горючий мрак вглядевщуюся душу.
А та и рада сгинуть в новизне,
сбежать во тьму, себя саму задувши,
повыплести всю внутреннюю—вне,
10 по завиткам и выгибам воздушным.

А если и светить, то лишь едва—
летучей, эфемерной порошиной.
И—числить этажи, сиречь—слова,
не «богом из машины», а машиной,
15 сказуемой из глотки божества,

где, знаками осмысленно блистая
(сим электронным мега-языком),
горит надчеловеческая тайна,
с которой ты дикарски не знаком,
20 но силишься вписаться в начертанья.

И странно—чем вольнее мысль о ней,
чем больше от нее отнумерован,
тем сущность домышляется полней,
и кем?—тобою, трепетным нейроном
25 с обрубленной мутовкою корней.

Здесь мига не отложено до завтра...
От первых нужд, чем живо существо,
до жгучего порока и азарта—
КРОМЕШНАЯ ПРИЕМЛЕМОСТЬ ВСЕГО
30 из черепа торчит у Градозавра.

Буквально самого себя прияв,
каков ты есть, ты по такой идее
неслыханно, неоспоримо прав,
из низких и нежнейших наслаждений
35 наслаивая опыт или сплав.

Вот потому-то, жизнью в усмерть пьяный,
в разгаре неувиденного дня
прошу: да не оплакивайте в яме
Мафусаила юного, меня,
40 исполненного звуками и днями.

into the soul that has locked its gaze on the burning gloom.
But that soul is happy to perish in novelty,
to flee into the darkness, having outwitted itself,
and to splash everything that is internal onto the outside,
10 along the curlicues and convolutions of the air.

And if it is going to be light, then only a little
like flying, ephemeral spots of snow.
And to count the stories, that is to say, the words
not like a "deus ex machina" but like a machine,
15 that can be pronounced from the throat of a divinity,

where, shining meaningfully with signs
(this electronic megalanguage),
there burns a superhuman secret,
with which like a savage you're not familiar,
20 but which you strain to write yourself into its inscribings.

And it's strange: the freer is one's thought about it,
and the further one is numbered off from it,
so its essence is thought of more fully,
and as whom?—As you, a trembling neuron
25 with a severed bunch of roots.

Here, the fleeting moment is not put off until tomorrow...
From the primal needs by which an existence is alive,
to fiery vice and risk,
THE HELLISH ACCEPTABILITY OF EVERYTHING
30 sticks out from the skull of the Cityosaur.

Literally having accepted itself
the way you are, in this idea you are
unheard-ofly, unarguably right,
from the base and the most tender pleasures
35 accumulating experience or alloy.

And this is why, made dead drunk by life,
in the busiest time of an unseen day
I ask: Do not weep in the pit
for the youthful Methusalah, me,
40 who is filled with sounds and days.

55

Надо же, есть такие места,
где и животным живется спроста.

Белочке—рай, коль не схватит енот:
с груш и орехов довольно щедрот.

5 Птичий почти: полу-свист, полу-щелк
выпустив, спрятался бурундучок.

Сколько ж тут, сладких для лис, барышей:
скользких лягушей и вкусных мышей!

Знаю: запасец, запрятанный впрок,
10 есть у особенных синих сорок.

Что же до нас, что тут бродят вдвоем—
как-нибудь эдак и мы проживем.

Май 1983

56 Поминки по живым, 1

Рассказать бы простым языком
о голом комке протоплазмы,
что под галстуком и пиджаком
бьется из—, невылазный...

5 Да, и маменькин гогочка, и
злой зверек, и амеба
тычется в закоулки свои
в жажде, в общем-то праведной, млека и меда.

Больно—значит, живешь. Больно жить.
10 Иногда—интересно.
И зарубкам излюбленным (чем же еще дорожить?)
за года не стереться.

55

There surely must be such places,
where animals too have a simple life.

The squirrel's in paradise if the raccoon doesn't catch her,
for there are enough bounties from pears and nuts.

5 A bird-like almost, half-whistle, half-click
utters the chipmunk and then he's hidden himself.

How much profit to be gained is here, sweet for the vixen
slippery frogs and tasty mice!

I know that something set aside, hidden for later use
10 those special dark-blue magpies have.

And as far as we're concerned, the two of us who wander here,
somehow or other we too will survive.

May 1983

56 A Wake for the Living, 1

One should speak in simple language
about this naked lump of protoplasm,
that beneath tie and jacket
beats to get out, but cannot sortie...

5 Yes, mommy's little boy, and
the nasty little beast, and the amoeba
thrust themselves into their hideaways
in their thirst, by and large just, for milk and honey.

If it hurts, it means you're alive. It hurts to live.
10 Sometimes it's interesting.
And the beloved scars (what else should we value?)
will not wear away with the years.

Тут и случай: «До встречи Нигде».
Почему-то припомнилось Волково Поле,
15 почему-то перо—в (никогда не растил) бороде,
и—не станем додумывать боле...

И—никак, никуда, никогда:
перекресток вот эдаких, лучших
в переперченной жизни—и как ни хотелось бы—да—
20 нет, не выйдет, голубчик.

Не того ли же солнца припек
и не те ли же зги вечерами?
А, как вышло-то вовсе не так, поперек:
чтó страну, мы себя потеряли.

25 И с пробоиной в ребрах, и черпая черта бортом,
держим курс на какой-то Канопус.
Ну и что: если даже потонем, так это потом.
Раскрутили мы все-таки глобус.

Июнь 1983

57 Жизнь Урбанская, 3

А если Вену, Рим, Берлин или Париж
ты сходу про: фу-фу в воздушном перемахе,
то это место—здесь, где оду ты родишь—
    американский супермаркет.

5 Что да, то да: дают... Дрозда, и вообще!
Вот это—торжище, до горизонта—снеди:
Хеопсы разных блюд, Кавказы овощей
    под блюз, и в мыслях об обеде.

Обрызган пырсью льда, курчавится летук;
10 пучками рдятся бело-пыпочки редиски;
темнозелёно-жгуч, и злющ, и связан: лук...
    Не оду—ты, а сам: родился...

Here's the occasion, "Until we meet again Nowhere."
For some reason I remembered Volkov Field,
15 and a feather in (never grew one) my beard,
and, but let's not strain our thoughts any more...

And—no way, to nowhere, never:
are there such crossroads, the best
in one's overseasoned life, and no matter how much one would like it to be
    yes,
20 no, it won't work, old fellow.

Is it not the warmth of that same sun
and that same darkness in the evenings?
But the way it's come out all wrong, back to front:
the country, ha! It's ourselves we've lost.

25 And with bruises on our ribs, and scooping up the devil with the gunwale,
we hold our course toward some kind of Canopus.
Anyway: even if we do go down, it will be later on.
After all, we did make the globe spin.

June 1983

57 Urbana Life, 3[*]

And if Vienna, Rome, Berlin or Paris
you've skipped as you speed over them in the air,
this place, though, is here, where you will give birth to an ode,
        an American supermarket.

5 What's yes is yes, they give you...the lot, everything in general!
This is a grand trading place, with provisions to the horizon,
Cheopses of various dishes, Caucasuses of vegetables
        to the accompaniment of the blues and thoughts about dinner.

Sprinkled with tufts of ice, the leek spreads its leaves;
10 in garlands glow the white-globes of the radish;
dark-green-burning, sharp, tied up are the onions...
        it's not you giving birth to an ode
        but that you've been born yourself...

В мороз, а и в жару всегда прохладнопуз,
то—оклубничен, то—в картечинах черники,
15 с пупами-дынями здесь бабится арбуз.
   Ему и козыри—не пики.

Не вини-козыри, но кстати о вине...
Всё серебро в Шабли, а золотишко—в Рейне:
калифорнийская лоза, она вполне...
20   Сама ползет в стихотворенье.

Как с нею хороши: креветок нежный хрящ
и жирных устриц слизь, что спрыснута лимоном;
с кедровым ядрышком форель: поджар хрустящ,
   а мякоть—с розовым изломом.

25 Там пальмовы сердца секутся на куски:
где спаржи пук—Шекспир, а Пруст—ростки фасоли;
и Джойсом артишок: то иглит лепестки,
   то с маринадом расфасован.

Вот лазает в воде чудовищный омар,
30 а, скинут с кипятка, зане прекрасен витязь,
что—красен, и в броне. Крушите, стар и мал,
   с топленым маслом насладитесь!

Вон кружка: бок в росе и пена набекрень—
отрадно-горек Пабст, и Огсбургер, и Пильзень.
35 Колбасный арсенал, ветчинный потетень!
   Копченых дрынов полный список...

Но если угощать—тогда в 2 пальца стейк,
и—5 минут на сторону—на гриле...
Прости мой англицизм—я точно не из тех,
40   кто б волапюком говорили.

А просто слов таких «в забавном слоге»—нет.
По-русски ли сказать: «бифштекс» и «на мангале»?
И прыщет сок мясной, когда мы с Каберне,
   а то—с Бургундским налегаем.

45 Жизнь в общем удалась. Плесни на дно коньяк,
давай расслабимся... Теперь стихи попросим

In frost and in the heat too always cool-bellied,
sometimes strawberried and sometimes in the grape-shot of bilberries,
15 the watermelon swaps old wives' tales with the navel-melons.
      For the watermelon trumps aren't spades.

And spades aren't trumps, but while we're on the subject of wine...
All silver is in the Chablis and all gold in the Rhine wine
the Californian grape is perfectly...
20   Gets into the poem without needing help.

And so good with it are the tender cartilage of prawns
and the slime of fatty oysters, sprinkled with lemon,
the trout with its cedar speckle, crackly where it's grilled,
      its soft meat with a pink fracture.

25 There are palm hearts cut in pieces,
    where there's a bunch of asparagus, there's Shakespeare, and Proust with the
      bean shoots;
and with Joyce the artichoke, its petals needling,
      then taken apart in marinade.

And here the monstrous lobster creeping in water,
30 but thrown out of the boiling water it's still a fair warrior,
red and in armor. Crack it, young and old,
      Enjoy it with rendered butter!

Over there's a mug, flanks dewy and foam leaning over,
joyfully bitter are Pabst and Augsburger and Pilsner.
35 An arsenal of sausages, a devil-dance of hams!
      A whole inventory of smoked fingers...

And if there are guests, then it's steak two fingers thick,
and five minutes each side on the grill...
Forgive my Anglicism, I'm certainly not one of those people
40   who would like to speak Volapuk.

Words like that simply don't exist in "the amusing style."
Should one say in Russian "bifshteks" and "on the mangal"?
And the meaty juice squirts when we with Cabernet
      or with Burgundy get down to business.

45 Life on the whole's a success. Splash cognac on the bottom of the glass,
let's relax... Now we'll request some poetry

друг друга почитать.—Полцарства за коня,
      за папиросу б! Да курить я—бросил.

Urbana, Illinois, 1986

58 Звери св. Антония. Бестиарий. 17. Собственное тело

Ты—это я; но ты и тоже—скот:
от лености в крестце
          лишь убыль, убыть...
Казнь—из тебя единственный исход,
но палачем я не могу быть!

5 Я бью тебя, но больно мне.
  —Ударь, ударь, ударь!
         Ударь!
      —Нет, не ударю.
Мучитель, да,—но не вполне
подобен
тела сюзерену, государю.

10 Поскольку тело—я; но тоже—зверь,
а им не покомандуешь,
         не потиранишь...
Вот медитируешь о вечном,
      а враз—и в тело врез,
и, напоровшись, себя же протаранишь.

Нет, мясо, ты—не я,
        но ты—моя же мразь:
15 как мерзко духу знать, что тело—гадит...
А—умирать? А вот еще маразм:
в кусты гипотенузу тянет катет.

Так: тянет иль катит?
         Что за гиль!
Откуда этот вычур интеллекта?
20 У кучера ли свихнуты мозги,
конь спятил,
        или с пят сошла телега?

from each other. Half my kingdom for a horse,
        for a cigarette! But I've stopped smoking.

Urbana, Illinois, 1986

58 The Beasts of St. Antony. A Bestiary. 17. My Own Body

You are I; but you are also cattle:
from laziness in the sacrum
             there is only loss, loss...
Execution is the only way out of you,
but I cannot be an executioner!

5 I strike you, but it's me who's hurt.
Strike, strike, strike!
           Strike!
           "No, I shall not strike."
A tormentor, yes, but not entirely
similar to
the suzerain and lord of my body.

10 In as much as the body is I; but also a wild beast,
you cannot command it
         or be tyrant over it...
You're meditating on the eternal,
        instantly there's a cut to your body,
and having cut yourself open you ram yourself.

No, you meat,—you are not I,
         but you are my very own rubbish,
15 for how revolting it is for the spirit to know that the body does vile things...
And what about dying? But here's another thing to make you mad:
the cathetus drags the hypotenuse into the bushes.

Thus, does it drag or roll it?
             What nonsense!
Where does this excess of the intellect come from?
20 Has the coachman got his brains addled,
the horse stepped back,
         or has the wagon come off its heels?

Кто спит? Никто. Но раз
                    пролившись вниз,
в прах—дух кипит бродильной грязью
25 и пьяной окисью;
                    и это—жизнь,
и—крах,
когда погрязнуть угораздит...

А в том и дело, чтоб
одухотворить коснеющее тело
30 с тем, что когда его загонят
                    в гвоздеватый гроб,
оно бы чуть светлее тлело...

Ты, тело, все же я, но мы не заодно.
Зачем я горнего взыскую,
когда ты похотью и страхом сведено,
35 и тухнет пыл моей молитвы—
                    вскую?

Ты рвешься с привязи,
                    ты лязгаешь, рычишь,
болеешь блажью, жаром, гладом,
чумою, чирьями и выпаденьем грыж...
А если в здравии—
                    так дышит дух на ладан!

40 Но до того, как: «ложись и умирай»,
где место для
                    мускулистого скелета?
Конечно же, ни—Ад, ни—Рай...
А вот оно—
                    зверинец, клетка!

Who can sleep? No one. But once
                              it's coursed downward,
into the dust, the spirit seethes like mobile mud
25 and drunken oxide;
                         and this is life,
and collapse,
when it sees fit to be besmirched...

But the whole point is, so as
to spiritualize the stagnating body
30 so that when it's herded
                     into the be-nailed coffin,
it'll be a little brighter as it decomposes...

You, O body, are nevertheless I, but we're not at one.
Why do I search for the sublime
when you are gripped by lust and fear
35 and the ardor of my prayer goes rotten,
                                   whatever?

You strain at the leash,
                     you kick and snarl,
suffer from caprice, fever, hunger,
plague, boils, and hernias...
And if you're in good health,
                     the spirit has one foot in the grave!

40 But before it's a matter of "lay me down and die,"
where is the place for
                     this muscled skeleton?
Of course—neither Hell nor Heaven...
But here it is,
               the menagerie, the cage!

Наталья Горбаневская

59

Вот она, *la vie quotidienne*,
в громыханьи грязных метро,
сонный взор куда ты ни день,
белый день вопьется остро,

5 белый день взовьется в зенит,
сонные прорежет глаза,
заведет тебя, заманит,
закружит, закружится, за-

вертится, катясь на закат
10 невеселым веретеном,
падающий свет из окна,
гаснущий закат за окном,

под мостами темь-чернота,
сигареты тень изо рта,
15 холодок гранитной скамьи,
хладные объятья мои.

60

О бедная, дряхлая, впавшая в детство
Европа, кому ты оставишь в наследство
последний кабак, и последний бордель,
и Хартию Вольностей—о, не в бреду ль

Natalya Gorbanevskaya

59

Here it is, *la vie quotidienne*,
in the thundering of dirty subway trains,
no matter where you turn your sleepy gaze,
the broad daylight will sharply bite into it,

5   the broad daylight will soar to the zenith,
will cut though your sleepy eyes,
will wind you up, lure you away,
spin you round, itself start spinning, start to

whirl, rolling away toward sunset
10   like an unhappy spindle,
falling light from the window,
fading sunset through the window,

dark blackness under bridges,
shadow of cigarette from mouth,
15   cold of granite bench,
my chilly embraces.

60

O my poor, senile, fallen into childhood
Europe, to whom will you leave
the last pub, and the last bordello,
and the Charter of Liberties—O, was it not in delirium

5 ее сочинили бароны и эрлы,
вином успокаивая нервы,
надтреснутые в треволненьях битв,
когда неизвестно, кто прав, кто побит...

О бедная, этот мой стих надмогильный
10 —лишь доказательство бессильной
и безысходной любви до конца
к последним судорогам лица

твоего, иссеченного сетью скважин
окопов, когда пехотинец неважен,
15 но столько свободы для сквозняков,
грузовиков и броневиков.

61

Не пропеть—прошепелявить, прошептать, прощебетать,
    прощелкать,
так щепотка соли, подлетая на ладони, не взлетает к потолку,
так щекотка обращает облик в зеркале в обмолвку,
так надерганное лыко, как ни лихо, а не пишется в строку.

5 Но не плачет раненая липа, что не всяко лыко в строку.
Соль ложится на пол, в щели, в землю, пусть она не соль
    земли, а прах.
Безголосая мелодия небесному чертогу
всё мила. И щекотливое блаженство сребрится в зеркалах.

Ничего не получается, а все-таки выходит что-то,
10 не такое, как хотелось бы, отнюдь не идеал, но не исходный
    нуль,
не кантата, но уже и не цитата, и болото
остается топью, но тропинки слабый след ему не затянуть.

Так-то, сея кляксы и огрехи, шепелявя, чертыхаясь,
из обмолвок извлекаешь облик нескольких не слишком
    кривобоких строк,
15 так-то сложишь из обломков печку, ибо через хаос
тянется и катится, слепой и спутанный, а катится клубок.

5 composed by barons and earls,
calming their nerves with wine,
overstrained in the alarums of battles,
when it's unknown who is right and who is beaten...

O my poor one, this my verse over your grave
10 is only a proof of my powerless
and perpetual love to the end
for the last shudders of your face

etched with a network of slits
of trenches, when the infantryman is unimportant,
15 but there is so much freedom for draughts,
trucks and armored cars.

61

Not to sing out—to lisp out, whisper out, chirrup out, trill out,
thus a pinch of salt, bouncing on your palm, won't fly up toward the ceiling,
thus a tickling feeling turns its aspect to the mirror, and becomes a slip of the
tongue,
thus a jerked piece of bark no matter how deftly done still won't fit into the
line.*

5 But the wounded lime tree doesn't weep that not every piece of bark will fit
the line.
The salt falls to the floor, into the cracks, the earth, even if it's not the salt of
the earth but dust.
A voiceless melody to the heavenly palace
is still sweet. And ticklish bliss shows silver in the mirrors.

Nothing turns out right, but something still emerges,
10 not what you would have wanted, by no means the ideal, but not the zero you
started with,
not a cantata, but still not a quotation, and the swamp
remains a quagmire, but it can't drag down the feeble trace of the path.

Like this, sowing blots and blemishes, lisping, cursing,
from the slips of the tongue you exhaust the aspect of a few not too lopsided
lines,
15 like this you put together a stove from shards, for through chaos
it stretches and rolls, blind and tangled, but it still rolls, the ball.

62

...где реки льются чище серебра,
не загрязненные мазутом и маслами,
где Бог нас не оставил и светла
адмиралтейская игла, где на соломе
5   лежит Младенец и глаголет бык
мудрее мудрого, наевшись чистотела,
где русский от побед давно отвык
и от войны, держась родимого предела,
где под покровом звездного плаща
10   к нам не крадутся государственные тати,
где, слоги долго в горле полоща,
но не раздумывая, кстати ли, некстати,
как сказку, пересказывая быль,
былую быль, былую боль, любовь былую,
15   ты в пыльный обращаешься ковыль,
а я по ветру одуванчиком белею.

63

Шел год недобрых предсказаний.
Гадалки, опасаясь мести,
ушли в подполье. Под Казанью
родились сросшиеся вместе
5   телята. Где-то за Уралом
болота поглотили вышку
нефтодобычи. Небывалым
огнем, забывши передышку,
зашлись камчатские вулканы
10   одновременно все. На Пресне
распространились тараканы
величиной со сливу. Вести
чудовищные умножались,
едва скрываемые прессой.
15   Ужас усиливался. Жалость
друг к другу становилась пресной,
почти формальною. На Охте
мать бросила дитя в трамвае
с запиской. Чаще рвали когти

62

...where rivers flow purer than silver,
not polluted by heavy oil and grease,
where God has not abandoned us and bright
is the Admiralty spire,* where on straw
5 lies the Infant and the bull makes utterances
wiser than the wise man, having eaten its fill of celandine,
where the Russian has long ago had enough of victories
and war, staying within his native bound,
where beneath the cover of a starry cloak
10 the state's robbers do not creep up on us,
where, rinsing the syllables for a long time in their throat,
but not contemplating whether it's to the point or not,
like a fairy tale, retelling something that really happened,
the real events of the past, past pain, past love,
15 you are transformed into dusty feathergrass,
and I show white in the wind, like a dandelion.

63

It was the year of evil predictions.
Fortune-tellers, fearing retribution,
went underground. Near Kazan
were born joined together
5 calves. Somewhere beyond the Urals
the swamps swallowed up the tower
of an oil well. With unheard-of
fire, forgetting to take a break,
the volcanoes of Kamchatka started up
10 all at the same time. In the Presnya district*
there were cockroaches
as big as plums.* Tidings,
monstrous ones, multiplied,
barely concealed by the press.
15 Horror was getting stronger. Pity
for one another was getting feeble,
almost a formality. On the Okhta*
a mother abandoned her baby in a tram
with a note. More often, people ran off

20 без ничего, без слов. В сарае
в одном нашли самоубийцу
девятилетнего. Загадку
никто не разгадал. Не бился
разгадывать. Призыв к порядку
25 порою свыше издавался,
печатался, передавался
по радио. Но в каждом ухе
звенели только слухи, слухи.

64

Произношу заученный рефрен,
произвожу заученные жесты,
в который раз выравниваю крен
от скошенного громыханья жести

5 заржавленной, заржавленным гвоздем
ее кой-как приковывая к балке,
чтоб и не снился ей ни окоем,
ни гвоздодер... Все в той же раздевалке

я надеваю старое пальто
10 на стертую залатанную кожу
и вновь произношу и сё, и то,
произвожу всё это же и то же,

происхожу оттуда же. Молва
меня рисует много интересней,
15 чем то, что есть, чем тою, какова
я есть, была и буду. И хоть тресни.

65

Это пето на заре
завтрашнего утра,
на затоптанной золе
от любви как будто.

20 without taking anything, saying nothing. In a hut
   they found a suicide,
   a nine-year-old male. The puzzle
   nobody solved. Nor did anyone make a great effort
   to solve it. A call for order
25 from time to time was issued from above,
   published, and broadcast
   on the radio. But in every ear
   resounded only rumors, rumors.

64

I pronounce the learned-by-heart refrain,
perform learned-by-heart gestures,
for the umpteenth time straighten out the tilt
of the rusty tin sheet, knocked crooked by its thundering,

5 with a rusty nail
fastening it any old how to the beam,
so it won't dream either of horizon
or pincers... and still in this same cloakroom

I put on my old overcoat
10 with its rubbed and patched leather lining
and once more pronounce this and that,
and perform yet again this and that same thing,

come from the same place. Gossip
paints me much more interesting
15 that what is, than the kind of woman
I am, was, and will be. For the life of me.

65

This is sung at dawn
of tomorrow's morning,
on the trampled ashes
of love that seemed to be.

5 Это пето с холодком,
   будто бы нетрудно
   разжигать костер тайком,
   а топтать прилюдно.

   Это пето кое-как,
10 не стараясь чище,
   словно жизнь была пустяк,
   а не пепелище.

66 К дискуссии о статистике

   Не будем спорить. Лишний миллион
   засуженных, замученных, забитых
   —всего лишь цифра. И мильон слезинок
   не слился, и не вызвал наводненья,
5 и не оттаял вечной мерзлоты.
   Допустим, этот миллион имен
   История накопит и предъявит,
   но кто же в четырех столицах мира
   прочтет подобный телефонной книжке
10 по весу и по скуке этот том?
   Кто это купит? На костяшках счетов
   махнуть и сбросить. Миллион слезинок,
   а не оттаял вечной мерзлоты.

67

   И, эту мелодию запев,
   мы не сочинили к ней припева,
   а как повели нас на расстрел,
   стало нам уже не до того,
5 под стеною стали мы, вспотев,
   и стена за нами запотела,
   и дрожащий дымчатый рассвет
   озарял чужое торжество.

   Но эта мелодия взошла
10 радугой на сером небосводе,
   стебельком, ломающим асфальт,
   дождичком в беспамятный четверг,

5 This is sung with a chill,
as if it's not hard
to light a bonfire in secret
and trample it in public.

This is sung any old how,
10 not trying to be in tune,
as if life had been a trifle,
not a burnt-out place.

66 Contribution to a Discussion of Statistics

We won't argue. An extra million
condemned, tortured, battered,
is no more than a number. The million tears
haven't flowed together, haven't caused a flood,
5 and haven't thawed the permafrost.
Let's allow that this million names
history will put together and present,
but who in the four capitals of the world
will read this volume, like a telephone book
10 in weight and tedium?
Who will buy this? At the beads of the abacus
wave dismissively and abandon it. A million tears,
but it hasn't thawed out the permafrost.

67

And, having started singing this melody,
we didn't compose a refrain for it,
and when we were led out to be shot,
we didn't feel like it any longer,
5 we stood under the wall, breaking into a sweat,
and the wall started sweating after us,
and the trembling misty dawn
lit up someone else's triumph.

But this melody went up
10 like a rainbow against the gray vault of the sky,
like a stalk breaking through asphalt,
like a shower one forgetful Thursday,

и скатилась пуля из ствола
крупною слезою о свободе,
15 и душа из ребер понеслась,
пятаком подпрыгивая, вверх.

and the bullet rolled down out of the barrel
like a huge teardrop about freedom,
15 and the souls rushed out of our ribs
bouncing like a five-kopek piece, upward.

Александр Кушнер

68 Воспоминания

Н. В. была смешливою моей
подругой гимназической (в двадцатом
она, эс-эр, погибла), вместе с ней
мы, помню, шли весенним Петроградом

5 в семнадцатом и встретили К. М.,
бегущего на частные уроки,
он нравился нам взрослостью и тем,
что беден был (повешен в Таганроге),

а Надя Ц. ждала нас у ворот
10 на Ковенском, откуда было близко
до цирка Чинизелли, где в тот год
шли митинги (погибла как троцкиста),

тогда она дружила с Колей У.,
который не политику, а пенье
15 любил (он в горло ранен был в Крыму,
попал в Париж, погиб в Сопротивленье),

нас Коля вместо митинга зазвал
к себе домой, высокое на диво
окно смотрело прямо на канал,
20 сестра его (умершая от тифа)

Ахматову читала наизусть,
а Боря К. смешил нас до упаду,
в глазах своих такую пряча грусть,
как будто он предвидел смерть в блокаду,

Aleksandr Kushner

68 Memories

N. V. was my giggling girlfriend
in high school (in '20,
being an S. R.,* she perished); with her,
I remember, I used to stroll through springtime Petrograd

5 in '17, and we met K. M.,
scurrying to give his private lessons,
we liked him for being grown-up and because
he was poor (hanged in Taganrog),*

and Nadya Ts. used to wait for us at the gate
10 on Kovenskaya Street, from there it was not far
to the Ciniselli Circus,* where that year
meetings were held (she perished as a Trotskyite),*

at that time she was friends with Kolya U.,
who loved not politics, but singing
15 (he was wounded in the throat in the Crimea,*
made it to Paris, perished in the Resistance),

and Kolya, instead of going to his meeting,
invited us home, where a marvelously high
window looked right down on the canal,
20 his sister (who died of typhus)

could declaim Akhmatova by heart,
and Borya K. made us laugh till we dropped,
his eyes hiding such grief,
as if they foresaw his death during the blockade,*

25 и до сих пор я помню тот закат,
жемчужный блеск уснувшего квартала,
потом за мной зашел мой старший брат
(расстрелянный в тридцать седьмом), светало...

69

История не учит ничему,
Но, как сказал историк—и ему
Не верить нет причины—за незнанье
История наказывает нас.
5 Не учит, а наказывает. Глаз
Да глаз за нами нужен, да вниманье.

Скорее воспитательница, чем
Учительница. Сколько страшных тем
В учебниках ее, в ее анналах...
10 Но мы, известно, тоже хороши.
Хоть кол на голове у нас теши—
Вот присказка учительниц усталых.
Подумай. Сядь. Не ерзай. Запиши.
Как двоечник, о трех мечтаем баллах.

70

Лет на семь раньше я родись—и жизнь иначе
Моя устроилась бы: я б стихи любил
Иные, с юностью б совпал моей горячей
Гнев государственный и коллективный пыл
5 Собраний в актовом, пахнущем пылью зале.
С языкознанием и крупной тяжбой в нем
При мне бы чью-нибудь моральную связали
Нестойкость, жгали б ее железом и огнем.

Лет на семь раньше я родись... В чертополохе
10 Людском и сам бы я лилов был и колюч.
Дух обличительный, как пух... Продукт эпохи,
Я, человек, от почв завишу и от туч,
Каким бы вымахал, подумать страшно, вроде

25 and even now I can remember that sunset,
   the pearly brilliance of the sleeping district,
   then my elder brother came to fetch me
   (he was shot in '37), and it was getting light…

69

   History teaches us nothing,
   But, as one historian said—and there's
   No reason not to believe him—for not knowing it
   History punishes us.
5 Not teaches, punishes. Eyes
   And more eyes are what we need, and to pay attention.

   It's more a governess than a
   Schoolmistress. So many fearsome themes
   In its textbooks, in its annals…
10 But we ourselves, you know, aren't all that great.
   We are so darned stubborn, as per
   The weary schoolmistress's opening words:
   "Think, will you. Sit. Don't fidget. Write this down."
   Bottom of the class, we dream of average grades.*

70

   If I'd been born about seven years earlier, my life
   Would have worked out differently: I would have liked
   Different poetry, and my hot youth would have coincided with
   The anger of the state* and the collective enthusiasm
5 Of meetings in the main university auditorium that smells of dust.
   In my presence they would have linked linguistics and that large-scale
      controversy
   With someone's moral turpitude
   And cauterized it with iron and fire.

   If I'd been born about seven years earlier, in the thistle
10 Of humankind I too would have been purple and prickly.
   A spirit to unmask, like thistledown… A product of the epoch,
   I, a human being, depend on the soils and the clouds,
   What I would be doing is awful to think—like

Тех, кто поглядывает искоса сейчас
15 На время мягкое и жаждет от мелодий
Звучанья громкого и непреклонных фраз.

71

Век, может быть, и атомный, но дети
Такими ж, как при Дарии, при Кире,
Рождаются на белом этом свете
И враждовать, и жить со всеми в мире—
5 Так думал я, идя по школе, классы
Начальные галдели в коридоре,
Извечные дразнилки и гримасы,
Все то же счастье ждет их, то же горе.

Кто ж сделает их мягче, милосердней,
10 Отзывчивей, добрей, великодушней—
Полузверят—к сыновней и дочерней
Любви приводит, сестринской и мужней,
Кто даст им смысл, кто мостик перекинет
От прежних бед к сегодняшней заботе—
15 Полина Львовна в синем крепдешине?
Да, и она, с указкой на отлете.

72

В стихах сверкает смысл, как будто перестрелка
В горах—и нелегко нам уследить за ним.
Вот так еще, обняв ствол, радуется белка:
Она уже не там, куда еще глядим.

5 Неуловимый взгляд и яркий мех опрятный.
А сидя, чем она так странно занята?
Как будто инструмент какой-то непонятный
Все время удержать старается у рта.

Ты к ней не подходи в своей широкой шубке.
10 Я вспомнить шкурки две в чужих стихах могу:
Две радости, два сна, две маленьких зарубки.
Мы третью проведем, чтоб нам не быть в долгу.

Those men who now look askance
15 At this soft time, and who thirst for melodies
With thundering sonorities and adamant phrases.

71

This may be the atomic age, but the children
Are just the same as under Darius or Cyrus,
They're born into this wide world
Both to make enemies and to live in peace with everyone in it—
5 This is what I was thinking as I walked around the school,
The bottom classes raising a rumpus in the corridor,
The age-old teasing and pulling of faces,
The same happiness awaits them, the same grief.

Who can make them softer, more merciful,
10 More responsive, kinder, more magnanimous,
These half-wild cubs; who can induce filial and daughterly,
Sisterly and husbandly love,
Who can give them sense, who can cast a bridge
From older troubles to today's concerns—
15 Polina Lvovna in her navy crepe de chine?
Yes, even she, her arm with pointer outstretched.

72

In verse, meaning sparkles like an exchange of gunfire
In the mountains, and it's hard for us to follow it.
In just the same way too a squirrel has fun as it hugs the trunk:
It's already gone from the place we're looking at.

5 Glance you can't catch and bright, cared-for fur.
When it sits down, what is it busy doing in that odd way?
It's as if it were trying to keep some unknown instrument
To its mouth all the time.

Don't you go near it in your wide fur coat.
10 There are two other pelts I remember in other people's poems:*
Two joys, two dreams, two small notches.
We'll make another, so we won't be indebted.

Я знаю, что сказать под занавес, шуршащий,
Сползающий в конце столетья, шелестя:
15 Нам все-таки связать с вчерашним настоящий
День рифмой удалось, по ельнику бродя.

Суровый выпал век, но белочка как дома
В нем чувствует себя: наверное, чутье
Подсказывает ей, что место перелома
20 Залечено, в когтях не флейта ль у нее?

73

Как раскапризничавшийся ребенок,
Что упирается, и канючит,
И тянет за руку мать, силенок
Откуда столько—так туча тучей
5 Душа глядит, ничего не хочет,
И блеску волн, и статье журнала
Сопротивляется что есть мочи,
А дело в том, что она устала.

Ругать не надо—сильней заплачет,
10 Отшлепать—господи, рев поднимет,
Спать, спать, скорее домой, в горячий
Сон, на руках уже спит, обнимет
За шею, спит, поскорей чулочки
Стянуть, в постель уложить—и всхлипы
15 Все реже, спит, родилась в сорочке—
И спит. Пусть клены шумят и липы.

74

Счастливые стихи писали мы,
Когда все, все препятствовало нам.
И волновали нити бахромы,
И взгляд тянулся к вышитым цветам
5 На скатерти—да здравствует пустяк,
Под подозреньем он у дураков!
Ты, солнца луч, ко мне на пальцы ляг,
Приди, прильни; скользнул—и был таков.

I know what to say at this curtain, rustling,
Coming down at the end of the century, swishing.
15 In spite of everything, we have been able to connect this day
With yesterday through rhyme, as we wander through the firs.

A stern century it's turned out to be, but the squirrel
Feels at home in it: probably, instinct
Is suggesting to it that the place where the break was
20 Is healed,* and isn't that a flute in its claws?

73

Like a child that's started to get really naughty,
And refuses to cooperate, and grumbles,
And drags its mother by the hand, where does
It get so much strength?—in a black mood
5 My soul looks, doesn't want anything,
And resists the brilliance of the waves, and the journal article,
resists as hard as it can,
But it's tired, that's what's the matter.

Don't curse it—it'll only cry harder,
10 Or spank it—Lord, it'll just howl,
Sleep, sleep, get home as soon as possible, into hot
Sleep, it's asleep in my arms already, holding on
Round my neck, sleeping, hurry and take off
Its stockings, put it to bed—and the sobs
15 Less and less, sleeping, born with a silver spoon—
Sleeping. Let maple trees sound, and lime trees.

74

We used to write happy poems
When everything, everything hindered us.
The threads of a fringe excited us,
And our glance was drawn to the embroidered flowers
5 On the tablecloth—long live the trivial,
For fools hold it in suspicion!
You, ray of the sun, fell on my fingers,
Come, be close—but it slipped away, was gone.

Пленяла жизнь, давленью вопреки.
10 Сейчас, когда все, все разрешено,
Еще посмотрим, что нам смельчаки
Преподнесут, какое нам кино
Подарят... Помню фильм «Жил певчий дрозд,»
Насквозь прошитый музыкой ночной,
15 Тбилисский дом, грузинский длинний тост,
Борьбу во сне уснувшего с луной.

Моя любовь, тебя я не отдам,
Вас, дни мои, в аду не прокляну...
Никто, никто читать по вечерам
20 Нам не мешал, я жизнь свою одну
Не поделю ни на две, ни на три.
Волшебный смысл то вспыхивал, то гас,
И сад не зря шумел, держу пари,
И с полуслова понимали нас!

75

Льется свет. Вода бредет во мраке.
И звезда с звездою говорит.
Как непрочны слов дневные браки!
Вот оно, рыданье аонид.

5 И душа с другим, ночным глаголом
В непроглядной тьме обручена,
Словно с богом, ласковым и голым,
Юным, захмелевшим от вина.

Ничего-то он не обещает,
10 И бессмертье дать не может ей.
Речь струится. Время? Время тает.
Дом глядит на нас из-за ветвей.

Странно жить, в виду имея темный
Край, конец, уступчатый обрыв.
15 Что ты хочешь там услышать: волны,
Жаркий шепот, вкрадчивый мотив?

Настежь смерть нестрашная открыта,
Смысл сидит у вечности в гостях,

Life was captivating, despite the oppression.
10 And now, when everything, everything is permitted,
Let's wait and see what the bold spirits
Will present us with, what kind of movies
They'll give us... I remember the film "There Once Was a Songthrush,"*
Stitched throughout by nocturnal music,
15 A house in Tbilisi, a long Georgian toast,
The dream struggle with the moon of a sleeping man.

My love, I will not give thee up,
And you, my days, I shall not curse in hell...
No one, no one tried to stop us reading in the evening,
20 This one and only life of mine
I shall not divide into two or three.
Magic meaning flared up sometimes, sometimes died,
And the garden rustled not in vain, I'll bet on it,
And people understood the hints we dropped!

75

Light flows. Water wanders in the darkness.
And star talks with star.*
How fragile are the daytime marriages of words!
And there it is, the sobbing of the Aonides.

5 And the soul with a different, nocturnal world
In the impenetrable gloom is betrothed.
As if with a god, affectionate and naked,
Young, and light-headed from wine.

He promises [the soul] nothing,
10 And cannot give it immortality.
Speech streams. Time? Time melts.
A house looks at us through the branches.

It's strange to live, having in mind a dark
Region, the end, a ledged ravine.
15 What do you want to hear there: waves,
An ardent whisper, an insidious motif?

Unfearful death is open wide.
Meaning is the guest of eternity.

Обсуждая с нею деловито
20 Все, что мы не поняли впотьмах.

76

Ничто так к смерти нас не приближает,
Как сбывшееся желанье.
Вот почему Венеция внушает
Не только радость, но и содроганье,
5 Не только счастье, но и опасенье.
Раскрывшиеся объятья
Навстречу нам—услада, и томленье,
И влажный луч... Надень, Даная, платье.

Втяни живот, а жаркие браслеты
10 Замкни в шкатулку... Вот они, отчасти
Пугающие приметы
Грозящей смерти: сбывшееся счастье,
Любимый труд, поездка за границу.
Китс умер в Риме,
15 И Баратынский музой смуглолицей
Обманут был, волнами голубыми.

Как нас томят и тешат перемены,
Свершающиеся сегодня!
За пологом, упрятана в глубь сцены,
20 История стоит, как эта сводня
На полотне, с неверною улыбкой...
Прислушаемся к поэту?
Ему все мнилось: счастлив он ошибкой.
Или поверим солнцу и браслету?

Discussing with it in a matter-of-fact way
20 Everything we didn't understand in the dark.

76

Nothing brings us closer to death
Than a wish come true.*
This is why Venice inspires
Not only joy, but a shudder,
5 Not only happiness, but apprehension too.
The embrace that's opened up
To meet us is delight, and anxiety,
And a moist ray of light… Put on, Danae, your dress.

Pull in your stomach, and those hot bracelets
10 Lock up in their box… There they are, partly
Frightening signs
Of threatening death: happiness come true,
Your favorite work, a trip abroad.
Keats died in Rome,
15 And Baratynsky* by a swarthy-faced muse
Was deceived, and by the sky-blue waves.

How they torment and console us, the changes
Taking place today!
Behind the arras, hidden deep backstage
20 History stands, like that procuress
In the picture, with a false smile…
Shall we pay heed to the poet?
He always thought that he was happy by mistake.
Or shall we trust the sun and the bracelet?

Белла Ахмадулина

77

Завидна мне извечная привычка
быть женщиной и мужнею женою,
но уж таков присмотр небес за мною,
что ничего из этого не вышло.

5 Храни меня, прищур неумолимый,
в сохранности от всех благополучий,
но обойди твоей опекой жгучей
двух девочек, замаранных малиной.

Еще смеются, рыщут в листьях ягод
10 и вдруг, как я, глядят с такой же грустью.
Как все, хотела—и поила грудью,
хотела—медом, а вспоила—ядом.

Непоправима и невероятна
в их лицах мета нашего единства.
15 Уж коль ворона белой уродится,
не дай ей бог, чтоб были воронята.

Белеть—нелепо, а чернеть—не ново,
чернеть—недолго, а белеть—безбрежно.
Все более я пред людьми безгрешна,
20 все более я пред детьми виновна.

1974

Bella Akhmadulina

77

I find enviable the age-old habit
of being a woman and a husband's wife.
But the heavens have been watchful over me in such a way
that nothing's come of it.

5 Keep me, inexorable narrow-eyed scrutiny,
safe from all kinds of well-being,
but let your burning guardianship pass by
these two young girls smeared with raspberries.

They're still laughing, scouring the leaves for berries,
10 and suddenly, like I, their glance has the same sadness.
Like everyone, I wanted to nourish with my breast,
I wanted to give honey, but I gave poison.

Incorrigible and improbable—
in their faces is the mark of our oneness.
15 For if a crow is born white,*
pray God she have no baby crows.

To be white is absurd, but to be black isn't new,
being black is not for long, but being white's unlimited.
I am ever more innocent before adults.
20 I am ever more guilty before children.

1974

78 Ночь упаданья яблок

Семену Липкину

Уж август в половине. По откосам
по вечерам гуляют полушалки.
Пришла пора высокородным осам
навязываться кухням в приживалки.

5 Как женщины глядят в судьбу варенья—
лениво-зорко, неусыпно-слепо—
гляжу в окно, где обитает время
под видом истекающего лета.

Лишь этот образ осам для пирушки
10 пожаловал—кто не варил повидла.
Здесь закипает варево покруче:
живьем съедает и глядит невинно.

Со мной такого лета не бывало.
—Да и не будет!—слышу уверенье.
15 И вздрагиваю: яблоко упало,
на «НЕ»—извне поставив ударенье.

Жить припустилось вспугнутое сердце,
жаль бедного: так бьется кропотливо.
Неужто впрямь небытия соседство,
20 словно соседка глупая, болтливо?

Нет, это—август, упаданье яблок.
Я просто не узнала то, что слышу.
В сердцах, что собеседник непонятлив,
неоспоримо грохнуло о крышу.

25 Быть по сему. Чем кратче, тем дороже.
Так я сижу в ночь упаданья яблок.
Грызя и попирая плодородье,
жизнь милая идет домой с гулянок.

1981

78 The Night of Falling Apples

To Semen Lipkin[*]

Halfway through August now. Over the cut fields
in the evenings the women's shawls wander.
The time has come for high-born wasps
to take up residence in the kitchens.

5 Like women watching over the fate of their preserves
with lazy watchfulness, with unwinking blindness,
I look through the window, where time dwells
disguised as the fading summer.

The only person who would begrudge this image
10 to the feasting wasps is someone who's never made jam.
Here a stronger brew is being boiled up,
which eats you up alive and looks on innocently.

I have never had a summer like this before.
"And you never will again!"—I hear an assurance.
15 And I shudder: an apple has fallen,
stressing the "never" from the outside.

My heart, made anxious, is living more intensely,
I'm sorry for the poor thing, beating so conscientiously.
Can the proximity of nonexistence really be
20 so voluble, like a stupid woman neighbor?

No, it's August, and the falling of the apples.
I simply didn't recognize what I had heard.
Annoyed that the person talking with them was slow to catch on,
it made an unarguable thundering on the roof.

25 So be it, then. The shorter, the more precious.
I sit like this during the night of falling apples.
Gnawing and trampling the fruitful bounty,
Sweet life is coming home from its merrymaking.

1981

79 Бабочка

День октября шестнадцатый столь тепел,
жара в окне так приторно желта,
что бабочка, усопшая меж стекол,
смерть прервала для краткого житья.

5 Не страшно ли, не скушно ли? Не зря ли
очнулась ты от участи сестер,
жаднейшая до бренных лакомств яви
средь прочих шоколадниц и сластен?

Из мертвой хватки, из загробной дремы
10 ты рвешься так, что, слух острее будь,
пришлось бы мне, как на аэродроме,
глаза прикрыть и голову пригнуть.

Перстам неотпускающим, незримым
отдав щепотку боли и пыльцы,
15 пари, предавшись помыслам орлиным,
сверкай и нежься, гибни и прости.

Умру иль нет, но прежде изнурю я
свечу и лоб: пусть выдумают—как
благословлю я хищность жизнелюбья
20 с добычей жизни в меркнущих зрачках.

Пора! В окне горят огонь-затворник.
Усугубилась складка меж бровей.
Пишу: октябрь, шестнадцатое, вторник—
и Воскресенье бабочки моей.

1979

80 Пашка

Пять лет. Изнежен. Столько же запуган.
Конфетами отравлен. Одинок.
То зацелуют, то задвинут в угол.
Побьют. Потом всплакнут: прости, сынок.

79 The Butterfly

This sixteenth day of October is so warm,
the heat in the window so too-sweetly yellow,
that a butterfly that had passed away between the panes
interrupted death for a short life.

5 Frightening, boring, isn't it? Isn't it pointless
for you to awake, abandoning your sisters' fate,
greediest for the fleeting dainties of wakening
among the other chocolate-faces and sweet-tooths?

From this deathly grip, from reverie beyond the tomb
10 you strain away so hard that if my hearing were sharper,
I would need, as if at an airfield,
to close my eyes and bend down my head.

To these unyielding invisible fingers
having given a pinch of pain and pollen,
15 soar! Surrendering to the eagle's designs,
glitter, luxuriate, perish and forgive.

If I die or not, before I do I'll wear out
my candle and my brow: let them think what they like—
how I shall bless the rapaciousness of love for life,
20 with life the prey in my fading pupils.

It's time! The hermit-fire is burning in the window.
The furrow between my brows is more pronounced now.
I write: October, the sixteenth, a Tuesday,
the Resurrection of my butterfly.

1979

80 Pashka

Five years old. Spoiled. And bullied equally.
Poisoned with candy. Solitary.
Kissed too much and then put in a corner.
Beaten. Then tears: forgive me, my little boy.

5 Учен вину. Пьют: мамка, мамкин дядя
и бабкин дядя—Жоржик-истопник.
—А что это?—спросил, на книгу глядя.
Был очарован: он не видел книг.

Впадает бабка то в болезнь, то в лихость.
10 Она, пожалуй, крепче прочих пьет.
В Калуге мы, но вскрикивает Липецк
из недр ее, коль песню запоет.

Играть здесь не с кем. Разве лишь со мною.
Кромешность пряток. Лампа ждет меня.
15 Но что мне делать? Слушай: «Буря мглою...»
Теперь садись. Пиши: эм—а—эм—а.

Зачем все это? Правильно ли? Надо ль?
И так над Пашкой—небо, буря, мгла.
Но как доверчив Пашка, как понятлив.
20 Как грустно пишет он: эм—а—эм—а.

Так мы сидим вдвоем на белом свете.
Я—с черной тайной сердца и ума.
О, для стихов покинутые дети!
Нет мочи прочитать: эм—а—эм—а.

25 Так утекают дни, с небес роняя
разнообразье еженощных лун.
Диковинная речь, ему родная,
пленяет и меняет Пашкин ум.

Меня повсюду Пашка ждет и рыщет.
30 И кличет Белкой, хоть ни разу он
не виделся с моею тезкой рыжей:
здесь род ее прилежно истреблен.

Как, впрочем, все собаки. Добрый Пашка
не раз оплакал лютую их смерть.
35 Вообще наш люд настроен рукопашно,
хоть и живет смиренных далей средь.

Вчера: писала. Лишь заслышав «Белка!»
я резво, как одноименный зверь,
своей проворной подлости робея,
40 со стула—прыг и спряталась за дверь.

5 Wise to drink. They all drink—his mother, her "uncle,"
and granny's "uncle," Georgii the janitor.
"What's this?" he asked, looking at a book.
He was entranced, he'd never seen books.

Sometimes his granny's ill, and sometimes wild.
10 She probably drinks harder than the others.
We're in Kaluga, but Lipetsk screams out
from deep inside her, when she starts singing.

There's no one to play with here. Except perhaps me.
The hell of hide-and-seek. My lamp awaits me.
15 But what can I do? "Listen: 'The storm with gloom…'*
And now sit down. Write: M, A, M, A."

What's all this for? Is it right? Or necessary?
But now over Pashka is heaven, storm, darkness.
But Pashka's so trusting, so quick on the uptake.
20 How sadly he writes: M, A, M, A.

And so we sit, the two of us in the wide world.
And I with my black secret of heart and mind.
Oh, the children abandoned for poetry!
I haven't the strength to read "M, A, M, A."

25 And so the days flow away, dropping from the heavens
the variety of each night's moon.
This outlandish speech, native to him,
captures and changes Pashka's mind.

Everywhere, Pashka waits and searches for me.
30 And calls me Belka, even though not once
has he ever seen the ruddy animal that shares my name:*
its kind has been assiduously exterminated here.

Like all the dogs, too, by the way. Good Pashka
has bewailed their savage death more than once.
35 In general, our folk are partial to hand-to-hand,
even though they live 'mid peaceful vistas.

It's yesterday; I'm writing. As soon as I hear "Belka!"
nimbly, like the animal of that name,
quailing at my adroit baseness
40 I'm off my chair and hidden behind the door.

Значенье пряток сразу же постигший,
я этот взгляд воспомню в крайний час.
В щель поместился старший и простивший,
скорбь всех детей вобравший Пашкин глаз.

45 Пустился Пашка в горький путь обратный.
Вослед ему все воинство ушло.
Шли: ямб, хорей, анапест, амфибрахий
и с ними дактиль. Что там есть еще?

81

Воскресенье настало. Мне не было грустно ничуть.
Это только снаружи больница скушна, непреклонна.
А внутри—очень много событий, занятий и чувств.
И больше гуляют, держась за перила балкона.

5 Одиночество боли и общее шарканье ног
вынуждают людей к (вдруг слово забыла) контакту.
Лишь покойник внизу оставался совсем одинок:
санитар побежал за напарником, бросив каталку.

Столь один—он, пожалуй, еще никогда не бывал.
10 Сочиняй, починяй—все сбиваемся в робкую стаю.
Даже хладный подвал, где он в этой ночи ночевал,
кое-как опекаем: я доброго сторожа знаю.

Но зато, может быть, никогда он так не был любим.
Все, кто был на балконе, его озирали не вчуже.
15 Сочастье любви на мгновенье сгустилось над ним.
Это ластились к тайне живых боязливые души.

Все свидетели скрытным себя осенили крестом.
За оградой—не знаю, а здесь нездоровый упадок
атеизма заметен. Всем хочется над потолком
20 вдруг увидеть утешный и здравоопрятный порядок.

Две не равных вершины вздымали покров простыни.
Вдосталь, мил-человек, ты небось доходил по Расее.
Натрудила она две воздетые к небу ступни.
Что же делать, прощай. Не твое это, брат, воскресенье.

That look, grasping immediately the meaning of this hide-and-seek,
I will remember when my last hour comes.
Pashka's eyes, grown older and forgiving,
containing all children's grief, looking through the crack.

45 Pashka set off on his bitter journey back.
And in his steps went all my armament.
Iamb, trochee, anapaest, amphibrach
and dactyl with them. What is there left?

81

Sunday came. I wasn't sad at all.
Only from the outside was the hospital boring and adamant.
But inside there were lots of events, tasks and feelings.
Patients strolling around, holding onto the rails of the balcony.

5 The loneliness of pain and this general shuffling of feet
force people into (I suddenly forgot the word) contact.
Only the dead man downstairs remained completely lonely:
the orderly had run off to fetch his assistant, abandoning the wheelchair.

Probably, he's never before been so alone.
10 When we're making things up, mending things, we all gather into a timid herd.
Even the cold basement where he had spent the night
we will somehow stand guard on: I know a goodhearted watchman.

But for all that, perhaps he has never been so loved before.
Everyone who was on the balcony watched over him, not alien.
15 The compassion of love grew dense above him for a moment.
Apprehensive souls snuggling up to the secret of the living.

All the witnesses crossed themselves without letting it be seen.
I don't know about the outside, but here the unhealthy decadence
of atheism can be noticed. Everyone suddenly wants to see
20 above the ceilings a consolatory and healthily tidy order.

Two unequal summits raising up the shroud of the sheet.
Dear man of mine, you probably did enough wandering around Russia.
She has worn out these two feet that point at the heavens.
What's to be done, farewell. It's not your resurrection, brother.

25 Впрочем, кто тебя знает. Вдруг матушка в церковь вела:
«Дево, радуйся!» Я—не умею припомнить акафист.
Санитары пришли. Да и сам ты не жил без вина.
Где душе твоей быть? Пусть побудет со мною покамест.

1984

82 Одевание ребенка

Ребенка одевают. Он стоит
и сносит—недвижимый, величавый—
угодливость приспешников своих,
наскучив лестью челяди и славой.

5 У вешалки, где церемониал
свершается, мы вместе провисаем,
отсутствуем. Зеницы минерал
до-первобытен, свеж, непроницаем.

Он смотрит вдаль, поверх услуг людских.
10 В разъятый пух продеты кисти, локти.
Побыть бы им. Недолго погостить
в обители его лилейной плоти.

Предаться воле и опеке сил
лелеющих. Их укачаться зыбкой.
15 Сокрыться в нем. Перемешаться с ним.
Стать крапинкой под рисовой присыпкой.

Эй, няньки, мамки, кумушки, вы что
разнюнились? Быстрее одевайте!
Не дайте, чтоб измыслие вошло
20 поганым войском в млечный мир дитяти.

Для посягательств прыткого ума
возбранны створки замкнутой вселенной.
Прочь, самозванец, званый, как чума,
тем, что сияло и звалось Сиеной.

25 Влекут рабы ребенка паланкин.
Журчит зурна. Порхает опахало.
Меня—набег недуга полонил.
Всю ночь во лбу неслось и полыхало.

25 But then, who knows? Suddenly, an old woman in the church led off:
"Rejoice, O Maid!" I can't remember the acathistus.
The orderlies have come. And you didn't live without drink, either.
Where will your soul abide? Let it abide with me for the time being.

1984

82 Dressing the Child

A child is being dressed. He stands there
and tolerates, motionless and stately,
the obsequiousness of his minions,
these menials who have bored him with flattery and glory.

5 Near the coat hangers, where this ceremonial
is being conducted, together we sag,
we're not there. The mineral of his pupils
is pre-primordial, fresh, impenetrable.

He looks into the distance, above human services.
10 Into the parted down hands and elbows are thrust.
I'd like to be him for a bit. To be a short-stay guest
in the abode of his lily-white flesh.

To abandon myself to the will and guardianship
of those who cherish. Unsteady, to be rocked to sleep by them.
15 To hide myself in him. To be intermingled with him.
To be a speck under the sprinkled baby powder.

I say, nannies, nurses, good women, what are you
sniveling for? Dress him as fast as you can!
Don't allow these figments to enter
20 like pagan troops into the milky world of the child.

To the infringements of my nimble mind
the folds of the closed universe have been forbidden.
Away, pretender, summoned like the plague,
by that which shone and was called Siena.

25 The slaves draw on the child's palanquin.
The zurna* babbles. The big fan flutters.
And I am captured by a raiding illness.
All night in my forehead things are shifting and blazing.

Прикрыть глаза. Сна гобелен соткать.
30 Разглядывать, не нагляжусь покамест,
палаццо Пикколомини в закат
водвинутость и вогнутость, покатость,

объятья нежно-каменный зажим
вкруг зрелища: резвится мимолетность
35 внутри, и Дева-Вечность возлежит,
изгибом плавным опершись на локоть.

Сиены площадь так нарек мой жар,
это его наречья идиома.
Оставим площадь—вечно возлежать
40 прелестной девой возле водоема.

Врач смущена:—О чем вы?—Ни о чем.
В раззор весны ступаю я с порога
не сведущим в хожденье новичком.
—Но что дитя?!—Дитя? Дитя здорово.

Репино, апрель 1990 года

I'll shut my eyes. Weave the tapestry of sleep.
30 View—I haven't had my fill of looking at it yet—
the palazzo Piccolomini, its into-the-sunset
insertion and concavity, its declevity,

the tender-stone clamp embraced
around this spectacle: transience gambols
35 inside, and the Maid Eternity reclines,
in a flowing curve leaning on her elbow.

My fever thus named the Siena square,
it is an idiom of my fever's dialect.
Let's leave the square, and leave eternally reclining
40 The charming maid by the cistern.

The doctor's concerned. "What are you talking about?" "Nothing."
Into the bursting light of spring I step from the entrance
like a beginner who knows nothing about walking.
"But how's the child?" "The child? It's healthy."

Repino, April 1990

Юнна Мориц

83

Вечно ждать кровавых новостей,
шепотом воспитывать детей,
рукописи прятать под пеленку.
Кто доносчик?—главный наш секрет.
5 Кто приходит в дом, когда нас нет?
Кто там в телефоне крутит пленку?
Сколько лет за это, сколько зим?
По какой наклонной мы скользим,
выпив рюмку чая с иностранцем?
10 Как не попадаться на глаза
тем, кому руки подать нельзя,
если полным ты не стал засранцем?
Как же нам отсутствовать везде?
Затаиться и дышать в воде
15 жабрами? За сколько дней, мгновений,
худшее предчувствуя, бежать?
И куда? И надо ли рожать
для тюрьмы так много поколений?

1975

84 Между Сциллой и Харибдой

Быть поэтессой в России—труднее, чем быть
поэтом: единица женской силы в русской
поэзии—1 ахмацвет.

Ходим в люльке с погремушкой,
Расцветаем, увядаем

Yunna Morits

83

Eternally to be waiting for bloody news,
to bring up children in a whisper,
to hide manuscripts under a diaper.
Who's the informer? is our main secret.
5 Who comes to the house when we're not there?
Who's that making a tape go round in the telephone?
How many years d'you get for this, how many winters?
Down what slope do we slide,
if we've drunk a glass of tea with a foreigner?
10 How not to avoid catching the eye
of people you must not give your hand to
if you're still not a complete shit?
How can we be absent everywhere?
Hide and breathe in water
15 with gills? For how many days, moments,
anticipating the worst, to flee?
And where to? And must we give birth
to so many generations for the prison?

1975

84 Between Scylla and Charybdis

> To be a woman poet in Russia is harder than to be a
> man poet: the unit of female force in Russian poetry
> is 1 *akhmatsvet.**

We walk around the cot with our rattle,
We flourish and we fade

Между Арктикой и Кушкой,
Между Польшей и Китаем.

5 Покидаем с вечным всхлипом
Облак над лицейским прудом—
Между Лиром и Эдипом,
Между Цезарем и Брутом.

Сохраняем здравый разум,
10 Маслим свет над фолиантом,
Строим ясли голым фразам—
Между Пушкиным и Дантом.

Поднося фонарь к репризам,
Связь находим колоссальной—
15 Между Блоком и Хафизом,
Между Музой и Кассандрой.

И, дыша гипербореем,
Проплываем каравеллой
Между Женей и Андреем,
20 Между Беллой и Новеллой.

Но кровавою корридой
Угрожает путь старинный
Между Сциллой и Харибдой—
Между Анной и Мариной.

25 Между Сциллой и Харибдой,
Между Анной и Мариной—
Кто проглочен был пучиной,
Тот и выплюнут пучиной.

Стало следствие причиной.
30 Объясняю образ странный:
Кто проглочен был Мариной,
Тот и выплюнут был Анной.

Золотою серединой
Отродясь не обладаем—
35 Между Анной и Мариной,
Между Польшей и Китаем.

Between the Arctic and Kushka,*
Between Poland and China.

5 With an eternal sob we abandon
The cloud over the lycée pond,
Between Lear and Oedipus,
Between Caesar and Brutus.

We preserve commonsense reason,
10 Dim the light over the folios,
Make a cradle for naked phrases
Between Pushkin and Dante.

Lifting up a lamp to the reprises,
We find the connection colossal
15 Between Blok and Hafiz,*
Between the Muse and Cassandra.

And, breathing like the Hyperborean,
We sail through like a caravel
Between Zhenya* and Andrei,*
20 Between Bella* and Novella.*

But like a bloody corrida
The ancient path threatens
Between Scylla and Charybdis—
Between Anna and Marina.

25 Between Scylla and Charybdis,
Between Anna and Marina,
Whoever was swallowed by the deep
Was spat out by the deep.

Consequence has become cause.
30 I explain this strange image:
Whoever was swallowed by Marina
Was spat out by Anna.

The golden mean
Has never in our born days been our possession,
35 Between Anna and Marina,
Between Poland and China.

И над бездною родимой—
Уж незнамо как!—летаем
Между Анной и Мариной,
40 Между Польшей и Китаем.

1975

85

Я с гениями водку не пила
И близко их к себе не подпускала.
Я молодым поэтом не была,
Слух не лелеяла и взоры не ласкала.

5 На цыпочках не стоя ни пред кем,
Я не светилась, не дышала мглою
И свежестью не веяла совсем
На тех, кто промышляет похвалою.

И более того! Угрюмый взгляд
10 На многие пленительные вещи
Выталкивал меня из всех плеяд,
Из ряда—вон, чтоб не сказать похлеще.

И никакие в мире кружева
Не в силах были напустить тумана
15 И мглой мои окутать жернова
И замыслы бурлящего вулкана.

Так Бог помог мне в свиту не попасть
Ни к одному из патриархов Музы,
Не козырять его любовью всласть,
20 Не заключать хвалебные союзы,

Не стать добычей тьмы и пустоты
В засиженном поклонниками зале...
Живи на то, что скажешь *только ты*,
А не на то, что о тебе сказали!

1979

And above our native abyss—
So unfathomably!—we fly
Between Anna and Marina,
40 Between Poland and China.

1975

85

I never drank vodka with geniuses,
And didn't let them get close to me.
I wasn't a young poet,
I didn't foster ears and fondle eyes.

5 Not standing on tiptoe before anyone,
I didn't shine, didn't breathe gloom,
And didn't ever waft freshness
On those who trade in praise.

And more than that! A sullen view
10 Of many entrancing things
Pushed me out of all pleiades,
Out of the ordinary run, to put it no more crudely.

And no lace fabrics in the world
Were strong enough to bring down mist
15 And wreathe my millstones in gloom
And the designs of my seething volcano.

Thus, God helped me not to join the suite
Of any of the patriarchs of the Muse,
Nor flaunt his love to my heart's content,
20 Nor forge laudatory alliances,

Nor become the prey of darkness and emptiness
In a hall packed with admirers...
Live on what *only you* will say,
And not on what's been said about you!

1979

86

Июль восьмидесятого. В Москве
вторые сутки льет, не умолкая,
тяжелый ливень. Кости, размокая,
в спине, в коленях ноют, в голове...

5 Пока в приемной очереди жду,
мой зонт, раскисший, станет суше трости,
а я спою или сыграю в кости,
или с ума от бешенства сойду.

А в это время—мать на костылях,
10 восьмидесятилетняя старуха,
к окну больничному приклеивает ухо,
и слышит ливня шорох в тополях,

и на единственной несломанной ноге
спешит в мечтах своих достигнуть совершенства,
15 последние изюминки блаженства
в житейском колупая пироге.

1980

87 Над телом смертным, над бессмертным идеалом

Памяти школьной учительницы Д. Я. Таран

Однажды в нашей средней женской школе,
что в Киеве стояла на Подоле,
где грохотал трамвай, как паровоз,
она возникла, юная такая,
5 и, девственностью грозною сверкая,
влила волненья огненный мороз.

Ее предмет—язык, литература.
Все влюблены! Никто не зубрит хмуро,
бушуют страсти, ревность, тайный бой—
10 за взор ее горящий, за улыбку,
за счастье искупить в письме ошибку
блестящим содержаньем! Боже мой,

86

July of '80. In Moscow
for the second day pours without pausing
a heavy downpour. Getting sodden, the bones
ache in my back and knees, and in my head...

5 While I wait my turn in the reception room,
my umbrella becomes limp and will get dryer than a twig,
and I'll start singing or playing dice,
or go crazy with rage.

And meanwhile, my mother on her crutches,
10 an old woman of eighty,
glues her ear to the hospital window,
and listens to the rustle of the downpour in the poplars,

and on her one unbroken leg
hurries in her dreams to reach perfection,
15 picking at the last raisins of bliss
in life's pie.

1980

87 Over the Mortal Body, Over the Immortal Ideal

In memory of my schoolteacher, D. Ya. Taran

One day in our middle school for girls,
which was in Kiev in the Podol district,
where trams racketed like locomotives,
she arose, so young a woman she was,
5 and, sparkling with fearful virginity,
poured in a fiery frost of agitation.

Her subject was language and literature.
Everyone fell in love! Nobody cramming gloomily,
passions, jealousy, secret battle boiled—
10 to win her burning look, her smile,
the happiness of redeeming a spelling mistake
by brilliant content! My God,

в каких мечтах возвышенно-жестоких
мы все, как самураи на Востоке,
15 без колебаний гибли за нее,
пьянея от греховного бесстрашья!
И преданность восторженная наша
воздела ту жар-птицу на копье—

бедняжка, ведь наедине с мужчиной
20 она была учительницей чинной
с воображеньем, слабым для греха,
и грозовая сладость королевы
окислилась, и облик старой девы
произошел, как проза от стиха.

25 Да разве мог мужчина—
                            хоть отчасти—
вернуть ей бескорыстье нашей страсти,
ревнивую отвагу наших душ
и преданности рыцарские латы?
Мы со своей любовью виноваты,
30 что на нее не отыскался муж.

И через тридцать лет, по смерти ранней,
когда замкнулся круг ее страданий
и роковой недуг ее убил,
я плачу над великим и над малым:
35 над телом смертным, над бессмертным идеалом—
над чем еще заплачет кто любил?

1983

88 На грани выдоха и вдоха

На грани выдоха и вдоха есть волна,
где жизнь от видимости освобождена,
упразденены тела и внешние черты,
и наши сути там свободно разлиты.

5 Там нет сосудов для скопления пустот,
и знак присутствия иной, чем здесь, и счет

in what elevated and cruel dreams
all of us, like samurai in the East,
15 would perish without hesitation for her sake,
intoxicated with sinful fearlessness!
And our rapturous devotion
heaved this firebird up on a spear—

poor woman—after all, alone with a man
20 she was a dignified schoolteacher
with an imagination too weak for sin,
and the stormy sweetness of this queen
turned sour, and the image of an old maid
came to pass, like prose from verse.

25 But then again, could a man—
                              even partly—
return the selflessness of our passion to her,
the jealous daring of our souls
and the knightly armor of devotion?
With our love we are guilty
30 that no husband was found for her.

And thirty years later, after her early death,
when the circle of her sufferings closed
and a fatal affliction killed her,
I weep over the great thing and the small:
35 over the mortal body, over the immortal ideal—
over what else will one who has loved weep?

1983

88 On the Edge of Breathing Out and Breathing In

On the edge of breathing out and breathing in is a wave,
where life is liberated from appearance,
bodies and external features are cast aside,
and our essences are freely poured out there.

5 No vessels for hoarding emptiness are there,
and the sign of presence is different than it is here, and the account

не лицевой, не именной, и только ритм
там раскаляется и звездами горит.

На грани выдоха и вдоха есть волна,
10 где жизнь, как музыка, слышна, но не видна.
И там поэзия берет свои стихи.
И там посмертно искупаются грехи.

1984

89

Поэзия жива свободой и любовью.
На каторге, в тюрьме, в изгнании—жива,
на бойне, где народ причислен к поголовью
и меньшинство идет в желудок большинства.

5 Но всюду—тайники, убежища, укрытья:
то щель в глухой стене, то свет в чужом окне.
В сугробе, в сапоге, во рту, в мозгу, в корыте
спасаются стихи—в копне и в дряхлом пне—

и спросит юный внук у бедного Адама:
10 —А где ты был, Адам, инструктор ПВО,
когда стерег Руслан безумье Мандельштама?
—Я был, где большинство, а он—где меньшинство.

У черта на рогах, в трубе и в готовальне
спасаются стихи по воле меньшинства,
15 чтоб совесть большинства была еще кристальней,
когда промчится слух: Поэзия—жива!...

...когда примчится весть о меньшинстве великом,
которое сожрал кровавый людофоб,
усатый лилипут с изрытым оспой ликом
20 и толпами рабов, его лобзавших гроб.

Ни мертвый, ни живой не прекратит свободу
поэзии, чей дух не брезгует бедой.
Поэты—меньшинство, дающее народу
дышать, дышать, дышать—
25 хоть в стебель под водой!

1982

is not a personal one nor by name, and only rhythm
is heated white-hot there and burns like stars.

On the edge of breathing out and breathing in is a wave,
10 where life, like music, can be heard, but not seen.
And there poetry takes its lines.
And there posthumously sins are atoned for.

1984

89

Poetry is alive through freedom and love.
At hard labor, in prison, in exile it's alive,
in the slaughterhouse where the people are numbered as cattle
and the minority goes into the stomachs of the majority.

5 But everywhere are hiding places, sanctuaries, shelters:
a crack in a blank wall, a light in someone else's window.
In a snowdrift, a boot, a mouth, a brain, a rut
verse finds refuge—in a haystack, an ancient tree stump—

And his young grandson asks poor Adam:
10 "And where were you, Adam, an AAD* instructor,
When Ruslan* stood guard over Mandelstam's madness?"*
"I was where the majority was, and he where the minority was."

At the back of beyond, in a chimney and in a case of drawing instruments,
verse finds a refuge through the will of the minority,
15 so that the conscience of the majority should be even more crystal clear,
when the rumor comes flying round that Poetry's alive!

…when the news comes flying in about the great minority
which the bloody anthrophobe* gobbled up,
the moustachioed Lilliputian with his pockmarked visage
20 and the crowds of slaves who kissed his coffin.

Neither the dead nor the living will put a stop to the freedom
of poetry, whose spirit isn't squeamish of calamity.
Poets are the minority who allow the people
to breathe, breathe, breathe—
25 if only through a stalk under water!

1982

90

...и придут дикари молодые—для
того, чтоб начать с нуля,
и будут они беспощадны,
их вкусы грубы, аппетиты громадны,
5 ничто им не свято, не дорого—
слишком все стоит дорого,
слишком велик разрыв
между тем, что им обещали,
и тем, как вы обнищали,
10 вкалывая навзрыд,
как ломовые лошади,
чтоб они наплясались, наплавались,
наплевали на страх и прославились
воем стихов на площади.
15 И не вздумайте корчить кислую мину,
вы—из очень прошлого века
и сами себе подложили мину,
глубоко унижаемый, желчный калека,
чья скорость равна нулю,
20 с которого все начинается—
все то, что вам уже не подчиняется,
как шторм—кораблю.
...лапшой свисают прогнившие снасти,
барахло такелажа идет на дно,
25 дикарям причиняя огромное счастье,
которое вам не дано.

1985

91

Аллеи душные в пыли,
окурки в лужах, вонь асфальта,
и туч отечные кули
в лучах, оскольчатых, как смальта.
5 У высших сил на поводу
собака лапою босою
скребет помойный бак в аду,

90

...and young savages will come, in
order to start from zero,
and they will be pitiless,
their tastes crude, their appetites enormous,
5 nothing sacred for them, nothing dear—
everything costs too dear,
too great is the gap
between what they were promised
and how impoverished you've grown,
10 slogging away until you sobbed,
like cart horses,
so they could dance and swim as much as they like,
not give a damn about fear and become famous
for the roar of verse on a square.
15 And don't you think of pulling a sour face,
you're from a very past age
and you've set a minefield for yourself,
you profoundly degraded,* peevish cripple,
whose speed is equal to zero,
20 from which everything begins—
everything that no longer submits to you,
like a storm to a ship.
...like noodles hangs down the rotted rigging,
the jumble of tackle is going to the bottom,
25 causing the savages enormous happiness,
which is not given to you.

1985

91

Stuffy avenues covered in dust,
butts in puddles, stink of asphalt,
dropsical sacks of clouds
in rays splintery like smalt.*
5 On a lead held by the higher powers
a dog with one unshod paw
scratches out a cesspool in hell,

где все стоят за колбасою,
виясь в кудрях очередей,
10 завитых чародеем пыток
клещами пламенных вождей,
которых здесь переизбыток.
Любимой сластью стал страшок,
что этот век, от крови пьяный,
15 еще себе на посошок
наполнит кладезь наш багряный.
Мы—главные поставщики
какой-то нови людоедской.
Что б ни болтали языки—
20 сильны мы лютостью простецкой,
для нас блаженство—сознавать,
что мы незрелы для свободы,
что взор не в силах оторвать
от наших ужасов народы.

1989

92

Когда все наши всех не наших перебьют,
а наших всех угробят все не наши,
когда все те порубят всех не тех,
а все не те зароют тех и этих—
5 тогда этническое равенство берцовых,
голеностопных, тазовых, височных,
не будет волновать дегенератов,
усопших в героической борьбе,
дегенералов, штаб дегенеральный
10 с дегенеральной линией не бу-
дет волновать такой дегенераль-
ный пух и прах, дегенеральный крах
рядов, сплоченных пищей из крахмала.

1989

where everyone stands in line for sausage,
winding in the curls of lines,
10 that have been waved by the magician of tortures
with the tongs of fiery leaders,
of whom there's a superabundance here.
Our favorite delight is now the fear
that this age, drunk with blood,
15 will still have one more for the road
and fill our crimson well.
We are the main purveyors
of a kind of cannibal virgin soil.
No matter what idle tongues chatter,
20 we're strong with a simpleminded savagery,
for us, bliss is to confess
that we're not mature enough for freedom,
and that the nations haven't the strength
to tear their eyes away from our horrors.

1989

92

When all of ours slaughter all of theirs,
and all of theirs do in all of ours,
when all those cut down all the not-those,*
and all the not-those bury those and these—
5 then the ethnic equality of tibials,
talocrurals, pelvics, temporals,
will not worry the degenerates
who've fallen in the heroic struggle;
the degenerals, the degeneral staff
10 with their degeneral line will not be
worried by this degener-
al rout, the degeneral collapse
of the ranks which are closed by food let down with starch.

1989

93

Плавучая тоска преджизненньх темнот,
мучительные сны, безумия истоки—
их ритмы вкрадчивы, их образы жестоки,
уже к пяти годам клубится этот флот
5   за шторой ветреной, за лунной полосой,
когда отец и мать вот-вот из мглы вернутся,
душа воспалена, и страшно блещет блюдце,
и блеска страшный звук вонзается осой
осеннею в висок, и опухоль кровит,
10   покуда сквозь нее отсасывают жало...
Годам к тринадцати все то, что набежало
с любовью матери, слоится и язвит
хвощами, прорастающими—сквозь
бессонницу видений, пену плоти,
15   униженность души, при перелете
разодранной о раскаленный гвоздь.
На рельсы! В петлю! К голым проводам!...
Быть может, там отыщется, кому бы
завыть, как воют, разрывая трубы—
20   как воют сны к семнадцати годам,
как воет день с виденьями картин
навязчивых, как мы не знаем лени,
преуспевая в самоистребленьи...
как в белоснежном входит господин
25   чтоб молоточком вызвонить колени,
в мозгу пересекающихся льдин
сверканье черное, и вызволить, как стон,
влеченье к смерти, твой зеркальный ужас
пред жизнью и безумьем... Я о том,
30   как, на мосту случайно обнаружась
в слезах, глядеть на реку под мостом.

1989

93

The floating anguish of pre-life darkness,
the tormenting dreams, sources of madness—
their rhythms are insidious, their images are cruel,
by five years old this fleet already billows
5 behind a windy shutter, behind a strip of moonlight,
when father and mother will come back any time from the dark,
the soul's inflamed, and a saucer glitters strangely,
and the frightening sound of its glitter plunges like a wasp
in autumn into your temple, and the swelling bleeds
10 while through it the sting is sucked out...
By about thirteen, everything that accumulated
with your mother's love becomes layered and stinging
with mare's tails that grow through
the sleeplessness of visions, the foam of the flesh,
15 the degradation of the soul, which while migrating
has been torn on a white-hot nail.
Onto the tracks! Into the noose! To the bare wires!
Maybe someone will be found there to whom
one can howl like howling that bursts the pipes—
20 the way your dreams howl when you're reaching seventeen,
the way the day howls with visions of scenes that are
obsessive, the way we know no idleness
as we prosper in self-destruction...
the way a gentleman in snowy white comes in
25 to sound your knee with a little hammer,
in the brain the black sparkle of
intersecting icebergs, and to help free like a groan
the attractiveness of death, your mirror horror
before life and madness... What I'm talking about
30 is how, if you happen to find yourself on a bridge
in tears, to look down at the water under the bridge.

1989

Лев Лосев

94

«Понимаю—ярмо, голодуха,
тыщу лет демократии нет,
но худого российского духа
не терплю»—говорил мне поэт.
5 «Эти дождички, эти березы,
эти охи по части могил»—
и поэт с выраженьем угрозы
свои тонкие губы кривил.
И еще он сказал, распаляясь:
10 «Не люблю этих пьяных ночей,
покаянную искренность пьяниц,
достоевский надрыв стукачей,
эту водочку, эти грибочки,
этих девочек, эти грешки
15 и под утро заместо примочки
водянистые Блока стишки;
наших бардов картонные копья
и актерскую их хрипоту,
наших ямбов пустых плоскостопье
20 и хореев худых хромоту;
оскорбительны наши святыни,
все рассчитаны на дурака,
и живительной чистой латыни
мимо нас протекала река.
25 Вот уж правда—страна негодяев:
и клозета приличного нет»—
сумасшедший, почти как Чаадаев,
так внезапно закончил поэт.
Но гибчайшею русскою речью

Lev Loseff

94

"I understand—yoke,* starvation,
a thousand years and no democracy,
but it's the rotten Russian spirit
I can't stand," said a poet to me.
5 "These sweet little rains, these birch trees,
these 'ohs' directed at graves,"
and the poet with a threatening expression
curled his delicate lips.
And further he said, getting worked up:
10 "I don't like these drunken nights,
the repentant sincerity of the drunks,
the dostoevsky* anguish of the informers,
this good old vodka, these dear old mushrooms,
these girlies, these cute little sins,
15 and as morning comes, instead of a wet towel,
there's Blok's watery doggerel;
the cardboard spears of our bards*
and their actor's hoarseness,
the flat-footedness of our empty iambs
20 and the lameness of our rotten trochees;
the things we hold sacred, they're an insult,
all calculated for the imbecile,
and the river of life-giving pure Latin
has flowed past us.
25 It's quite true—it's the land of nogoodniks;*
there isn't even a decent WC."
Out of his mind, almost like Chaadaev,*
the poet suddenly concluded.
But with his most supple Russian speech

30 что-то главное он огибал
и глядел словно прямо в заречье,
где архангел с трубой погибал.

95

...в *Костре* работал. В этом тусклом месте,
вдали от гонки и передовиц,
я встретил сто, а, может быть, и двести
прозрачных юношей, невзрачнейших девиц.
5 Простуженно протискиваясь в дверь,
они, не без нахального кокетства,
мне говорили: «Вот вам пара текстов».
Я в их глазах редактор был и зверь.
Прикрытые немыслимым рваньем,
10 они о тексте, как учил их Лотман,
судили как о чем-то очень плотном,
как о бетоне с арматурой в нем.
Все это были рыбки на меху
бессмыслицы, помноженной на вялость,
15 но мне порою эту чепуху
и вправду напечатать удавалось.

Стоял мороз. В Таврическом саду
закат был желт, и снег под ним был розов.
О чем они болтали на ходу,
20 подслушивал недремлющий Морозов,
тот самый, Павлик, сотворивший зло.
С фанерного портрета пионера
от холода оттрескалась фанера,
но было им тепло.

               И время шло.
25 И подходило первое число.
И секретарь выписывал червонец.
И время шло, ни с кем не церемонясь,
и всех оно по кочкам разнесло.
Те в лагерном бараке чифирят,
30 те б Бронксе с тараканами воюют,
те в психбольнице кычат и кукуют,
и с обшлага сгоняют чертенят.

30 he was omitting something important,
  and looking, it seemed, directly to a land across the river
  where an archangel with his trumpet was dying.

95

  ...I used to work on *The Campfire.** In this dismal place,
  far away from the rat race and leading articles,
  I met one, or perhaps even two, hundred
  transparent youths and most uncomely maids.
5 Chilled to the bone, they squeezed through the door,
  and not without haughty flirtatiousness
  they would say to me: "Here's a couple of texts for you."
  In their eyes I was an editor and a beast.
  Covering themselves with unimaginable tatters,
10 they would refer to "the text," as Lotman* taught them,
  as if it were something very corporeal,
  like concrete with an armature inside.
  All this was like fish with fur on,
  senselessness multiplied by slackness,
15 but from time to time I actually
  managed to print this nonsense.

  There was a frost. In the Tauride Garden*
  the sunset was yellow and the snow below was pink.
  And the things they chattered about as they walked
20 were eavesdropped on by the ever-vigilant Morozov,*
  that same Pavlik Morozov who did evil.
  From the chipboard portrait of the pioneer
  from the cold the chipboard had chipped off,
  but they felt warm.

     And time went on.
25 And the first of the month approached.
  And the secretary signed over my tenner.
  And time went by, asking nobody's permission,
  and swept them all away to various tussocks.
  Some get high on extra-strong tea in labor camp huts,
30 or do battle with cockroaches in the Bronx,
  others make turkey and cuckoo noises in the mental home,
  and brush the baby devils off their cuffs.

96 Путешествие. 4. У женевского часовщика

С. Маркишу

В Женеве важной, нет, в Женеве нежной,
в Швейцарии вальяжной и смешной,
в Швейцарии со всей Европой смежной,
в Женеве вежливой, в Швейцарии с мошной,
5 набитой золотом, коровами, горами,
пластами сыра с каплями росы,
агентами разведок, шулерами,
я вдруг решил: «куплю себе часы.»

Толпа бурлила. Шла перевербовка
10 сотрудников КЦГРБУ.
Но все разведки я видал в гробу.
Мне бы узнать, какая здесь штамповка,
какие на рубиновых камнях,
водоупорные и в кожаных ремнях.

15 Вдруг слышу из-под щеточки усов
печальный голос местного еврея:
«Ах, сударь, всё, что нужно от часов,
чтоб тикали и говорили время.»

«Чтоб тикали и говорили время...
20 Послушайте, вы это о стихах?»
«Нет, о часах, наручных и карманных...»
«Нет, это о стихах и о романах,
о лирике и прочих пустяках.»

97 Стансы

Расположение планет
и мрачный вид кофейной гущи
нам говорят, что Бога нет
и ангелы не всемогущи.

5 И все другие письмена,
приметы, признаки и знаки

96 A Journey. 4. At a Watchmaker's in Geneva

To Shimon Markish

In Geneva the solemn, no, in Geneva the tender,
in Switzerland the imposing and laughable,
in Switzerland that adjoins the whole of Europe,
in Geneva the polite, in Switzerland with its pouch
5 crammed with gold, cows, mountains,
layers of cheese with dewdrops,
secret service agents, cardsharps,
I suddenly decided: "I'll buy myself a watch."

The crowd seethed. Re-recruitment was going on
10 of collaborators with the KCGIBA.
But I've had it with all secret services.
What I need to know is what kind of cheapos they have here,
which ones have rubies for their jewels,
which are water-resistant and which have leather straps.

15 Suddenly I hear from under the brush of his moustache
the sad voice of a local Jew:
"Ach, my dear sir, all you need from a watch
is that it should tick and tell the time."

"Tick and tell the time...
20 Listen, are you talking about poetry?"
"No, about watches, wrist- and pocket-..."
"No, that's about poems and novels,
the lyric, and other trifles."

97 Stanzas

The disposition of the planets
and the gloomy aspect of coffee grounds
tell us there's no God
and the angels are not almighty.

5 And all other written characters,
omens, signs, and marks

не проясняют ни хрена,
а только топят все во мраке.

Все мысли в голове моей
10 подпрыгивают и бессвязны,
и все стихи моих друзей
безо́бразны и безобра́зны.

Когда по городу сную,
по делу или так гуляю,
15 повсюду только гласный У
привычным ухом уловляю.

Натруженный, как грузовик,
скулящий, как больная сука,
лишен грамматики язык,
20 где звук не отличим от звука.

Дурак, орущий за версту,
болтун, уведший вас в сторонку,
все произносят пустоту,
слова сливаются в воронку,

25 забулькало, совсем ушло,
уже слилось к сплошному вою.
Но шелестит еще крыло,
летящее над головою.

98

Грамматика есть бог ума.
Решает все за нас сама:
что проорем, а что прошепчем.
И времена пошли писать,
5 и будущее лезет вспять
и долго возится в прошедшем.

Глаголов русских толкотня
вконец заторкала меня,
и, рот внезапно открывая,
10 я знаю: не сдержать узду,

don't clarify a damned thing,
but just drown everything in gloom.

All the thoughts in my head
10 hop around and are disconnected,
and all the poetry of my friends
is formless and malformed.

When I'm getting around town,
on business or just strolling,
15 everywhere the single vowel "u"
I catch with my accustomed ear.

Worn out with work like a truck,
grinning like a sick bitch,
language has lost its grammar,
20 and one sound can't be distinguished from another.

The idiot yelling from a mile away,
the yacker who takes you to one side,
all enunciate emptiness,
the words flow together in a funnel,

25 which gurgles and then disappears altogether,
and has now merged with the unbroken howl.
But still a wing rustles,
flying overhead.

98

Grammar is the god of mind.
It decides everything for us on its own:
what we'll yell and what we'll whisper.
The tenses have all gone to hell,
5 and the future tries to go into reverse
and messes about for a long time in the past.

The jostling of Russian verbs
eventually choked me up,
and, suddenly opening my mouth,
10 I know that I can't rein it in,

и сам не без сомненья жду,
куда-то вывезет кривая.

На перегное душ и книг
сам по себе живет язык,
15 и он переживет столетья.
В нем нашего—всего лишь вздох,
какой-то ах, какой-то ох,
два-три случайных междометья.

99 Один день Льва Владимировича

Перемещен из Северной и Новой
Пальмиры и Голландии, живу
здесь нелюдимо в Северной и Новой
Америке и Англии. Жую
5 из тостера изъятый хлеб изгнанья
и ежеутренне взбираюсь по крутым
ступеням белокаменного зданья,
где пробавляюсь языком родным.
Развешиваю уши. Каждый звук
10 калечит мой язык или позорит.

Когда состарюсь, я на старый юг
уеду, если пенсия позволит.
У моря над тарелкой макарон
дней скоротать остаток по-латински,
15 слезою увлажняя окоем,
как Бродский, как, скорее, Баратынский.
Когда последний покидал Марсель,
как пар пыхтел и как пилась марсала,
как провожала пылкая мамзель,
20 как мысль плясала, как перо писало,
как в стих вливался моря мерный шум,
как в нем синела дальняя дорога,
как не входило в восхищенный ум,
как оставалось жить уже немного.

25 Однако что зевать по сторонам.
Передо мною сочинений горка.
«Тургенев любит написать роман
Отцы с Ребенками». Отлично, Джо, пятерка!
Тургенев любит поглядеть в окно.

and not without doubt I wait
to see which way I'll get out of this mess.

In the humus of souls and books
the language lives of its own accord,
15 and it will outlive the centuries.
In it there is only a sigh of what is ours,
some sort of "ah," some sort of "oh,"
two or three random interjections.

99 One Day in the Life of Lev Vladimirovich

Displaced from the Northern and New
Palmyra* and Holland,* I live
here unsociably in North and New
America and England. I chew
5 the bread of exile, extracted from a toaster,
and every morning clamber up the steep
steps of a white-stone building,
where I support myself with my native language.
My jaw drops. Every sound
10 cripples my language or insults it.

When I grow old, to the old south
I'll away, if my pension permits.
By the sea over a plate of pasta
to while away the rest of my days in Latin,
15 moistening my horizon with a tear,
like Brodsky—or rather Baratynsky.*
When the latter was leaving Marseilles,
how the steam puffed and the Marsala went down,
how that passionate mamselle saw him off,
20 how his thoughts danced, how his pen wrote,
how the measured sound of the sea flowed in his verse,
how the distant road was dark blue in it,
and how it didn't enter his rapt mind,
how little he had left to live.

25 But why yawn around.
Before me is a mound of student papers.
"Turgenev loves to wrote the novel
Fathers with Childs." Excellent, Joe, top marks!
Turgenev loves looking out the window.

30 Увидеть нив зеленое рядно.
Рысистый бег лошадки тонконогой.
Горячей пыли пленку над дорогой.
Ездок устал, в кабак он завернет.
Не евши, опрокинет там косушку...

35 И я в окно—а за окном Вермонт,
соседний штат, закрытый на ремонт,
на долгую весеннюю просушку.
Среди покрытых влагою холмов
каких не понапрятано домов,
40 какую не увидишь там обитель:
в одной укрылся нелюдимый дед,
он в бороду толстовскую одет
и в сталинский полувоенный китель.
В другой живет поближе к небесам
45 кто, словеса плетя витиевато,
с глубоким пониманьем описал
лирическую жизнь дегенерата.

Задавши студиозусам урок,
берем газету (глупая привычка).
50 Ага, стишки. Конечно, «уголок»,
«колонка» или, сю-сю-сю, «страничка».
По Сеньке шапка. Сенькин перепрыг
из комсомольцев прямо в богомольцы
свершен. Чем нынче потчуют нас в рыг-
55 -аловке? Угодно ль гонобольцы?
Все постненькое, Божии рабы?
Дурные рифмы. Краденые шутки.
Накушались. Спасибо. Как бобы
шевелятся холодные в желудке.

60 Смеркается. Пора домой. Журнал
московский, что ли, взять как веронал.
Там олух размечтался о былом,
когда ходили наши напролом
и сокрушали нечисть помелом,
65 а эмигранта отдаленный предок
деревню одарял полуведром.
Крути, как хочешь, русский палиндром
барин и раб, читай хоть так, хоть этак,
не может раб существовать без бар.
70 Сегодня стороной обходим бар.

30 And seeing the green burlap of the cornfields.
   The trotting gait of a fine-legged horse.
   The film of hot dust over the road.
   The rider's tired and drops into an inn.
   Without eating, he downs a half-bottle of vodka.

35 I too look out of the window—and there's Vermont,
   my neighboring state, closed for repairs,
   for its long springtime drying-out.
   Among these moisture-shrouded hills
   every last kind of house is hidden,
40 you'll see every last kind of abode:
   in one, unsociable grandpa has gone to ground,
   he's dressed in a Tolstoy beard
   and Stalin semi-military tunic.
   In another there lives, nearer to the heavens,
45 someone who, weaving words* ornately,
   with profound understanding has described
   the lyric life of a degenerate.

   Having given our studiosi their lesson,
   we pick up the newspaper (stupid habit).
50 Oho, some verse. Of course, a "corner,"
   "column" or (lithp-lithp) "little page."
   Banner headline on Senka* (serve him right!). Senka's leap
   out of the komsomols straight into the godly
   is complete. What's on offer these days in the burp-
55 -orium? Would you care for fast-time berries?
   Everything nice and unleavened, slaves of God?
   Rotten rhymes. Stolen jokes.
   We've had enough. Thanks. Like beans
   shifting cold in your stomach.

60 It's getting dark. Time for home. A magazine
   from Moscow, maybe, take for sleeping pills?
   There, some dunderhead dreaming of what used to be,
   when our lads would go through thick and thin
   and smite the scum clean away,
65 and the distant ancestor of an émigré
   bestowed half a barrel on his village.
   Juggle whichever way you like the Russian palindrome
   barin i rab [master and slave], read it this way or that,
   the slave cannot exist without the masters.
70 Today we'll give the bar a wide berth.

Там хорошо. Там стелется, слоист,
сигарный дым. Но там сидит славист.
Опасно. До того опять допьюсь,
что перед ним начну метать свой бисер
75 и от коллеги я опять добьюсь,
чтоб он опять в ответ мне пошлость высер:
«Ирония не нужно казаку,
you sure could do with some domestication,[1]
недаром в вашем русском языку
80 такого слова нет—sophistication».[2]

Есть слово «истина». Есть слово «воля».
Есть из трех букв—«уют». И «хамство» есть.
Как хорошо в ночи без алкоголя
слова, что невозможно перевесть,
85 бредя, пространству бормотать пустому.
На слове «падло» мы подходим к дому.

Дверь за собой плотней прикрыть, дабы
в дом не прокрались духи перекрестков.
В разношенные шлепанцы стопы
90 вставляй, поэт, пять скрюченных отростков.
Еще проверь цепочку на двери.
Приветом обменяйся с Пенелопой.
Вздохни. В глубины логова прошлепай.
И свет включи. И вздрогни. И замри:

95 ...А это что еще такое?

А это—зеркало, такое стеклецо,
чтоб увидать со щеткой за щекою
судьбы перемещенное лицо.

1. "You sure could do with some domestication"—«уж вам бы пошло на пользу малость
дрессировки».
2. Sophistication—очень приблизительно: «изысканность».

100

Поэт есть перегной, в нем мертвые слова
сочатся, лопаясь, то щелочно, то кисло,
звук избавляется от смысла, а
аз, буки и т.д. обнажены, как числа,

5 улыбка тленная уста его свела,
и мысль последняя, как корешок, повисла.

In there it's good. There spreads out, layered,
cigar smoke. But in there sits a Slavist.
Dangerous. Will I once more have so much to drink
that I'll start casting my pearls before him
75 and compel my colleague once more
to drawl out a vulgar platitude once more in answer:
"The Cossack needs no irony,
you sure could do with some domestication,
not without reason in your russky lingo
80 there's no such word as 'sophistication.'

There is the word *istina* [truth]. There is the word *volya* [will, freedom].
And three-lettered *uyut* [cosiness]. And *khamstvo* [rudeness].
How good at night sans alcohol,
rambling words that can't be translated,
85 to mumble them to empty space.
On the word *padlo* [crap] we approach the house.

Let's close the door tight behind us, that
the spirits of the crossroads not steal into the house.
Into your worn-out slippers, poet, insert
90 your foot's five gnarled appendages.
Check the door chain once more.
Exchange greetings with Penelope.
Sigh. Trundle off into the depths of your lair.
Turn on the light. Shudder. And freeze.

95 …Now what on earth is that?

But that's a mirror, just a piece of glass,
so as to see with brush behind cheek
the displaced person of fate.

100

The poet is humus, within him dead words
ooze, bursting, alkaline then acid,
sound gets rid of sense, but
A, B, etc. are laid bare, like numerals,

5 a mortal smile then draws his lips together,
and the final thought hangs there like a rootlet.

Потом личинка лярвочку прогрызла,
бектерия дите произвела.

Поэт есть перегной.
10 В нем все пути зерна,
то дождик мочит их, то солнце прогревает.

Потом идет зима,
и белой пеленой
пустое поле покрывает.

101 Самодеятельность

Джон в сафьяновы сапожки обут.
У него подбит гвоздями каблук.
Так топочет, что доскам каюк.
А у меня на душе кошки скребут.

5 Самодеятельность танцует гопак.
Джон и Джейн одеты в красный кумач.
Если тошно, пойди да поплачь.
Я и рад бы—не выходит никак.

Я и сам бы эту душу скрёб, скрёб.
10 Я бы язву эту в кровь расчесал.
В такт прихлопывает топоту зал,
точно гвозди загоняют в гроб, в гроб.

102 Двенадцать Коллегий. Элегия в трех частях

*

Бог умер.
            Ницше.
Ницше умер.
            Бог.[1]
В уборной стонет сизый голубок.
За дверью 00 (два нуля) хорал воды проточной
и посетитель беспорточный
5 средь мрамора сидит, как полубог.

Then the larva nibbles through the caul,
the bacteria have brought forth the child.

The poet is humus.
10 In him are all the ways of the grain,*
a shower soaks them, then the sun warms them.

Then comes winter,
and with a white shroud
covers the empty field.

101 Amateur Theatricals

John is shod in morocco leather boots.
His heels are studded with nails.
He stamps so hard the boards have had it.
But it's as if cats were scratching at my heart.

5 The amateur theatricals are dancing the gopak.
John and Jane are dressed in red calico.
If it sickens you, go and have a cry.
I would like to, but it just won't come.

I myself would like to scratch, scratch this soul.
10 I would like to worry this sore until it bleeds.
The audience claps in time to the stamping,
as if driving nails into a coffin, a coffin.

102 The Twelve Colleges.* An Elegy in Three Parts

*

God is dead.
       Nietzsche.
Nietzsche is dead.
       God.[1]
In the toilet groans the gray-blue dove.*
Behind door 00 (two zeroes) is a chorale of running water,
and the deunderpanted visitor
5 sits midst the marble, like a demigod.

Усвоив шутку с зеркалом внутри,
неспешным оком осмотри
сырые стены мраморной пещеры.
Здесь части тел ведут свою войну,
10 забыв предохранительные меры,
ужасные в длину и ширину.

...бог умер ницше: ницше умер бог...
Напухших пушек дула смотрят вбок
поверх бойниц курчавых. Из бойниц же,
15 раскрытых между ног, как третий глаз,
на нас глядит не Бог, не Ницше,
незнамо что глядит на нас.

* *

Дом, именуемый глаголом—«лгу»,
пустынных волн стоял на берегу
20 и вдаль глядел. Пред ним неслись «победы»,
троллейбусы, профессоры, народ,
красавицы и наоборот,
и будущие эзоповеды.

За чтенье на картошке «Also sprach...»
25 ах, некогда мне было там sehr schwach.
Я там узнал, что комсомол неистов,
что, что бы я им там ни плел, козел,
из этих алкашей и онанистов
со мной никто б в разведку не пошел,

30 что я—змея, побег дурной травы,
что должен быть растоптан и раздавлен.
Но тут примчался папа из Москвы,
просил, и я был, так и быть, оставлен.

Я на допросе препирался с про-
35 (зачеркнуто)—на зачете с Проппом.
Я думал, сказки—то, се, зло, добро,
а Пропп считал избушку гробом.[2]

И Пропп был прав, а я неправ. И вот
ко мне избушка повернулся задом.
40 В разведку не был послан я отрядом,
но поворот мне вышел от ворот,
где забивает целый день козла,

Having assimilated the joke with the mirror inside,
with unhurried eye inspect
the damp walls of the marble cave.
Here the parts of the body wage their war,
10 forgetting preventative measures,
horrible in length and breadth.

...god is dead nietzsche: nietzsche is dead god...
The barrels of swollen cannon look to one side
above curly-haired loopholes. From these loopholes,
15 opened between legs, like a third eye,
at us looks not God, not Nietzsche,
something unbeknownst looks at us.

* *

The building named by the verb "I lie,"*
stood on the banks of the desolate waves
20 and looked afar.* Before it rushed "victories,"*
trolleybuses, professors, the people,
beautiful women and the opposite,
and future Aesop scholars.*

For reading *Also sprach...* while on potato picking duty*
25 For me it was once *sehr schwach* there.
I learned there that the Komsomol was furious,
that, no matter what stories I told them, dummy,
of these alkies and wankers
not one would go out on recce* with me,

30 that I was a serpent, a shoot of bad grass,
that needed to be trampled and crushed.
But then daddy came running from Moscow,
asked, and I was, let it be so, left alone.

At interrogation I wrangled with a pro-
35 (crossed out)—at examination with Propp.*
I thought that fairy tales were this, that, evil, good,
but Propp thought the hut was a coffin.[2]

And Propp was right, and I was wrong. And so
the hut showed me its backside.*
40 I was not sent on recce with the detachment,
but I was turned away from the gates
where all day long they play dominoes,

а польт не принимает гардеробщик,
где темная Нева под льдами ропщет
45 извне добра и зла.

* * *

Университет похмельной лиги.
На железных полках дрыхнут книги.
Перестрелка теннисных мячей.
Все всегда кончается ничьей.

50 Старички в штанишках сухопары
и старушки (смешанные пары).
Скованный склероз телодвиже-
ний, как пары рифм: две М, две Ж.

Теннисная схватка без ракетки.
55 Пишущая машинка без каретки.
Пыльное, без форточки окно.
Темновато. Впрочем, не темно.

Прогуляться возле стадиона.
Не студено? Вроде не студено.
60 Но нельзя сказать, чтобы тепло.
Два овала вялых на табло.

1. Граффити, часто встречающееся на стенах университетских уборных в США.
2. См.: В. Я. Пропп. «Исторические корни волшебной сказки».

the cloakroom man won't take coats,
where the dark Neva complains beneath her ice
45 beyond good and evil.

* * *

A hop-league university.
On metal shelves the books flake out.
Crossfire of tennis balls.
Everything always ends in a draw.

50 The old men in their shorts are lean,
the old women too (mixed doubles).
Constrained sclerosis of body
movements, like pairs of rhymes: two M, two F.

Tennis skirmish without a racket.
55 Typewriter without a carriage.
Dusty window with no opening part.
Darkish. Not dark, though.

Maybe take a walk by the stadium.
Not too chilly? Prob'ly not too chilly.
60 But one can't say it's warm.
Two feeble ovals on the scoreboard.

1. Graffiti frequently found on the walls of university toilets in the USA.
2. See V. Ya. Propp, *The Historical Roots of the Fairy Tale*.

Олег Чухонцев

103

Этот город деревянный на реке
словно палец безымянный на руке;
пусть в поречье каждый взгорок мне знаком,
как пять пальцев—а колечко на одном!

5 Эко чудо—пахнет лесом тротуар.
Пахнет тесом палисадник и амбар;
на болотах, где не выстоит гранит,
деревянное отечество стоит.

И представишь: так же сложится судьба,
10 как из бревен деревянная изба;
год по году—не пером, так топором—
вот и стены, вот и ставни, вот и дом.

Стой-постой, да слушай стужу из окон,
да поленья знай подбрасывай в огонь;
15 а окна запотеют от тепла—
слава Богу! Лишь бы крыша не текла!

104 Двойник

...А если это символ, то чего?

В тени платана, рядом с «Ореандой»,
сидел он у киоска и курил.
(Не знаю что, наверно, как обычно,
5 «Герцеговину Флор». Или «Памир».)

Oleg Chukhontsev

103

This wooden town on the river
is like the ring finger on my hand;
down by the river every little hillock may be as familiar to me
as my five fingers… But my ring is only on one!

5 What a miracle, the sidewalk smells of the forest.
Fence and barn smell of planks;
on the marshes, where granite would not remain standing,
there stands a wooden fatherland.

And imagine, fate is put together in the same way,
10 as a wooden hut is from logs;
year by year—if not by the pen then by the ax—
here are walls, and here are shutters, and here's a house.

But wait a minute, and listen to the hard frost from the windows,
why don't you add some logs to the fire;
15 if the windows run with sweat from the heat
thank God! As long as the roof doesn't leak!

104 The Double

…But if this is a symbol, then of what?

In the shade of a plane tree, next to the "Oreanda,"
he sat by his kiosk smoking.
(I don't know what, probably, as usual,
5 "Herzegovina Flor." Or "Pamir."*)

Цвели сады, и острый запах шторма
стоял, не просыхая, на бульваре,
и свежие газеты тяжелели
от йодистых паров и новостей.
10 Он докурил и развернул газету
так широко, что сделался невидим,
лишь сапоги с защитною фуражкой
обрамили невидимый портрет.
Но по рукам, по напряженной позе
15 я с ясностью увидел, что он *думал*
и даже *что* он думал (мысль была
отчетлива, вещественна, подробна
и зрима так, как если бы он был
индуктором, а я реципиентом,
20 и каждый оттиск на листе сознанья
был впечатляющ): баржи затопить
цыплят разделать и поставить в уксус
разбить оппортунистов из костей
и головы бараньей сделать хаши
25 сактировать любимчика купить
цицматы и лаваш устроить чистку
напротив бани выселить татар
из Крыма надоели Дон и Волгу
соединить каналом настоять
30 к женитьбе сына чачу на тархуне
Венеру перед зеркалом продать
поднос пустить по кругу по подаркам
и угощать нацелить микроскоп
на рисовое зернышко отправить
35 на Темзу бочку паюсной икры
засохший гуталин подскипидарить
примерить в мавзолее саркофаг
с мощами Геловани как нажрутся
так языки развяжут приказать
40 Лаврентию представить докладную
о языке Марр против Маркса вырвать
кого-чего кому-чему плевать
на хачапури главное цицматы
и чача больше чачи дать отпор
45 троцкистам вейсманистам морганистам
и раком поползут как луноход
на четвереньки встав от поясницы
достать змеиный яд и растирать
и растирать и чистить чистить чистить
50 до солнечного глянца—он сложил

The gardens were in flower, and the sharp scent of a squall
remained, not drying out, on the boulevard,
and the latest papers were heavy
with iodine fumes and the news.
10 He finished his cigarette and opened the paper
so wide that he became invisible,
only his jackboots and his khaki peaked cap
framed the invisible portrait.
But from his hands, from his tense posture
15 I could see clearly that he was *thinking*
and even *what* he was thinking (his thought was
clear-cut, substantial, detailed
and visible, as if he were
an inductor and I the thing induced,
20 and every single imprint on the page of consciousness
made an impression): sink barges*
carve up the chickens and put them in vinegar
smash the opportunists from the bones
and head of a sheep make *khashi**
25 sign arrest order for a favorite buy
*tsitsmaty** and *lavash** set up a purge
opposite the baths deport the Tartars
from the Crimea fed up with them the Don and Volga
join by a canal marinade
30 for my son's wedding *chacha** with *tarkhun**
sell Venus Before the Looking-Glass*
send round a tray for gifts
and help yourselves focus the microscope
on a grain of rice send off
35 to the Thames a barrel of pressed caviar
to the dried-out shoe polish add turpentine
measure up the sarcophagus in the mausoleum
with the remains the Gelovanis will feed their faces
that's how tongues are loosened order
40 Lavrentii* to submit a memorandum
on language Marr* versus Marx tear out
somebody-something to someone-something forget about
the *khachapuri* the main thing's *tsitsmati*
and *chacha* lots of *chacha* repulse
45 the Trotskyites* Weissmanites* Morganists*
they'll crawl on their bellies like a lunar vehicle
getting up on all fours from the waist
get some snake poison and rub
and rub and clean clean clean*
50 till it gleams like the sun—he folded

газету и зачем-то огляделся,
и мы глазами повстречались... (Так
на парагипнотическом сеансе
посылкой встречной размыкают цепь).
55 Он усмехнулся и усы пригладил.
И злость меня взяла—я подошел
и, выставив башмак, сказал:—Почистить!—
Он как-то странно на меня взглянул,
и молча поднял перст, и черным ногтем
60 мне показал: «Закрыто на обед».

Каких нам знамений ни посылает
судьба, а мы и явного не ждем!
Стучало море, высекая искры,
и вспыхивала радуга то здесь,
65 то там на берегу, удар—и брызги!
...Но для чего же этот маскарад?
Тщеславье? Вряд ли. Мелкое позерство?
Едва ли. Это сходство, думал я,
не может быть случайностью. А если
70 намек, и очевидный? Но на что?

—Волна!—я услыхал у парапета
и загадал. И ухнул водный столб!
Я пробежал, а парочку накрыло.
Ну и прекрасно, вот он и ответ.

75 Я должен быть лирическим поэтом,
а чистильщик пусть драит башмаки
или сдирает кожу с мирных граждан,
а двое любят. Каждому свое!

Как непосильно быть самим собой.
80 И он, и я—мы, в сущности, в подполье,
но ведь нельзя же лепестками внутрь
цвести—или плоды носить в бутоне!
Как непосильно жить. Мы двойники
убийц и жертв. Но мы живем. Кого же
85 в тени платана тень маньяка ждет
и шевелит знакомыми усами?
Не все ль равно, молчи. И ты был с ним?...
И я, и он—и море нам свидетель.
Ну что ж, еще волна, еще удар—
90 и радуга соленая, и брызги!...

his paper and looked round for some reason,
and our eyes met... (Thus
at a parahypnotic session
they break the chain by sending a parcel the wrong way.)
55 He grinned and stroked his moustache.
And I was filled with malice—I walked up to him
and sticking out my shoe, I said: "Clean it!"
He gave me a kind of funny look,
and silently lifted his finger, and with a black fingernail
60 pointed out to me: "Closed for lunch."

No matter what portents are sent to us
by fate, we don't expect the obvious!
The sea hammered, carving out sparks,
and a rainbow puffed up first here
65 then there on the shore, bang, then a shower of spray!
...But what is this masquerade for?
Vanity? Hardly. Petty striking of attitudes?
Unlikely. This similarity, I thought,
cannot be an accident. And what if
70 it's a hint, and an obvious one? But of what?

"Wave!" I heard by the parapet
and guessed it. And a column of water crashed in!
I ran out of the way, but a couple was engulfed.
Splendid, then, that's the answer.

75 I have to be a lyric poet,
but let the shoe cleaner polish shoes
or take the hide off peaceable citizens,
and the couple be in love. To each his own!

How insupportable to be oneself.
80 Both he, and I—we in essence are underground,
but after all it's impossible with petals pointing inward
to bloom, or to wear the fruit as a buttonhole!
How insupportable to live. We are doubles
of murderers and victims. But we're alive. For whom then
85 in the shade of the plane tree is the shade of the maniac waiting for
and twisting his familiar moustache?
But isn't it all the same, be quiet. And you were with him?...
Both I and he—and the sea is our witness.
Well then, one more wave, more more blow—
90 and the salty rainbow, and the spray!...

105 О той земле

А в той земле, где Рыбинское море
теперь шумит, где белый теплоход
кричит в тумане, чувствуя в моторе
живую боль, и сбрасывает ход,
5 как бы поклон последний отдавая,
и вторят криком встречные суда
да чайки, и волна береговая
в глухую память плещется, когда
решили землю сделать дном и Волгу
10 пустили в эти поймы и луга,
на дольный мир, крестьянскую двуколку
колхозом тянущий, и облака
из мутных вод, как саван погребальный,
всплыть не могли, и только монастырь
15 еще стоял, как в день первоначальный,
холодную высвечивая ширь
и поднимая купола и стены,
расписанные фресками внутри,
но и они, темнея постепенно,
20 туда бы перешли, где пескари
уже ходили, чудищ пучеглазых
напоминая, если бы не те
художники, из бывших богомазов,
которые, на козлах и в воде
25 по щиколотку стоя, по колено,
работали не покладая рук,
и сняли роспись, и спасли от тлена,
и умерли—так вот, какой-то звук
о той земле, какой-то призвук резкий,
30 как бы пилой по камню, все стоит,
стоит в ушах...

        Я видел эти фрески
в Донском монастыре. Тяжелых плит,
как бездны, распечатанные книги:
Ной у ковчега с парами зверей
35 и белым голубем—я слышу крики,
и рев, и плеск, и рокот кораблей
уже других, шелка и багряницы

105 About That Land*

But in that land where the Rybinsk sea
now sounds, where the white steamer
cries out in the mist, feeling in its engine
living pain, and drops its speed,
5   as if making a final bow,
and boats it meets echo with their cry
and seagulls too, and the wave at the shore
splashes into distant memory, when
they decided to make the earth the bottom and the Volga
10 was let into these wetlands and meadows
into the valley world, which pulled the peasant cart
all together like a kolkhoz, and the clouds
from the turbid waters, like a burial shroud,
could not swim out, and only the monastery
15 still stood, as on the very first day,
lighting up the cold expanse
and raising up its cupolas and walls
decorated with frescoes on the inside,
but they too, gradually growing darker,
20 would have gone to the same place where gudgeon
already went, reminiscent of walleyed
monsters, if it had not been for those
artists, former icon painters,
who, on trestles and in the water
25 standing up to their ankles, up to their knees,
worked without stopping
and took down the painting, saved it from decay,
then died—anyway, some kind of sound
about that land, a kind of cutting echo,
30 like saw on stone, still remains,
remains in my ears...

                    I have seen these frescoes
in the Monastery of the Don.* The unsealed books
of the heavy slabs, like abysses:
Noah by his ark with the pairs of beasts
35 and the white dove—I can hear the cries,
and roaring, and splashing, and the rumbling of boats,
different ones now, silks and purples

везущих в трюмах, вина и виссон,
вот Вавилон, великая блудница,
40 сидящая на водах и верхом
на звере семиглавом и багряном,
жена с блестящей чашею в руке,
паскудством переполненной и срамом,
я вижу обмеревших вдалеке
45 купцов, и корабельщиков, и кормчих
пред той, великолепной и нагой,
вмиг рухнувшей и околевшей в корчах,
а вот и бес пятнистый с кочергой,
пытающий свидетелей Христовых,
50 и сонмы их, полегших, как снопы,
в одеждах белых, и на всех просторах,
на всех морях—громовый глас трубы:
се—Первенец из мертвых и Владыка
царей земных на облаке грядет
55 с небесным воинством Своим, и дико
трепещет в злобе сатанинский сброд;
и—белый конь, и на коне Сидящий
в одежде окровавленной, и меч
из уст его исходит злоразящий,
60 то Слово Божье, огненная речь
возмездия!—но столько страсти грешной
в виденьях кисти, страсти и стыда,
что это уж не Страшный суд, конечно,
не суд, а Праздник Страшного суда.

65 Не убоимся же десницы гнева
Господнего, а возблагодарим
Дарующего урожай посева—
веселье праведным и гибель злым!

И вижу я на утреннике тусклом,
70 как вскрылись реки и очнулся лед,
крошась на льдины, и пошел по руслам
широкий шорох, как вселенский сход,
и схлынул за два дня, и две недели
снега сгоняло с обморочных нив,
75 а в третью, за ручьями вслед, запели
и птицы, и когда двойной разлив
все затопил—о, что́ с тобою стало,
вдруг вырвалось само, земля моя,
ты столько лучших в бездны покидала
80 и вот застыла, словно бы ничья,

carrying in their holds, wines and byssus,
here's Babylon, the great whore,
40 sitting on the waters and riding
on a seven-headed crimson beast,
a woman with a shining chalice in her hand,
full of filthiness and shame,
I can see far off the immobile
45 merchants, and boatbuilders, and helmsmen
before that woman, magnificent and naked,
who immediately crashed down and went rigid in spasms,
and here is a spotted devil with his poker,
torturing the witnesses of Christ,
50 and their legions who have lain down like sheaves
in white raiment, and on all expanses,
on all seas—is the thunderous voice of the trumpet:
behold, the Firstborn from the dead and the Lord
of earthly tsars comes on a cloud
55 with His heavenly troops, and savagely
the satanic rabble trembles in malice;
and there's a white steed, and on that steed a Man sitting
in bloodied raiment, and a sword,
evil-smiting, issuing from his lips,
60 this is the Word of God, the fiery speech
of retribution!—but there is so much sinful passion
in the visions of this brush, so much passion and shame,
that it's no longer the Last Judgment, of course,
not a judgment, but the Feast of the Last Judgment.

65 Let us not fear the anger of the right hand
of the Lord, but let us give thanks
to Him who gives a harvest after sowing—
joy to the just and destruction to the evil!

And I see in the dim morning time
70 rivers opening up and ice coming to life,
grinding itself against icebergs, and down the furrows
has started a broad rustle, like the gathering of the universe,
and flung it away in two days, and for two weeks
has driven the snows from the swooning cornfields,
75 and in the third week, following the streams, the birds
have started singing too, and when the double flood
engulfed everything—O, what happened to you,
suddenly it just burst out, my land,
you have tossed so many of the best into the abyss
80 and now come to rest, as if belonging to no one,

у паводковых вод, где кружит голубь
над островком невестящихся верб
и дебаркадером, где серп и молот,
перекрестившись, сочетались в герб.

85 Плывите, корабли, путями века,
венозной синью сухопутных карт
над лесом строевым, где Ян Сапега
поляков положил, где Волго-Балт
провел на Север шлюзы и заводы,
90 систему мариинских лагерей,
где плещут воды, многие народы,
плывите же дорогою своей
с победным маршем, поднимайте якорь
над жизнью той, что под воду ушла,
95 над косточками русскими, где пахарь
почил на дне, и пусть колокола—
подводные—звонят, пусть бьются била
у побережий новых атлантид,
над Китежем, вздымающим стропила,
100 где хриплый петушок еще кричит...

Что сделано, то сделано, но в силе
все кровное останется и впредь.
Мы заплатили больше, чем просили.
Зачем же плакать, если можно петь!
105 Пой, Муза, пой, пустые бросим споры,
унынье от лукавого—и пусть
проходят за кормою Переборы
и Пошехонь отвеивает грусть.
А где язык запнется у поэта,
110 при свете дня или ночной звезды
пусть встанет, как восьмое чудо света,
белеясь, колокольня из воды...

106

Вот деревушка на краю оврага:
полдюжины антенн над головой,
за каждым палисадником собака,
кой-где цветы—и ни души живой.

by the waters of melted snow, where the dove circles
over the little island of affiancing willows
and the landing stage, where the sickle and hammer,
crossed, have combined into a coat of arms.

85 Sail, boats, by the routes of the age,
like venous blue on the maps of inland transport
above the timber, where Jan Sapega*
laid low the Poles, where the Volga-Baltic
brought locks and factories northward,
90 the Mariinsk camp system,
where the waters splash, and to many peoples,
sail, then, on your route
with a victory march, raise the anchor
over that life that has gone under the water,
95 over Russian bones, where the plowman
has found his rest on the bottom, and may the bells—
underwater bells—ring out, may the beaters beat
by the shores of the new atlantides,
over Kitezh* heaving up its rafters,
100 where the hoarse rooster still cries...

What's done is done, but in force
will remain everything of the blood, henceforth.
We have paid more than we asked.
Why then weep, if we can sing?
105 Sing, Muse, sing, let's drop these empty arguments,
Dejection's from the Evil One—so let
Perebory* pass behind the stern
and Poshekhone* disperse sadness.
But where the poet's tongue stammers,
110 in the light of day or the night star
may there arise, like the eighth wonder of the world
white-shining, the bell tower from under the water...

106

Here's a little village on the edge of a ravine:
half a dozen TV aerials overhead,
behind every fence a dog,
here and there flowers—and not a living soul.

5 Хозяева, должно быть, горожане,
народ наезжий, гостевой народ.
Одна корова на переднем плане,
одна как целый молокозавод.

Четыре камеры ее желудка,
10 рубец и сетка, книжка и сычуг,
пока не гукнет из машины дудка,
поточно переваривают луг.

А к вечеру работницей уставшей,
мослами задевая за сосцы,
15 она идет деревней забрехавшей,
и тренькают на шее бубенцы.

Боднув калитку, в сумерках соловых
идет во двор она слепым шажком
поить своих хозяев непутевых,
20 кормить сметаной их и творожком.

107

По гиблому насту, по талой звезде
найдешь меня там, где не будет нигде.

Есть дальняя пристань, последний приют,
где скорби не знают и мертвых не чтут.

5 Кто был для единого слова рожден,
пусть ветром и пеплом развеян, но он

как кочет туда безголовый взлетел,
а это, скажу вам, не худший удел.

5 It must be that the owners are townsfolk,
  people who just visit, people who are guests.
  One cow in the foreground,
  on its own like a whole milk factory.

  The four chambers of its stomach,
10 —paunch and net, third stomach and abomasum—
  until the horn sounds from the car
  digest the meadow like a production line.

  But toward evening like a tired woman worker,
  its joints catching against its nipples,
15 it goes through the village that's started yelping,
  and the little bells tinkle at its neck.

  Having butted the gate, in the light bay dusk
  it goes into the yard with its blind gait
  to give drink to its good-for-nothing owners,
20 and feed them with sour cream and cottage cheese.

107

  By corroded snow crust, by melted star
  you will find me where there won't be anywhere.

  There is a distant refuge, a final haven,
  where they know no grief and the dead are not honored.

5 Whoever was born for the word alone,
  though blown about like wind and ashes, he still

  like a headless rooster has flown up there,
  and this, I'll tell you, is not the worst lot.

Иосиф Бродский

108 Пятая годовщина (4 июня 1977)

Падучая звезда, тем паче—астероид
на резкость без труда твой праздный взгляд настроит.
Взгляни, взгляни туда, куда смотреть не стоит.

*

Там хмурые леса стоят в своей рванине.
5 Уйдя из точки «А», там поезд на равнине
стремится в точку «Б». Которой нет в помине.

Начала и концы там жизнь от взора прячет.
Покойник там незрим, как тот, кто только зачат.
Иначе среди птиц. Но птицы мало значат.

10 Там в сумерках рояль бренчит в висках бемолью.
Пиджак, вися в шкафу, там поедаем молью.
Оцепеневший дуб кивает лукоморью.

*

Там лужа во дворе, как площадь двух Америк.
Там одиночка-мать вывозит дочку в скверик.
15 Неугомонный Терек там ищет третий берег.

Там дедушка в упор рассматривает внучек.
И к звездам до сих пор там запускают жучек
плюс офицеров, чьих не осознать получек.

Там зелень щавеля смущает зелень лука.
20 Жужжание пчелы там главный принцип звука.
Там копия, щадя оригинал, безрука.

Joseph Brodsky

108 Fifth Anniversary (4 June 1977)[*]

A falling star, or even more so, an asteroid
without difficulty will attune your idle glance to awareness.
Look, look, in that direction where it's not worth looking.

*

There, gloomy forests stand in their tatters.
5 Departing from point A, there a train along the plain
hurries to point B. Of which there is no trace.

There, life hides beginnings and ends from your gaze.
A dead man there is invisible, like one who has just been conceived.
It's different among birds. But birds don't count for much.

10 There in the dusk a piano strums in your temples flat-keyedly.
A jacket, hanging in the cupboard, is nibbled there by moths.
The enchained oak* nods to the seashore.

*

There a puddle in the courtyard is like the area of two Americas.
There, a single mother takes her daughter to the playground.
15 The rebellious Terek there seeks a third bank.

There, a granddad examines his granddaughters at point-blank range.
And toward the stars still, there, they blast off little dogs
plus officers, whose wages can't be conceived.

There, the green of sorrel embarrasses the green of onions.
20 The buzzing of a bee, there, is the main principle of sound.
There, the copy, taking mercy on the original, has no hands.

*

Зимой в пустых садах трубят гипербореи,
и ребер больше там у пыльной батареи
в подъездах, чем у дам. И вообще быстрее

25 нащупывает их рукой замерзшей странник.
Там, наливая чай, ломают зуб о пряник.
Там мучает охранника во сне штыка трехгранник.

От дождевой струи там плохо спичке серной.
Там говорят «свои» в дверях с усмешкой скверной.
30 У рыбьей чешуи в воде там цвет консервный.

*

Там при словах «я за» течет со щек известка.
Там в церкви образа коптит свеча из воска.
Порой дает раза соседним странам войско.

Там пышная сирень бушует в палисаде.
35 Пивная цельный день лежит в глухой осаде.
Там тот, кто впереди, похож на тех, кто сзади.

Там в воздухе висят обрывки старых арий.
Пшеница перешла, покинув герб, в гербарий.
В лесах полно куниц и прочих ценных тварей.

*

40 Там лёжучи плашмя на рядовой холстине
отбрасываешь тень, как пальма в Палестине.
Особенно—во сне. И, на манер пустыни,

там сахарный песок пересекаем мухой.
Там города стоят, как двинутые рюхой,
45 и карта мира там замещена пеструхой,

мычащей на бугре. Там схож закат с порезом.
Там вдалеке завод дымит, гремит железом,
ненужным никому: ни пьяным, ни тверезым.

*

Там слышен крик совы, ей отвечает филин.
50 Овацию листвы унять там вождь бессилен.
Простую мысль, увы, пугает вид извилин.

*

In winter in empty gardens the hyperboreans trumpet,
and there are more ribs, there, on dusty radiators
in entrance halls than on the ladies. And on the whole quicker

25 the traveler gropes for them with his freezing hand.
There, pouring out tea, they break their teeth on gingerbread.
There, the triple face of his bayonet tortures the sentry in his sleep.

From the streaming of the rain there it's bad for the sulphur match.
There, they say "one of ours" at the door with an evil grin.
30 The scales of fish in water, there, have the color of tin cans.

*

There, upon the words "I'm in favor" lime flows from the cheeks.
There, in the church, the icons are smoked by candles made of wax.
From time to time the troops show neighboring countries what's what.

There, luxuriant lilac storms in enclosures.
35 The beer stall all day is under close siege.
There, he who is in front resembles those who are behind.

There, in the air hang scraps of old arias.
Wheat has moved, abandoning the coat of arms, into the herbarium.
The forest is full of pine martens and other valuable creatures.

*

40 There, lying prone on a routine canvas
one throws a shadow like a palm tree in Palestine.
Especially when one is asleep. And, in the manner of the desert,

there, granulated sugar is traversed by a fly.
There, cities stand, as if gobsmacked,
45 and the map of the world, there, is replaced by a brindled cow,

mooing on a mound. There, the dawn is similar to a cut.
There, in the distance a factory smokes, rattles with metal,
that nobody needs, neither the drunk nor the sober.

*

There, the cry of the owl is heard, and it is answered by the eagle owl.
50 The ovation of the leaves, there, the leader is powerless to keep down.
Simple thought, alas, is frightened by the sight of convolutions.

Там украшают флаг, обнявшись, серп и молот.
Но в стенку гвоздь не вбит и огород не полот.
Там, грубо говоря, великий план запорот.

55 Других примет там нет—загадок, тайн, диковин.
Пейзаж лишен примет и горизонт неровен.
Там в моде серый цвет—цвет времени и бревен.

*

Я вырос в тех краях. Я говорил «закурим»
их лучшему певцу. Был содержимым тюрем.
60 Привык к свинцу небес и к айвазовским бурям.

Там, думал, и умру—от скуки, от испуга.
Когда не от руки, так на руках у друга.
Видать, не рассчитал. Как квадратуру круга.

Видать, не рассчитал; зане в театре задник
65 важнее, чем актер. Простор важней, чем всадник.
Передних ног простор не отличит от задних.

*

Теперь меня там нет. Означенной пропаже
дивятся, может быть, лишь вазы в Эрмитаже.
Отсутствие мое большой дыры в пейзаже

70 не сделало; пустяк: дыра—но небольшая.
Ее затянут мох или пучки лишая,
гармонии тонов и проч. не нарушая.

Теперь меня там нет. Об этом думать странно.
Но было бы чудней изображать барана,
75 дрожать, но раздражать на склоне дней тирана,

*

паясничать. Ну что ж! на всё свои законы:
я не любил жлобства, не целовал иконы,
и на одном мосту чугунный лик Горгоны

казался в тех краях мне самым честным ликом.
80 Зато столкнувшись с ним теперь, в его великом
варьянте, я своим не подавился криком

и не окаменел. Я слышу Музы лепет.
Я чувствую нутром, как Парка нитку треплет:
мой углекислый вздох пока что в вышних терпят,

There, the flag is adorned by hammer and sickle embraced.
But into the wall the nail is not driven and the vegetable garden is unweeded.
There, crudely speaking, the great plan is full of holes.

55 There are no other omens there, such as enigmas, secrets, marvels.
The landscape is devoid of features and the horizon is uneven.
There, in fashion is the color gray, the color of time and logs.

*

I grew up in those parts. I used to say "Let's have a smoke"
to their best singer. I was the contents of prisons.
60 Got used to the lead of the skies and to Aivazovsky-type* storms.

There, I used to think, I would die—from boredom, from fright.
If not by the hand, then in the arms, of a friend.
It looks as if I got it wrong. Like squaring the circle.

It looks as if I got it wrong; for in the theater the backdrop
65 is more important than the actor. Space is more important than the horseman.
Space will not distinguish the forelegs from the back ones.

*

I'm not there now. At the loss indicated above
only the vases in the Hermitage, perhaps, show surprise.
My absence has made no big hole in the landscape;

70 it's a trifle: a hole, but not a big one.
It will be covered over with moss or tufts of lichen,
not spoiling the harmony of the tones, etc.

I'm not there now. It's odd to think of that.
But it would be stranger still to act the sheep,
75 to tremble, but annoy the tyrant in his declining days,

*

to act the clown. Well then! Everything has its laws:
I didn't care for crude behavior, didn't kiss icons,
and the cast-iron visage of the Gorgon on one of the bridges

seemed to me in those parts to be the most honest visage.
80 Though, being confronted by it now, in its great
variant, I did not choke on my own cry

and didn't turn to stone. I hear the purling of the Muse.
I feel in my insides Fate twitching the thread:
my carbon-dioxide sigh is tolerated on high for the time being,

*

85 и без костей язык, до внятных звуков лаком,
судьбу благодарит кириллицыным знаком.
На то она—судьба, чтоб понимать на всяком

наречьи. Предо мной—пространство в чистом виде.
В нем места нет столпу, фонтану, пирамиде.
90 В нем, судя по всему, я не нуждаюсь в гиде.

Скрипи, мое перо, мой коготок, мой посох.
Не подгоняй сих строк: забуксовав в отбросах,
эпоха на колесах нас не догонит, босых.

*

Мне нечего сказать ни греку, ни варягу.
95 Зане не знаю я, в какую землю лягу.
Скрипи, скрипи, перо! переводи бумагу.

109 Йорк

To W. H. A.

Бабочки Северной Англии пляшут над лебедою
под кирпичной стеной мертвой фабрики. За средою
наступает четверг, и т.д. Небо пышет жаром,
и поля выгорают. Города отдают лежалым
5 полосатым сукном, георгины страдают жаждой.
И твой голос—«Я знал трех великих поэтов. Каждый
был большой сукин сын»—раздается в моих ушах
с неожиданной четкостью. Я замедляю шаг

и готов оглянуться. Скоро четыре года,
10 как ты умер в австрийской гостинице. Под стрелой перехода
ни души: черепичные кровли, асфальт, известка,
тополя. Честер тоже умер—тебе известно
это лучше, чем мне. Как костяшки на пыльных счетах,
воробьи восседают на проводах. Ничто так
15 не превращает знакомый подъезд в толчею колонн,
как любовь к человеку; особенно если он

мертв. Отсутствие ветра заставляет тугие листья
напрягать свои мышцы и нехотя шевелиться.
Танец белых капустниц похож на корабль в бурю.

*

85 and my boneless tongue, partial to comprehensible sounds,
thanks destiny through the Cyrillic sign.
Its purpose as destiny is to comprehend in every

dialect. Before me is space in pure form.
Within it there is no place for pillar, fountain, or pyramid.
90 In it, taking things all together, I do not need a guide.

Squeak away, my pen, my little talon, my crook.
Don't herd in these lines: skidding on the garbage,
this wheeled epoch won't catch up with us, the barefooted ones.

*

I have nothing to say to the Greek or the Varangian.
95 Since I no longer know what earth I will lie in.
Squeak away, squeak away, pen! Use up the paper.

109 York

To W. H. A.*

The butterflies of Northern England dance over the goosefoot
under the brick wall of a dead factory. After Wednesday
comes Thursday, and so on. The sky blazes with heat,
and the fields are getting parched. The towns give off musty
5 striped cloth, dahlias suffer from thirst.
And your voice, saying "I have known three great poets.* Each one
was a real son of a bitch," resounding in my ears
with surprising clarity. I slacken my stride

and am ready to take a look round. Soon it'll be four years
10 since you died in that Austrian hotel. Under the pointer of the crossing
there's not a soul: tiled roofs, asphalt, lime,
poplars. Chester's* dead too; you know that
better than I do. Like the counters on a dusty abacus,
sparrows sit enthroned on the wires. Nothing so
15 turns a familiar entrance into a bunch of columns,
as love for someone; especially if he is

dead. The absence of wind makes the taut leaves
flex their muscles and unwillingly stir.
The dance of the cabbage-white butterflies resembles a ship in a storm.

20 Человек приносит с собою тупик в любую
точку света; и согнутое колено
размножает тупым углом перспективу плена,
как журавлиный клин, когда он берет
курс на Юг. Как всё движущееся вперед.

25 Пустота, поглощая солнечный свет на общих
основаньях с боярышником, увеличивается наощупь
в направленьи вытянутой руки, и
мир сливается в длинную улицу, на которой живут другие.
В этом смысле он—Англия. Англия в этом смысле

30 до сих пор Империя и в состояньи—если
верить музыке, булькающей водой—
править морями. Впрочем—любой средой.

Я в последнее время немного сбиваюсь: скалюсь
отраженью в стекле витрины; покамест палец

35 набирает свой номер, рука опускает трубку.
Стоит закрыть глаза, как вижу пустую шлюпку,
замершую на воде посредине бухты.
Выходя наружу из телефонной будки,
слышу голос скворца, в крике его—испуг.

40 Но раньше, чем он взлетает, звук

растворяется в воздухе. Чьей беспредметной сини
и сродни эта жизнь, где вещи видней в пустыне,
ибо в ней тебя нет. И вакуум постепенно
заполняет местный ландшафт. Как сухая пена,

45 овцы покоятся на темно-зеленых волнах
йоркширского вереска. Кордебалет проворных
бабочек, повинуясь невидимому смычку,
мельтешит над заросшей канавой, не давая зрачку

ни на чем задержаться. И вертикальный стебель

50 иван-чая длинней уходящей на Север
древней Римской дороги, всеми забытой в Риме.
Вычитая из меньшего большее, из человека—Время,
получаешь в остатке слова, выделяющиеся на белом
фоне отчетливей, чем удается телом

55 это сделать при жизни, даже сказав «лови!»

Что источник любви превращает в объект любви.

1977

20 Man brings with him his dead end to any
    point in the world; and the bent knee
    multiplies with its obtuse angle the perspective of captivity,
    like a wedge of cranes, when it sets
    course for the South. Like everything that is moving forward.

25 Emptiness, swallowing up the sunlight on the same
    basis as the hawthorn, expands, feeling its way,
    in the direction of the outstretched arm, and
    the world flows into the long street, on which other people live.
    In this sense [the world] is England. England in this sense
30 is still an Empire and is capable—if
    one is to trust the music that gurgles like water—
    of ruling the waves. Any other medium, for that matter.

    Lately, I've been getting a bit muddled: I pull faces
    at my reflection in shop windows; while my finger
35 is dialing my number, my hand lets the receiver drop.
    I only need to shut my eyes, and I see an empty sloop
    motionless on the water in the middle of a bay.
    Going out of the phone booth,
    I hear the voice of the starling, and in its cry there is fear.
40 But before he takes flight, the sound

    dissolves in the air. To whose deep blue, devoid of objects,
    this life is akin, where things are more visible in the desert,
    for there's no you in it. And a vacuum gradually
    fills up the local landscape. Like dry foam,
45 the sheep take their rest on the dark-green waves
    of the Yorkshire heather. The corps-de-ballet of sprightly
    butterflies, obeying an invisible violin bow,
    flutter over the overgrown ditch, giving the eye's pupil

    nothing to linger on. And the vertical stalk
50 of the fireweed is longer than the, going away to the North,
    ancient Roman road, forgotten by everyone in Rome.
    Subtracting the greater from the lesser, Time from man,
    the remainder is words, which stand out against a white
    background more distinctly than the body succeeds
55 in doing while one is alive, even when you say "Catch!"

    Which turns the source of love into an object of love.

1977

110

Ты, гитарообразная вещь со спутанной паутиной
струн, продолжающая коричневеть в гостиной,
белеть а ля Казимир на выстиранном просторе,
темнеть—особенно вечером—в коридоре,
5 спой мне песню о том, как шуршит портьера,
как включается, чтоб оглушить полтела,
тень, как лиловая муха, сползает с карты,
и закат в саду за окном точно дым эскадры,
от которой осталась одна матроска,
10 позабытая в детской. И как расческа
в кулаке дрессировщика-турка, как рыбку—леской,
возвышает болонку над Ковалевской
до счастливого случая тявкнуть сорок
раз в день рожденья—и мокрый порох
15 гасит звезды салюта, громко шипя, в стакане,
и стоят графины кремлем на ткани.

22 июля 1978

111

Я входил вместо дикого зверя в клетку,
выжигал свой срок и кликуху гвоздем в бараке,
жил у моря, играл в рулетку,
обедал черт знает с кем во фраке.
5 С высоты ледника я озирал полмира,
трижды тонул, дважды бывал распорот.
Бросил страну, что меня вскормила.
Из забывших меня можно составить город.
Я слонялся в степях, помнящих вопли гунна,
10 надевал на себя что сызнова входит в моду,
сеял рожь, покрывал черной толью гумна
и не пил только сухую воду.
Я впустил в свои сны вороненый зрачок конвоя,
жрал хлеб изгнанья, не оставляя корок.
15 Позволял своим связкам все звуки, помимо воя;
перешел на шопот. Теперь мне сорок.

110

You, guitar-shaped thing with a tangled spider's web
of strings, continuing to show brown in the drawing room,
to show white à la Kazimir* on the laundered expanse,
to show dark—especially in the evening—in the corridor,
5 sing me a song about a portiere rustling,
fitting in so as to engulf half a body,
a shadow like a lilac fly crawling down off a map,
and the sunset in the garden through the window like the smoke of a
    squadron,
from which there survives just one sailor suit,
10 forgotten in the nursery. And the comb
in the fist of the Turkish trainer, like a fish with the rod,
lifting up a lapdog above Kovalevskaya*
until a lucky occasion to yap forty
times on the birthday—and the wet gunpowder
15 putting out the stars of the salute, hissing loudly, in a glass,
and the decanters standing like a kremlin on the cloth.

22 July 1978

111

I have entered a cage in place of a wild beast,
burned my sentence and nickname with a nail in a prison hut,
lived by the sea, played at roulette,
dined the devil knows with whom in a tailcoat.
5 From the height of a glacier I have surveyed half the world,
three times drowned, twice was ripped apart.
Abandoned the country that had nurtured me.
From those who have forgotten me it is possible to make a city.
I have hung around steppes that remember the wail of the Hun,
10 put on that which once more is coming back into fashion,
planted rye, covered with black tar paper the threshing floor
and haven't drunk only dry water.
I have let into my dreams the blued pupil of the warder,
chewed the bread of exile, leaving no crusts.
15 Allowed my [vocal] cords all sounds apart from a howl;
Gone over to a whisper. Now I am forty.

Что сказать мне о жизни? Что оказалась длинной.
Только с горем я чувствую солидарность.
Но пока мне рот не забили глиной,
20 из него раздаваться будет лишь благодарность.

24 мая 1980 г.

112

Я был только тем, чего
ты касалась ладонью,
над чем в глухую, воронью
ночь склоняла чело.

5 Я был лишь тем, что ты
там, внизу, различала:
смутный облик сначала,
много позже—черты.

Это ты, горяча,
10 ошую, одесную
раковину ушную
мне творила, шепча.

Это ты, теребя
штору, в сырую полость
15 рта вложила мне голос,
окликавший тебя.

Я был попросту слеп.
Ты, возникая, прячась,
даровала мне зрячесть.
20 Так оставляют след.

Так творятся миры.
Так, сотворив, их часто
оставляют вращаться,
расточая дары.

25 Так, бросаем то в жар,
то в холод, то в свет, то в темень,

What should I say about [my] life? That it's turned out a long one.
Only with grief I feel solidarity.
But until [they] cram my mouth with clay,
20 from it will resound only gratitude.

24 May 1980

112

I was only that which
you touched with your palm,
over which in the deep, raven
night you inclined your brow.

5 I was merely that which you
there, below, could distinguish:
a vague outline to begin with,
much later, features.

It was you, burning hot,
10 at dexter and sinister,
the shell of my ear
created for me, whispering.

It was you, picking at
the blind, into the damp orifice
15 of my mouth put a voice for me,
which called unto you.

I was simply blind.
You, arising, hiding,
made me a present of sight.
20 Thus a trace is left.

Thus are created worlds.
Thus, having created them, often
they are left to turn,
generously bestowing gifts.

25 Thus, plunged now into heat,
now into cold, or light, or darkness,

в мирозданьи потерян,
кружится шар.

1981

113

Как давно я топчу, видно по каблуку.
Паутинку тоже пальцем не снять с чела.
То и приятно в громком кукареку,
что звучит как вчера.
5 Но и черной мысли толком не закрепить,
как на лоб упавшую косо прядь.
И уже ничего не снится, чтоб меньше быть,
реже сбываться, не засорять
времени. Нищий квартал в окне
10 глаз мозолит, чтоб, в свой черед,
в лицо запомнить жильца, а не
как тот считает, наоборот.
И по комнате точно шаман кружа,
я наматываю как клубок
15 на себя пустоту ее, чтоб душа
знала что-то, что знает Бог.

114 К Урании

И. К.

У всего есть предел: в том числе, у печали.
Взгляд застревает в окне, точно лист—в ограде.
Можно налить воды. Позвенеть ключами.
Одиночество есть человек в квадрате.
5 Так дромадер нюхает, морщась, рельсы.
Пустота раздвигается, как портьера.
Да и что вообще есть пространство, если
не отсутствие в каждой точке тела?
Оттого-то Урания старше Клио.
10 Днем, и при свете слепых коптилок,
видишь: она ничего не скрыла,
и, глядя на глобус, глядишь в затылок.
Вон они, те леса, где полно черники,

lost in the firmament,
the sphere spins.

1981

113

How long I've been tapping around, you can see by the heel [of my shoe].
The spider's web also can't be removed from my brow with a finger.
Though what's pleasant in the noisy cock-a-doodle-do,
is that it sounds like it did yesterday.
5 But a black thought too can't be properly kept in its place,
like the strand of hair that falls aslant my forehead.
And now I can dream of nothing, so as to exist less,
to come to pass less often, not to clutter up
time. The poor part of town through the window
10 offends my sight, in order, in its turn,
to memorize the tenant by his face, and not
as he thinks, the other way round.
And circling around the room like a shaman
I wind round like a ball of wool
15 upon myself its emptiness, so that my heart
might know something that God knows.

114 To Urania*

To I. K.

There is a limit to everything: including grief.
One's glance catches in the window, like a leaf in a fence.
You may pour some water. Make keys ring.
Loneliness is man squared.
5 Thus the dromedary sniffs, wrinkling, the railway line.
Emptiness parts like a portiere.
And so what in general is space, if
not the absence at every point of a body?
For this reason Urania is older than Clio.
10 In daylight, and by the light of blind oil lamps,
one sees: she has hidden nothing
and looking at the globe, one looks at the back of the head.
There they are, those woods, where it's full of bilberries,

реки, где ловят рукой белугу,
15 либо—город, в чьей телефонной книге
ты уже не числишься. Дальше, к югу,
то есть, к юго-востоку, коричневеют горы,
бродят в осоке лошади-пржевали;
лица желтеют. А дальше—плывут линкоры,
20 и простор голубеет, как белье с кружевами.

115

Кончится лето. Начнется сентябрь. Разрешат отстрел
утки, рябчика, вальдшнепа. «Ах, как ты постарел»,
скажет тебе одна, и ты задерешь двустволку,
но чтоб глубже вздохнуть, а не спугнуть перепелку.
5 И легкое чутко дёрнется: с лотков продают урюк.
Но и помимо этого мир вокруг
меняется так стремительно, точно он стал колоться
дурью, приобретенной у смуглого иногородца.

Дело, конечно, не в осени. И не в чертах лица,
10 меняющихся, как у зверя, бегущего на ловца,
но в ощущении кисточки, оставшейся от картины,
лишенной конца, начала, рамы и середины.
Не говоря—музея, не говоря—гвоздя.
И поезд вдали по равнине бежит, свистя,
15 хотя, вглядевшись как следует, ты не заметишь дыма;
но с точки зренья ландшафта, движенье необходимо.

Это относится к осени, к времени вообще,
когда кончаешь курить и когда еще
деревья кажутся рельсами, сбросившими колеса,
20 и опушки ржавеют, как узловые леса.
И в горле уже не комок, но стопроцентный ёж—
ибо в открытом море больше не узнаёшь
силуэт парохода, и профиль аэроплана,
растерявший все нимбы, выглядит в вышних странно.

25 Так прибавляют в скорости. Подруга была права.
Что бы узнал древний римлянин, проснись он сейчас? Дрова,
очертания облака, голубя в верхотуре,

rivers where they fish for sturgeon with bare hands,
15 or—a town, in whose telephone book
one no longer figures. Further on, to the south,
that is, to the southeast, mountains show brown,
there wander among the alders Przeval-horses;*
faces show yellow. And further on battleships sail,
20 and the wide expanse is sky blue, like linen edged with lace.

115

Summer will end. September will begin. There will be open season
on duck, grouse, woodcock. "Oh, how you've aged"
one woman will say to you, and you'll jerk up your double-barrels,
but so as to take a deeper breath, and not so as to scare the quail.
5 And your lung will twitch sensitively: dried apricots being sold from
        hawker's trays.
But besides this the world around
is changing with such a rush, as if it had begun injecting itself
with shit acquired from a swarthy man from another town.

It's not, of course, a matter of autumn. And not the features of a face,
10 changing like that of a beast running at the hunter,
but in the sensation of a brush left behind after a painting,
deprived of an end, beginning, frame, and middle.
Not to mention a museum, not to mention a nail.
And a train in the distance runs through the plain, whistling,
15 although, when you look properly, you won't notice any smoke;
but from the point of view of a landscape, movement is essential.

This applies to autumn, to time in general,
when you finish smoking and when still
the trees seem to be railway lines that have thrown off the wheels,
20 and the fringe of the woods is rusting like the main forest.
And in your throat it isn't a lump now, but a one-hundred-percent
        hedgehog—
for on the open sea you will no longer recognize
the silhouette of a steamboat; and the profile of an airplane,
leaving all nimbus behind, looks strange in the empyrean.

25 Thus speed is increased. My woman friend was right.
What would an Ancient Roman recognize if he were to awaken now?
        Firewood,
the outlines of a cloud, showing sky blue in the up above,

плоскую воду, что-то в архитектуре,
но—никого в лицо. Так некоторые порой
30 ездят еще за границу, но, лишены второй
жизни, спешат воротиться, пряча глаза от страха,
и, не успев улечься от прощального взмаха,

платочек трепещет в воздухе. Другие, кому уже
выпало что-то любить больше, чем жизнь, в душе
35 зная, что старость—это и есть вторая
жизнь, белеют на солнце, как мрамор, не загорая,
уставившись в некую точку и не чужды утех
истории. Потому что чем больше тех
точек, тем больше крапинок на проигравших в прятки
40 яйцах рябчика, вальдшнепа, вспугнутой куропатки.

1987

116

Только пепел знает, что значит сгореть дотла.
Но я тоже скажу, близоруко взглянув вперед:
не все уносимо ветром, не все метла,
широко забирая по двору, подберет.
5 Мы останемся смятым окурком, плевком, в тени
под скамьей, куда угол проникнуть лучу не даст,
и слежимся в обнимку с грязью, считая дни,
в перегной, в осадок, в культурный пласт.
Замаравши совок, археолог разинет пасть
10 отрыгнуть; но его открытие прогремит
на весь мир, как зарытая в землю страсть,
как обратная версия пирамид.
«Падаль» выдохнет он, обхватив живот,
но окажется дальше от нас, чем земля от птиц,
15 потому что падаль—свобода от клеток, свобода от
целого: апофеоз частиц.

1986

the flat water, something in the architecture,
but no one by their face. Thus certain people from time to time
30 still go abroad, but, deprived of a second
life, they hurry to return, hiding their eyes with fear,
and, without having time to recover from the gesture of farewell,

flutter their handkerchiefs in the air. Others, whose fate it has already
been to love something more than life, in their hearts
35 knowing that old age is actually a second
life, show white in the sun, like marble, not getting tanned,
fixing their gaze on a certain point and not alien to the delights
of history. Because the more there are of those
points, the more speckles there are on the lost at hide and seek
40 eggs of the grouse, woodcock, and scared partridge.

1987

116

Only ashes know what it means to be burned out.
But I too will say as I look shortsightedly ahead:
not everything is carried away by the wind, not everything the broom,
taking a wide sweep across the courtyard, will pick up.
5 We will remain as a crumpled cigarette end, a gob of spit, in the shadow
under a bench where the corner does not permit a ray to penetrate.
And we will lie down in an embrace with the dirt, counting the days,
into humus, deposit, cultural layer.
Fouling his trowel, the archaeologist will open wide his craw
10 to belch; but his discovery will be thundered
worldwide, like a passion buried in the ground,
like a reversed version of the pyramids.
"Carrion!" he'll breathe, grabbing his stomach,
but he'll turn out to be further from us than the earth from the birds,
15 because carrion is freedom from cells, freedom from
the whole: an apotheosis of particles.

1986

117

М. Б.

Дорогая, я вышел сегодня из дому поздно вечером
подышать свежим воздухом, веющим с океана.
Закат догорал на галерке китайским веером,
и туча клубилась, как крышка концертного фортепьяно.

5 Четверть века назад ты питала пристрастье к люля и к финикам,
рисовала тушью в блокноте, немножко пела,
развлекалась со мной; но потом сошлась с инженером-химиком
и, судя по письмам, чудовищно поглупела.

Теперь тебя видят в церквях в провинции и в метрополии
10 на панихидах по общим друзьям, идущих теперь сплошною
чередой; и я рад, что на свете есть расстоянья более
немыслимые, чем между тобой и мною.

Не пойми меня дурно: с твоим голосом, телом, именем
ничего уже больше не связано; никто их не уничтожил,
15 но забыть одну жизнь человеку нужна, как минимум,
еще одна жизнь. И я эту долю прожил.

Повезло и тебе: где еще, кроме разве что в фотографии,
ты пребудешь всегда без морщин, молода, весела, глумлива?
Ибо время, столкнувшись с памятью, узнает о своем бесправии.
20 Я курю в темноте и вдыхаю гнилье отлива.

117

To M. B.

My dear, I left the house today late in the evening
to have a breath of fresh air wafting in from the ocean.
The sunset was burning out in the gods like a Chinese fan,
and a cloud was gathering like the lid of a concert grand piano.

5 A quarter of a century ago you were partial to lyulya-kebabs and dates,
you did charcoal sketches in a notebook, did a bit of singing,
had fun with me; but then you took up with a chemical engineer
and, to judge from your letters, you grew monstrously stupid.

Now people see you in churches in the provinces and the capital
10 at the funeral services for mutual friends, which are going on now in an
     unbroken
succession; and I'm glad that in this world there are distances more
unthinkable than the one between you and me.

Don't take what I say badly: with your voice, your body, your name
nothing is connected any more; nobody has destroyed them,
15 but to forget one life a person needs, as a minimum,
one more life. And I've lived through that portion.

You've been lucky too: where else, besides maybe in a photograph,
will you always be unwrinkled, young, happy, mocking?
For time, when it comes into collision with memory, finds out about its lack
     of rights.
20 I smoke in the darkness and inhale the rottenness of the ebb tide.

Дмитрий Пригов

118

Я устал уже на первой строчке
Первого четверостишья
Вот дотащился до третьей строчки
А вот до четвертой дотащился

5 Вот дотащился до первой строчки
Но уже второго четверостишья
Вот дотащился до третьей строчки
А вот до конца, Господи, дотащился

119

Когда здесь на посту стоит Милицанер
Ему до Внуково простор весь открывается
На Запад и Восток глядит Милицанер
И пустота за ними открывается
5 И центр, где стоит Милицанер—
Взгляд на него отсюду открывается
Отсюду виден Милиционер
С Востока виден Милиционер
И с Юга виден Милиционер
10 И с моря виден Милиционер
И с неба виден Милиционер
И с-под земли...
                    Да он и не скрывается

1976

Dmitrii Prigov

118

I'm tired already on the first line
Of the first quatrain
Now I've reached the third line
And now the fourth I've reached

5 Now I've reached the first line
But already of the second quatrain
Now I've reached the third line
And now the end, O Lord, I've reached

119

When here on duty stands a Pliceman
For him an expanse opens up as far as Vnukovo*
To West and East looks the Pliceman
And emptiness opens up behind them
5 And the center, where the Pliceman stands
From evrywhere a sight of him opens up
From evrywhere can be seen the Policeman
From the East can be seen the Policeman
And from the South can be seen the Policeman
10 Also from the sea can be seen the Policeman
Also from the sky can be seen the Policeman
Also from under the earth...
                                    But he isn't trying to hide, is he

1976

120

В буфете Дома литераторов
Пьет пиво милиционер
Пьет на обычный свой манер
Не видя даже литераторов

5 Они же смотрят на него
Вокруг Него светло и пусто
И все их разные искусства
При Нем не значат ничего

Он представляет собой Жизнь
10 Явившуюся в форме Долга
Жизнь кратка, а Искусство долго
И в схватке побеждает Жизнь

121

Народ он ведь не только пьет
Хоть это знают и немногие
Он трудится и он живет
Не как букашки многоногие

5 И за подвалами газет
Где пишется, что он работает
Читай, что он не только пьет
Но и действительно—работает

1976

122

Орел над землей пролетает
Не Сталин ли есть ему имя?
Да нет же—орел ему имя
А Сталин там не летает
5 Вот лебедь летит над землею

120

In the buffet of the House of Writers*
A policeman is drinking beer
He drinks in his usual fashion
Not even seeing the writers

5 They though are looking at him
Around Him it's bright and empty
And all their various arts
Mean nothing in the presence of Him

He represents Life
10 Manifested in the form of Duty
Life is short, but Art is long
And in the combat Life is victorious

121

The people after all doesn't only drink
Although not many people know that
It labors and it lives
Not like the little insects with lots of legs

5 And into the bottom-of-the-page articles in newspapers
Where they write that it works
You should read that it doesn't only drink
But that in fact it does work

1976

122

An eagle flies over the earth
Isn't Stalin its name?
'Course not, its name is eagle
And Stalin doesn't fly up there
5 There's a swan flying over the earth

Не Пригов ли есть ему имя?
Не Пригов, увы, ему имя
И Пригов там не летает
А Пригов?—сидит на земле он
10 И в небо украдкой глядит
Орла он и лебедя видит
А Сталин?—в земле он лежит

123

Известно, что можно жить со многими женщинами и в то же
время душою той единственной не изменять
Как же в этом свете измену Родине понимать?

Ведь Родину мы любим не плотью, а душой
Как ту единственную, или не любим—тогда тем более измены
нет никакой

5 Но все это справедливо, конечно, если Родину, как у Блока, как
женщину понимать
Но нет никакого оправданья, кроме расстрела, если она—Мать!

124

Когда я в Калуге по случаю был
Одну калужанку я там полюбил

Была в ней большая народная сила
Меня на руках она часто носила

5 А что я?—москвич я, я хрупок и мал
И вот что однажды всердцах ей сказал:

Мужчина ведь мужественней и сильней
Быть должен—на том и расталися с ней.

Isn't Prigov its name?
No, Prigov, alas, isn't its name
And Prigov isn't flying up there
What about Prigov? he sits on the earth
10 And steals a look up at the sky
The eagle and the swan he sees
And Stalin? He's lying in the earth

123

It's well known that you can live with many women and at the same time in
    your soul not betray that only one
How then in this world is one to understand betrayal of the Motherland?

After all we love the Motherland not with the flesh but with the soul
Like we do that only one, or else we don't love her—and then there's no
    betrayal even more so

5 But all this is just, of course, if one understands the Motherland to be a
    woman, like Blok did
But there's no justification apart from execution by firing squad, if she's the
    Mother!

124

When I once happened to be in Kaluga
I fell in love with a Kaluga woman

There was in her the great strength of the people
She often carried me in her arms

5 But what about me? I come from Moscow, I'm frail and small
And here's what I said to her once in anger:

A man after all more masculine and strong
Must be, and on that I parted from her

125

Вот я, предположим, обычный поэт
А тут вот по прихоти русской судьбы
Приходится совестью нации быть
А как ею быть, коли совести нет
5 Стихи, скажем, есть, а вот совести—нет
Как тут быть

126

Когда я размышляю о поэзии, как ей дальше жить
То понимаю, что мои современники должны меня больше, чем
    Пушкина любить
Я пишу о том, что с ними происходит, или происходило, или
    произойдет—им каждый факт знаком
И говорю им это понятным нашим общим языком
5 И если они все-таки любят Пушкина больше, чем меня, так это
    потому что
я добрый и честный: не поношу его не посягаю на его стихи,
    его славу и честь
Да как же я могу поносить все это, когда я тот самый Пушкин
    и есть

127

Премудрость Божия пред Божим лицом
Плясала безнаказная и пела
А не с лицом насупленным сидела
Или еще каким таким лицом

5 Вот так и ты, поэт, перед лицом народа
Пляши и пой перед его лицом
А то не то что будешь подлецом
Но неким глубокомысленным уродом
Будешь

125

Here's me, an ordinary poet let's assume
But the thing is that by the whim of Russian fate
I have to be the conscience of the nation
But how to be that thing, if there is no conscience
5 Poems, maybe, there are, but a conscience—no
What to do

126

When I think about poetry, how it should live from now on
I understand that my contemporaries ought to love me more than Pushkin
I write about what happens to them, or has happened, or will happen, they're
  familiar with every fact
And I say this to them in our comprehensible common language
5 And if they still love Pushkin more than me, then it's because
I'm good and honest, I don't put him down don't make allegations about his
  poetry, his fame and honor
But how could I put all this down when I am that same Pushkin

127

God's wisdom before the face of God
Danced with impunity and sang
And didn't sit with cast-down face
Or with some other kind of face

5 Just like this you too, poet, before the face of the people
Dance and sing before its face
Or else it's not that you'll be a bastard
But a kind of profoundly thinking monster
You will be

128 Банальное рассуждение на тему:
быть знаменитым некрасиво

Когда ты скажем знаменит—
Быть знаменитым некрасиво
Но если ты незнаменит
То знаменитым быть не только
5 Желательно, но и красиво
Ведь красота—не результат
Твоей возможной знаменитости
Но знаменитость результат
Есть красоты, а красота спасет!
10 А знаменитым быть, конечно, некрасиво
Когда уже ты знаменит

1982

129

Женщина в метро меня лягнула
Ну, пихаться—там куда ни шло
Здесь же она явно перегнула
Палку и все дело перешло
5 В ранг ненужно-личных отношений
я, естественно, в ответ лягнул
Но и тут же попросил прощенья—
Просто я как личность выше был

130

Известно нам от давних дней
Что человек сильнее смерти
А в наши дни уже, поверьте—
И жизни тоже он сильней

5 Она его блазнит и манит
А он ей кажет голый шиш

128 A Banal Disquisition on the Subject "To Be Famous Isn't Beautiful"*

When you're let's say famous
It's not beautiful to be famous
But if you're not famous
To be famous is not only
5 Desirable, but also beautiful
For beauty, after all, is not the result
Of your possible famousness
But famousness is the result
of beauty, and beauty will save!*
10 But to be famous, of course, isn't beautiful
When you're already famous

1982

129

A woman in the subway kicked me
What's using your feet, though—it happens
But in this case she clearly went too
Far, and the whole business went over
5 To the level of unnecessarily personal relations
naturally, in response I kicked
But immediately said I was sorry—
It's just that I as an individual was superior

130

We've known since ancient times
That man is stronger than death
But in our times, believe me—
He's stronger than life as well

5 Life tempts and beckons him
But he just gives it the finger

Его ничем не соблазнишь—
Он нищенствует и ликует
Поскольку всех уже сильней

131

Висит на небе ворон-птица
А под землей лежит мертвец
Они друг другу смотрят в лица
Они друг друга видят сквозь
5 Все, что ни есть посередине
О ты, земля моя родная!
Меня ты держишь здесь певцом
Меж вороном и мертвецом

There is nothing that can seduce him—
He lives in poverty and rejoices
Since he's stronger than anyone

131

A raven-bird hangs in the sky
And under the earth lies a dead man
They look each other in the face
They see each other through
5 everything that may be in the middle
O thou, my native earth!
You hold me here as a singer
Between raven and dead man

Юрий Кублановский

132 Этюд

Д. Б.

Копыта над корчью змеиной.
Под тонкою тогой—плеча́,
покрытые свежей патиной,
родителя и палача.
5 Мы сироты власти Петровой,
что ласковой кажется нам.
Под стенами крепости новой
навстречу торосам и льдам
он терпит едва на престоле
10 одряблой кагал татарвы,
все цепче держа на приколе
летучее устье Невы.

1979

133

Ростовщичьи кленовые грабки
зажимают парижскую мглу,
и навряд ли доходны и зябки
сны взлохмаченных астр на углу...
5 Ночью в лаковом логове чарку
исчерпав на глубоком хлебке,
наконец подношу зажигалку
настоящую—к сонной строке

Yurii Kublanovsky

132 Study[*]

to D. B.

Hooves above the serpent's writhe.
Under the thin toga are the shoulders,
covered with a fresh patina,
of the father and executioner.
5 We are the orphans of Peter's power,
which seems to us kind.
Beneath the walls of the new fort
[moving] toward ice hummocks and flat stretches of ice
he barely tolerates on the throne
10 the limp-grown kahal of the heathen swine,
holding ever more tightly at its mooring
the flying mouth of the Neva.

1979

133

The usurious rakes of the maples
squeeze the Paris gloom,
and hardly profitable, and chilled
are the dreams of the bedraggled asters at the corner…
5 At night in a varnished lair, a goblet
having emptied with a deep gulp,
at last I bring a lighter,
a real one, up to the sleepy line

и сквозь желтое марево вижу
10 как ершится неоновый еж.
И люблю и вдвойне ненавижу
неродной европейский грабеж.
И кофейная мгла полотенца
неизменно сливается с той,
15 с коей вы Робеспьера-младенца
и убийцу—везли на убой.

Как не вспомнить родную берлогу,
где давно начала плесневеть
на тиране, закутанном в тогу,
20 бессловесная русская медь.
Чем глядеть, как убойной десницей
указует он жертву орлам,
лучше б впрямь хитроумной лисицей
обернуться в курятнике нам.

17.X.83

134

Не спеши отрешаться—утешимся,
нам не век у чужих куковать,
молодясь, на экзаменах срежемся,
станем шапками птицам махать

5 по весне, когда воду грабастая,
у придавленных камнем плотин
собираются с шумом зубастые
аллигаторы тающих льдин.

Будем чай зверобоем заваривать,
10 кочергою угар ворошить,
уминая бумажное зарево,
и Великим постом—не грешить.

...Только надо поджаться, дыхания
поднабрать в терпеливую грудь,
15 чтобы вольно менять очертания
облаков, преграждающих путь.

and through a yellow glow I see
10 a neon hedgehog rise.
And I love and doubly hate
the alien European robbery.
And the coffee gloom of a towel
invariably blends with the one
15 with which you took baby Robespierre
and the murderer away to be slaughtered.

How not to remember that native den,
where long ago began to grow musty
on the tyrant, robed in his toga,
20 the wordless Russian copper.
Why watch him with his slaughtering right hand
pointing his eagles toward the victim,
better indeed like the cunning vixen
for us to turn our backs in the henhouse.

17.X.1983

134

Don't rush to abdicate—we'll be consoled,
not forever are we to cry cuckoo among aliens,
growing younger, we'll plough our exams,
we'll wave our caps at birds

5 in the spring, when the water raking
next to dams squashed by stones,
there gather noisily the toothy
alligators of the melting ice lumps.

We will brew tea with St. John's wort,
10 stir the brew with a poker,
kneading the paper glow
and not sin during Lent.

…All you need is to hunch up, taking breath
into your patient breast,
15 so as freely to change the outlines
of the clouds that block your path.

Не беда, что ты тоже беспечная,
стало быть, уцелеем верней.
Европейская ночь бесконечная,
20 слава Богу, не будет черней.

12.X.83

135

Судьба стиха—миродержавная,
хотя его столбец и краток,
коль в тайное—помимо явного
заложен призрачный остаток.

5 Нерукотворное содеется
и до конца не дастся в руки,
спасется—не уразумеется
ни встреченное, ни в разлуке.

Казалось бы, давно за скобками
10 судьбы—Отечество и вера
в орла с змеиными головками,
как всякая земная мера,

ан, с вьюгою разноголосою
скольженье по тропе неровной,
15 что танец с голубоволосою
Елизаветою Петровной.

...Когда и тайное и явное
в силке забьются шелкокрыло,
на воле уцелеет—главное,
20 чья неопределимость—сила.

Участники того тревожного
дворцового переворота
—мы, алчущие невозможного
ползка, броска и перелета.

31 декабря 1987

It's no calamity that you're also carefree, my girl,
if it's so, then more certainly will we survive.
The endless European night*
20 thank God, will not get blacker.

12.X.1983

135

The fate of verse is world-sovereign,
though the column it makes be short,
if into the mysterious, missing the manifest,
its spectral remnant is inserted.

5 What is not made by hands will still be fashioned,
and won't allow itself to be entirely grasped,
it will escape, will not be comprehended
either in what is encountered, or what is apart.

It would seem that for ages enclosed in the parenthesis
10 of fate has been the Fatherland and faith
in the eagle with the serpentine heads,
like any earthly measure,

but on the contrary, with a discordant snowstorm
it slips along an uneven path,
15 like a dance with blue-haired
Elizaveta Petrovna.*

...When both what is secret and what is manifest
thrash silk-winged in the snare,
the main thing will remain at liberty intact,
20 its indefinability being its strength.

The participants in this disquieting
palace coup d'etat
are we, who thirst for the impossible
crawling approach, attack, and flight across.

31 December 1987

136

Под снегом тусклым, скудным
первопрестольный град.
Днём подступившим, судным
чреват его распад.
5 На тёмной, отсыревшей
толпе, с рабочих мест
вдруг снявшейся, нездешний
уже заметен крест.

Но в переулках узких
10 доныне не погас
тот серый свет из русских
чуть воспалённых глаз.
И у щербатой кладки
запомнил навсегда
15 я маленькой перчатки
пожатье в холода.

Москва, ты привечала
среди своих калек
меня, когда серчала.
20 Почто твой гнев поблек?
Кто дворницкой лопатой
неведомо кому
расчистил путь покатый
к престолу твоему?

25 ...Напротив бакалеи
еще бедней, чем встарь,
у вырытой траншеи
нахохленный сизарь
о падаль клювик точет,
30 как бы в воинственной
любви признаться хочет
к тебе, единственной.

Январь 1990

136

Under wan, meager snow
is the first capital city.*
With an imminent day of judgment
its decline is pregnant.
5 On the dark, dampened
crowd, from its places of work
suddenly breaking away, an other-worldly
cross is already to be seen.

But in the narrow side streets
10 hitherto has not been extinguished
that gray light from Russian
slightly inflamed eyes.
And by some gap-toothed brickwork
I remembered forever
15 a little glove's
clasp in the cold.

Moscow, you included me
among your cripples
when you were angry.
20 Wherefore has your anger faded?
Who with a yardsman's spade
for someone unknown
has cleared a sloping path
toward your throne?

25 …Opposite a grocer's shop
that's even poorer than of old,
by an excavated trench
a ruffled-up pigeon
sharpens its bill on some carrion
30 as if it wanted to confess
a militant love
for you, unique as you are.

January 1990

137

Каким Иоаннам, Биронам
И Стенькам поклонимся мы,
провидит, должно быть, ворона,
игуменья здешней зимы,
5 раз каркает властно над нами:
мол, дети, о чем разговор?
И красными сосны стволами
нас манят в кладбищенский бор...

Всевышний, прости наши долги.
10 Прощаем и мы должникам
—в верховьях отравленной Волги
клубящимся облакам.
Скудны по-евангельски брашна
и тленна скудельная нить.
15 Как стало таинственно, страшно
и, в общем, невесело жить.

Усопшие взяты измором,
кто водкой, кто общей бедой.
Хлам старых венков за забором,
20 пропитанный снежной водой:
воск роз, посеревший от ветра,
унылый слежавшийся сор
—как будто распахнуты недра
отечества всем на позор.

137

Before what Ivans, Birons,
and Stenkas* we will cringe,
the crow, probably, will see,
the mother superior of the winter here,
5 since it croaks commandingly over us,
saying "Children, what are you talking about?"
And with their red trunks the pines
lure us into the forest by the cemetery...

Almighty, forgive us our debts.
10 We also forgive our debtors—
the swirling clouds
at the upper reaches of the poisoned Volga.
Meager are our repasts, as in the Gospel,
and frail the weak thread.
15 How it has become mysterious, frightening,
and, in general, unhappy to live.

The deceased have been taken by starvation,
some by vodka, some by the general catastrophe.
Trash of old wreaths behind the fence,
20 soaked in water from melted snow:
wax of roses grown gray from the wind,
dismal rubbish that's lain until it rotted
—as if the depths of our fatherland
have been thrown open to the shame of everyone.

Алексей Цветков

138

На лавочке у парковой опушки,
Где мокнет мох в тенистых уголках,
С утра сидят стеклянные старушки
С вязанием в морщинистых руках.
5 Мне по душе их спорая работа,
Крылатых спиц стремительная вязь.
Я в этом сне разыскивал кого-то,
И вот на них гляжу, остановясь.
Одна клубки распутывает лихо,
10 Другая вяжет, всматриваясь в даль,
А третья, как заправская портниха,
Аршинных ножниц стискивает сталь.

Мгновение неслышно пролетело,
Дымок подернул времени жерло.
15 Но вдруг они на миг прервали дело
И на меня взглянули тяжело.
В пустых зрачках сквозила скорбь немая.
Квадраты лиц—белее полотна.
И вспомнил я, еще не понимая,
20 Их греческие злые имена.
Они глядели, сумеречно силясь
Повременить, помедлить, изменить.
Но эта, третья, странно покосилась
И разрубила спутанную нить.

Aleksei Tsvetkov

138

On a bench by the edge of the park,
Where the moss dampens in the shady corners,
From morning on sit glassy old women
With knitting in their wrinkled hands.
5 I feel sympathy with their goodly work,
The headlong curlicue of their winged needles.
I was looking for someone in this dream,
And now, stopping, I look at them.
One of them nimbly unravels balls of wool,
10 The second knits, looking into the distance,
And the third, like a true tailor woman,
Grips the steel of her *arshin**-long needles.

The moment flew past inaudibly,
The maw of time twitched a smoke ring.
15 But suddenly they interrupted their business for a second
And gave me a weighty look.
Through their empty pupils showed dumb grief.
The squares of their faces were whiter than cloth.
And I recalled, still not understanding,
20 Their malign Greek names.
They looked on, in a twilight way making an effort
To wait a while, to slow down, to change things.
But she, the third one, gave a strange sidelong glance
And sundered the tangled thread.

139

Судьба играет человеком
До смертной сырости на лбу.
Но человек берет из шкафа
Свою красивую трубу.

5 Она лежит в его ладонях,
Умелой тяжестью легка,
И полыхают над эстрадой
Ее латунные бока.

Как он живет, как он играет
10 В приемной Страшного Суда!
Он в каждой песне умирает
И выживает навсегда.

Он звездной родиной заброшен
На землю драки ножевой,
15 Такой потерянный и детский,
Еще живой, еще живой...

140

отверни гидрант и вода тверда
ни умыть лица ни набрать ведра
и насос перегрыз ремни
затупился лом не берет кирка
5 потому что как смерть вода крепка
хоть совсем ее отмени

все события в ней отразились врозь
хоть рояль на соседа с балкона сбрось
он как новенький невредим
10 и язык во рту нестерпимо бел
видно пили мы разведенный мел
а теперь его так едим

бесполезный звук из воды возник
не проходит воздух в глухой тростник

139

Fate plays with man
To the point of mortal damp on the brow.
But man takes from the cupboard
His beautiful trumpet.

5 It lies in his hands,
Light with its skilled weight,
And glimmering over the stage
Are its brass flanks.

How he lives, how he plays
10 In the waiting room of the Last Judgment!
In every song he dies
And comes back to life forever.

He's been abandoned by his starry homeland
Onto earth with its knife fighting,
15 So lost and so childish,
Still alive, still alive…

140

turn on the hydrant and the water's hard
you can't wash your face or fill a pail
and the pump has chewed right through its hose
the crowbar's dull and the pick won't bite
5 because like death water is tough
though you abolish it altogether

all events are reflected in it separately
even toss a piano from the balcony on your neighbor
like a new man he's invulnerable
10 and the tongue in your mouth is unbearably white
looks as if we'd been drinking a solution of chalk
and now we're eating it like that

a useless sound from the water arose
the air will not pass down the hollow reed

15 захлебнулась твоя свирель
прозвенит гранит по краям ведра
но в замерзшем времени нет вреда
для растений звезд и зверей

потому что слеп известковый мозг
20 потому что мир это горный воск
застывающий без труда
и в колодезном круге верней чем ты
навсегда отразила его черты
эта каменная вода

141

(не притязая на глубину ума
в скобках замечу в последнее время не с кем
словом обмолвиться ни обменяться веским
взглядом ввиду отсутствия слова в карма-
5 не обольщен кругосветным застольем одесским
а в остальные покуда не вхож дома

бывший герой перестрелки бульварных мо
нынче за словом в проруби шарю донкой
наедине с собой словно кот в трюмо
10 перестаю разбираться в оптике тонкой
понаторевший во всем помыкать в семье
с детства уже ничем не взорву этот плоский
стиль и пишу с анжамбман как иосиф бродский
чтоб от его лица возразить себе

15 даже дефектом оптики не страдая
свет отраженья не удержать в горстях
это понятно по вечерам когда я
сам у себя безуспешно сижу в гостях
впору в трюмо огласить манифест и будто
20 дело к реформе но как обойтись без бунта
где-то под тверью в неведомых волостях)

15 it has choked, thy flute
    granite will ring out on the side of the pail
    but in frozen time is no harm
    to plants stars and beasts

    because the limestone brain is hard
20 because the world is mountain wax
    that congeals without difficulty
    and in the well's circle more faithfully than you
    its features have been reflected forever
    by this stone water

141

    (making no claim to profundity of intellect
    in parenthesis i note lately no one
    to have a word with or exchange a weighty
    glance in view of the absence of a word in the pock-
5   -et charmed by the roundworldly feasting of odessa
    but into the remaining insofar as not received homes

    the former hero of skirmishes with boulevard mots
    nowadays searching for a word in the icehole i rummage bottomy
    all alone with myself like a cat in a pier glass
10 i am ceasing to know something about optics subtle
    being ground down in everyday bumming around the family
    since childhood nothing to use to explode this flat
    style and i write with enjambman like joseph brodsky
    so as on his behalf to object to myself

15 even no optical defect suffering from
    the world of a reflection can't hold in cupped hands
    understandable in the evenings when i
    to my own home unsuccessfully pay a visit
    right time into the pier glass to proclaim the manifest and as if
20 things're moving toward reform but how to manage it without an uprising
    somewhere near tver and in unknown ridings)

142

предмет наблюденья природа
в любое взгляни озерцо
в извилистой шкурке микроба
особая жизнь налицо
5 в ином носороге отдельном
всемирная совесть тяжка
как самоубийца в отельном
окне накануне прыжка

я сам на людей удивляюсь
10 какие у жизни сыны
когда в туалет удаляюсь
неловко присесть у стены
зачем нас рожает утроба
отцовская учит лоза
15 когда у простого микроба
научных идей за глаза

143

куранты в зените ковали века
река соблюдала блокаду
ходил на гитарные курсы в дэка
потом подучился вокалу
5 с трибун присягали твердили в трубу
напрячься и времени больше не бу

досуги и дни пропадают в дыму
куранты лютуют далече
в хрустальном пейзаже проело дыру
10 жуков перелетное вече
раздолье зенита реки ширина
проснешься и времени больше не на

нас в кадре росы ненароком свело
биенье немецкой пружинки
15 из туч левенгук наставляет стекло

142

an object of study is nature
look down into any small pond
in the rippling hide of the microbe
a life of its own is at hand
5 in the odd selected rhinoceros
universal conscience weighs deep
like a suicide framed in a hotel
window on the eve of his leap

i too am astonished at people
10 the offspring that life can deploy
when i take myself off to the toilet
and awkwardly crouch by the wall
but why from the womb we're delivered
the paternal rod still our guide
15 when no more than a simple microbe
has ideas scientific inside

143

the chimes at the zenith were forging the ages
the river maintained a blockade
i went to guitar classes at the DK*
then i had some voice lessons
5 from podiums they swore allegiance repeatedly trumpeted
make an effort and time will be no mo

leisures and days go up in smoke
the chimes rage on afar
in the crystal landscape a hole's been corroded
10 by a passing *veche** of beetles
the expanse of the zenith the river's breadth
one will awake and time will no longer be nec

we've been accidentally brought together in a frame of dew
by the beat of a german spring
15 from the clouds leeuwenhoek* focuses his glass

на тщетные наши ужимки
в теснине проспекта удобно видна
оставшихся дней небольшая длина

144

вот дедушка сторонник мидий
поживу рыщет из песка
ему как стронцию рубидий
морская фауна близка
5 годами он господствует над пляжем
куда и мы как трилобиты ляжем

но впредь как миносу соваться на весы
чем гостье в пасть как эскарго на вилке
я жив я тоже гражданин весны
10 земную жизнь дойдя до половинки
и дальше в лес
а дед в пределе узком
свой геноцид ведет моллюскам

мать мидия мы свидимся в раю
15 прощай в зобу его свирепом
я мал мне тоже жаль идти в рагу
и умереть и быть скелетом
бог вещества я существую лес
любую сойку в нем и росомаху
20 им не бывать покуда я исчез
как эта устрица к салату
глядящая печально изо рта
как в радамантовы врата

145

в ложбине станция куда сносить мешки
всей осени макет дрожит в жару твердея
двоюродных кровей проклятия смешны
не дядя-де отнюдь тебе я

5 в тромбозном тамбуре пристройся и доспи
на совесть выстроили вечности предбанник

on our vain grimaces
in the ravine of the avenue can conveniently be seen
the not great length of remaining days

144

here's the old fellow advocate of the mussels
seeking his living in the sand
as rubidium to strontium
marine fauna are close to him
5 for years he's lorded it over the beach
where we too will lie down like trilobites

from hence to minos* jump onto the scales
by which into a lady guest's maw like escargot on fork
i'm alive i too am citizen of spring
10 this earthly life reaching the just a half please
further into forest
and granddad in his close domain
does his genocide on the mollusks

mother mussel we'll meet in paradise
15 farewell inside his savage craw
i'm small i'm sorry too making me too into ragout
and die and be a skeleton
god of matter i exist forest
any old jay in it or wolverine
20 will not be while i've disappeared
like this oyster to make salad
glancing sadly from mouth
as into rhadamanthine gates

145

down in a gulch a whistle-stop where to dump the sacks
all autumn's mock-up quakes in the heat as it hardens
of once-removed bloods the curses are absurd
no uncle quote to you at all am i

5 in the thrombotic tambour settle in and sleep
conscientiously they've built eternity's locker room

что ж дядю видимо резон убрать с доски
пржевальский зубр ему племянник

ты царь живи один правительство ругай
10 ажурный дождь маршрут заштриховал окрестный
одна судьба сургут другая смерть тургай
в вермонте справим день воскресный

я знаю озеро лазурный глаз земли
нимроды на заре натягивают луки
15 но заполночь в траве прибрежные зверьки
снуют как небольшие люди

нет весь я не умру душа моя слегка
над трупом воспарит верни ее а ну-ка
из жил же и костей вермонтского зверька
20 совокупит себе наука

се дяде гордому вся спесь его не впрок
нас уберут равно левкоем и гвоздикой
и будем мы олень и вепрь и ныне дикий
медведь и друг степей сурок

well now looks like good cause to remove uncle from plaque
przevalsky's bison* to him the kinsman

thou tsar live on thy own* badmouth the government
10 tracey rain routeplan has sketched in neighboring
one fate is surgut* the other death is turgai*
in vermont we'll celebrate the sabbath

i know a lake the azure eye of earth
the nimrods in the dawn are pulling taut their bows
15 but aftermidnight in grass the shoreline little creatures
scurry around like small people

no all i will not die* my soul will slightly
above my corpse rise up give it me back come on
from veins though and the bones of little vermont creature
20 science will go on coupling away

lo to proud uncle all his arrogance a waste
they'll clear us up the same as gillyflower and pink
and we will be the deer and boar and for the nonce savage*
bear and friend of steppe the marmot

Елена Шварц

146 Невидимый охотник

Может быть—к счастью или позору—
Вся моя ценность только в узоре
Родинок, кожу мою испещривших,
В темных созвездьях, небо забывших.
5 Вся она—карточка северной ночи—
Лебедь, Орел, Андромеда, Возничий,
Гвозди и гроздья, и многоточья...
Ах—страшны мне эти отличья!
Нет, что ни дар, ни душа, ни голос,
10 Кожа—вот что во мне оказалось ценнее.
И невидимый меткий охотник,
Может, крадется уже за нею.
Бывают такие черепахи
И киты такие бывают—
15 Буквы у них на спине и знаки,
Для курьезу их убивают.
Не на чем было, быть может, флейтисту,
Духу горнему, записать музы́ку,
Вот он проснулся средь вечной ночи,
20 Первый схватил во тьме белый комочек
И нацарапал ноты, натыкал
На коже нерожденной, бумажно-нежной...
Может, ищет—найдет и срежет.
Знают ли соболь, и норка, и белка
25 Сколько долларов стоит их шкурка?
Сгниет ли мозг и улетит душа...
Но кожу—нет—и червь не съест,
И там—мою распластанную шкурку
Глядишь, и сберегут, как палимпсест
30 Или как фото неба-младенца.

Elena Shvarts

146 The Invisible Hunter

Perhaps—good for me or shame for me—
My entire value is only in the pattern
of birthmarks spattering my skin,
in these dark constellations that have forgotten the sky.
5 All [my skin] is a chart of the northern night—
Swan, Eagle, Andromeda, Charioteer,
clusters and bundles and dot-dot-dots...
Agh, these distinguishing marks frighten me!
No, no matter what my gift, my soul, or my voice—
10 my skin, that's what's more valuable in me.
And an invisible efficient hunter
may already be stalking me for it.
There are certain turtles
and certain whales too,
15 that have letters and signs on their backs,
they get killed as curiosities.
Perhaps, that flutist—that celestial spirit—
had nothing to write his music on,
and he woke up amid the eternal night,
20 and seized the first white scrap in the dark
and scratched out his notes, pricked them
into that unborn, paper-snowy skin...
Perhaps he's looking for it, he'll find it and slice it off.
Do the sable, the mink, and the squirrel know
25 how many dollars their pelt is worth?
If my brain rots and my soul flies away...
But my skin, no—the worm won't eat it up,
and then my spreadeagled pelt
will be preserved—just you see, like a palimpsest
30 or a photo of the sky in its infancy.

Куда же мне спрятаться, смыться бы, деться?
Чую дыханье, меткие взоры...
Ах, эти проклятые на гибель узоры.

март 1975

147 Воспоминание о странном угощении

Я отведала однажды
молока моей подруги,
молока моей сестры—
не для утоленья жажды,
5 а для вольности души.
Она выжала из груди
левой в чашку молоко,
и оно в простой посуде
пело, пенилось легко.
10 Оно пахло чем-то птичьим,
чем-то волчьим и овечьим,
больше вечным, чем путь Млечный,
было теплым и густым.
Так когда-то дочь в пустыне
15 старика-отца поила,
став и матерью ему,
силой этой благостыни
в колыбель гроб превратила,
белизной прогнала тьму.
20 Из протока возле сердца
напоила ты меня—
не вампир я—ой ли—ужас—
оно пенилось, звеня,
сладким, теплым, вечным, мягким,
25 время в угол, вспять тесня.

май 1976

148

Я бы вынула ребро свое тонкое,
из живого вырезала бы тела я.
Сотвори из него мне только Ты

Where can I hide myself, flee to, put myself?
I feel his breathing, his accurate gaze...
Agh, those patternings doomed to die.

March 1975

147 Memory of a Strange Refreshment

I tasted once
the milk of a woman friend,
the milk of a sister—
not to slake my thirst
5 but for the liberty of my soul.
She squeezed the milk from her left
breast into a cup,
and in this simple vessel
it sang, foamed slightly.
10 It smelled of something bird-like,
something wolf-like and sheep-like,
more eternal than the Milky Way,
it was warm and thick.
Thus once a daughter in the desert
15 gave her old father to drink,
becoming a mother to him,
and by the force of these alms
turned a coffin into a cradle,
drove away the dark with whiteness.
20 From the duct next to your heart
you gave me to drink,
I'm no vampire—what a horror—
it foamed, ringing,
sweet, warm, eternal, soft,
25 crowding time back into the corner.

May 1976

148

I would take out my delicate rib,
would cut it out of my living body.
O Thou, create out of it for me only

друга верного, мелкого, белого.
5 Ни мужа, ни жену, ни среднего,
а скорлупою одетого ангела,
чтоб он песни утешные пел
и сидел бы ночами на лампочке,
на паучьих звенел бы струночках.
10 Не Адам я—но его еще одиночей.
Трудно ли, если захочешь?
Сотвори.
Уж так-то рада я тут была бы,
ах, друга светлого, тонкого, мелкого
15 из капли крови, из кости слабой.

1978

149

Снова сунулся отец с поученьем:
—Надо жить, мол, не так, а этак.
—Хорошо, говорю ему, папа,
Больше этого не будет, папаша.

5 Смотрю я, кроткая, на голову седую,
На руки скрюченные, слишком красный рот.
Говорю я рабам—немедля
Киньте дурака в бассейн.

Волокут его по мраморному полу,
10 Он цепляется, а не за что цепляться,
Кровь течет по лицу и слезы:
—Доченька, кричит, прости, помилуй!

Нет! Некормленным муренам на съеденье
Ты пойдешь, развратник и ханжа.
15 Или представлю—как лев в цирке
Дожевывает его печень.

Ладно, ладно—говорю—я исправлюсь,
Ах ты бедный мой, старый папа.
Когда тигр вылизал даже пар от крови,
20 Мне стало его чуточку жалко.

a faithful, tiny, white friend.
5 Not a husband, not a wife, not something between,
but an angel dressed in a shell,
who would sing consolatory songs
and sit at nights on the lamp,
and ring the spiders' strings.
10 I am not Adam—but I'm even more alone than he.
Would it be hard, if You wanted to?
Create.
I would be so, so happy here,
Agh, a bright, subtle, tiny friend
15 out of a drop of blood, out of a weak bone.

1978

149

Once again father interfered, exhorting:*
"That's not the way to live, this is."
"Fine," I say to him, "dad,
There will be no more of it, dear daddy."

5 I look, meek, at his gray head,
At his gnarled hands, his too-red mouth.
I tell the slaves immediately
To throw the fool into the swimming pool.

They drag him across the marble floor,
10 He clutches, but there's nothing to clutch,
Blood flows down his face, and tears,
"Dear daughter," he shouts, "forgive me, have mercy!"

No! To be devoured by unfed lampreys
You will go, debauchee and hypocrite.
15 Or I can imagine a lion in the circus
Chewing the last of his liver.

"All right, all right," I say, "I'll reform,
Oh my poor thing, my old dad."
When the tiger licked up even the steam from his blood
20 I felt a little bit sorry for him.

В уме казню его по-разному—тыщу
Раз и еще раз тыщу—
Чтоб однажды и в самом деле
Молоток подняв—по виску не стукнуть.

1978

150 Обрезание сердца

Значит, хочешь от меня
Жертвы кровавой.
На, возьми—живую кровь,
Плоть, Любовь и славу.

5 Нет, не крайнюю плоть—
Даже если была б—это мало,
А себя заколоть
И швырнуть Тебе в небо.

Хоть совсем не голубица—
10 Захриплю я голубицей.
Миг еще пылает Жизнь,
Плещет, пляшет и струится.

Думала я—Ангел схватит
В миг последний лезвие,
15 Но Тебе желанна жертва—
Сердца алое зерно.

151 Ворон

Старый Ворон сердце мое просил,
Воронятам своим отнести—
«А то закопают в землю тебя,
Мне уж не выскрести».
5 «Злая птица—ему отвечала я—
Ты Илью кормил и святых,
А меня ты сам готов сожрать,
Хоть, конечно, куда мне до них».
Отвечала птица: «Вымерзло все кругом.
10 Холодно, греться-то надо.

In my mind I execute him in different ways—a thousand
times and another thousand—
So as one day in actual fact,
Raising the hammer, not to hit him in the temple.

1978

150 Circumcision of the Heart*

So, you want from me
A bloody sacrifice.
Here, take it—living blood,
Flesh, Love and fame.

5 No, not the prepuce—
Even if I had one, that would be too little,
But to stab myself
And hurl [myself] to You in the heavens.

Although I'm no innocent dove at all,
10 I will speak hoarsely like an innocent dove.
For one more instant Life glows,
Plashes, dances and flows.

I thought that an Angel would seize
The blade at the last instant,
15 But the sacrifice is desired by Thee,
The crimson grain of the heart.

151 The Raven*

An old Raven asked for my heart
To take away to its baby ravens,
"Or else they'll bury you in the ground,
And I won't be able to scratch you up."
5 "Evil bird," I replied to him,
"You fed Elijah and the saints,
But me you yourself are ready to eat up,
Although, of course, I'm no match for them."
The bird replied, "Everything around is frozen.
10 It's cold, and I have to get warm.

Я сердце снесу в ледяной свой дом,
Поклюют пусть иззябшие чада
Не шутка—три сына и дочь...»
Я палку швырнула в него: «Прочь!»
15 Ночью проснулась от боли в груди—
О, какая боль—в сердце боль!
Спрыгнул Ворон с постели, на столик, к дверям—
С клюва каплет на пол кровь.

152

Мне снилось—мы плывем по рисовым полям
(Из риса делают бумагу),
По блеску мокрому, по зеркалам,
Болотному архипелагу.
5 В бумажной лодке, лодке бледной,
Не слышно плеска—весла так легки,
В тумане лодка мокнет, утопает
И мелкие дождятся огоньки.
Метелки риса, вставши из воды,
10 Корейскими косят глазами—дабы
Я поняла—предмет любви бе ты—
Они. Любви ветвится канделябр.
Органной песней, как труба в трубе,
(Естественно любить и всех и сразу),
15 Смотри—уходит память о себе
На дно неловким мертвым водолазом.
Смотри—дождем кружатся огоньки,
Не падая на землю—это души,
Которых неутешная любовь
20 К Творенью и Творцу, душа, не тушит.
О как давно я это знала все—
Еще когда была двуногой
И вот тону и вот лежу на дне
Любви мильоноруким осьминогом.

25 На мелком дне, на рисовых полях,
Принадлежа земле, воде и небу,
Томлением живым—и сладкий страх—
Меня полюбят те, кто думает—«я не был».

I'll take your heart away to my icy home,
Let my freezing offspring peck it,
No joke—three sons and a daughter…"
I threw a stick at him, "Away!"
15 That night I woke up from a pain in the chest,
Oh, what pain, a pain in the heart!
The Raven hopped off the bed, onto the table, toward the door—
From its beak blood drips onto the floor.

152

I dreamed we were sailing through rice fields
(they make paper out of rice),
Along a wet brilliance, along mirrors,
Along a marshy archipelago.
5 In a paper boat, a pale boat,
No splashing could be heard, the oars were so light,
In the mist the boat gets wet, is sinking,
And tiny lights will appear soon.
The shoots of rice, standing out of the water,
10 Look askance with their Korean eyes—so that
I should understand—an object of love be thou—
They are. The candelabrum of love branches out.
With an organ song, like a pipe inside a pipe,
(It's natural to love everyone and immediately too),
15 Look: memory of oneself is going away
To the bottom like a clumsy dead diver.
Look: the lights are spinning round like rain,
Not falling to the earth—these are souls
Whose inconsolable love
20 For the Creation and the Creator, the soul will not extinguish.
Oh, how long ago I knew all this—
When I was still a two-legged woman
And now I'm drowning, now I'm lying on the bottom
Of love, like a million-armed octopus.

25 On the shallow bottom, in the rice fields,
Belonging to earth, water and sky,
With a living longing—and sweet fear—
Those will fall in love with me who think "I was not there."

153

Когда за мною демоны голодные помчались
Косматыми и синими волками,
Ах, что тогда мне, бедной, оставалось—
Как с неба снять луны холодный камень
5 И кинуть в пасть им—чтоб они взорвались.

От блеска взрыва вмиг преобразились,
Ягнятами ко мне они прижались
(Я рядом с ними теменью казалась)
И даже шерсть их снежная светилась
10 И я их сожрала—какая жалость!

Я стала рядом с ними великаном—
Сторуким, торжествующим в печали,
По одному брала, рвала и ела,
Они же только жалобно пищали.

15 Но я им говорила—не вопите
И ничего не бойтесь. Вы
Там в животе немного полежите
И выпрыгнете вон из головы.

Но светом их набив свою утробу
20 Сама я стала ясной и двурукой,
И новых демонов семья в голодной злобе
Учуяла меня. Все та же мука.

1982

153

When hungry demons came chasing after me
Like shaggy, dark-blue wolves,
Ah, what then was left to poor me—
How to take down from the sky the cold stone of the moon
5 And hurl it in their jaws, so they explode.

From the brilliance of the explosion they immediately were transfigured,
Like lambs they nestled up to me
(By the side of them I seemed to be the darkness)
And even their snowy coats shone
10 And I ate them up—indeed a pity!

I stood by their side like a giant,
Hundred-armed, triumphing in his sorrow,
One by one took them, tore them, ate them,
And they only cheeped piteously.

15 But I said to them, "Do not cry out
And don't be afraid of anything. You
Just lie there a little in my stomach
And then jump out of my head."

But having stuffed my womb with their light
20 I myself became clear and two-handed,
And a family of new demons in hungry rage
Caught my scent. Still the same torment.

1982

Иван Жданов

154 Портрет отца

И зеркало вспашут. И раннее детство
вернется к отцу, не заметив его,
по скошенным травам прямого наследства,
по желтому полю пути своего.

5 И запах сгорающих крыльев. И слава
над желтой равниной зажженных свечей.
И будет даровано каждому право
себя выбирать, и не будет ночей.

Но стоит ступить на пустую равнину,
10 как рамкой резной обовьется она,
и поле увидит отцовскую спину
и небо с прямыми углами окна.

А там, за окном, комнатенка худая,
и маковым громом на тронном полу
15 играет младенец, и бездна седая
сухими кустами томится в углу.

И мак погремушкой ударит по раме
и камешком чиркнет, и вспыхнет она,
и гладь фотоснимка сырыми пластами,
20 как желтое поле, развалит до дна.

Прояснится зеркало, зная, что где-то
плывет глубина по осенней воде,
и тяжесть течет, омывая предметы,
и свет не куется на дальней звезде.

Ivan Zhdanov

154 Portrait of My Father

And the mirror will be ploughed up. And early childhood
will return to my father without noticing him,
over the scythed grasses of direct inheritance,
over the yellow field of its path.

5 And the smell of wings burning up. And glory
over the yellow plain of lit candles.
And there will be gifted to each man the right
to choose himself, and there will be no nights.

But one only needs to set foot on the empty plain,
10 and it will entwine like a carved window frame,
and the field will see my father's back
and the sky with the right angles of a window.

And there through the window a mean little room,
and on the throne floor with poppyseed thunder
15 plays a baby, and a grizzled abyss
pining for dry bushes in the corner.

And the poppy like a rattle will bang into the frame
and strike like a pebble, and it will burst into fire,
and the shiny expanse of a photograph in damp layers
20 like a yellow field will collapse to the bottom.

The mirror will clear up, knowing that somewhere
deepness is floating over the autumn water,
and heaviness flows, lapping over objects,
and light is not being forged on a distant star.

155 Стихи на песке, 2

Березовый ли сок дымится или рана?
Бросай монету в щель—и вздрагивает автомат,
и, форму переняв граненого стакана,
дохнут в лицо туман и жидкий виноград.
5 И кажется, внутри жестянки-автомата
деревья, разломав по косточкам стволы,
срывая кожу с лиц и кошениль с заката,
торопятся назад сквозь черноту золы.
Торопятся назад, разъединяя запах
10 ромашки и воды, спешат обратно в прах.
И вот уже стакан на перебитых лапах,
облепленный листвой, расплескивает страх.
Торопимся и мы. Куда? Еще не смыта
со стенок бытия запекшаяся кровь.
15 Мы падаем в стакан—в стеклянное корыто,
и век глотает нас за славу и любовь.

156 Гроза

Храпя, и радуясь, и воздух вороша,
душа коня, как искра, пролетела,
как будто в поисках утраченного тела,
бросаясь молнией на выступ шалаша.
5 Была гроза. И, сидя в шалаше,
мы видели: светясь и лиловея,
катался луг за шиворот по шее,
как конский глаз разъятый, и в душе
мы всех святых благодарили—три,
10 три раза столб огня охватывал одежду,
отринув в пустоту спасенье и надежду,
как выстрел гибельный чернея изнутри.
Был воздух кровью и разбоем напоен,
душа коня лилась и моросила,
15 какая-то неведомая сила
тащила нас в отечество ворон.
Кто вынул меч? Кто выстрел распрямил?
Чья это битва? Кто ее расправил?
Для этой битвы нет, наверно, правил—

155 Lines Written in the Sand, 2

Is it birch sap steaming or a wound?
Drop your coin in the slot, and the vending machine shudders,
and, taking the form of the thick glass tumbler,
mist and watery grapes will breathe in your face.
5 And it seems that inside the tin can of the slot machine
trees, having smashed their trunks on the pips,
tearing the skin from faces and cochineal from the sunset,
hurry back, through the black of ashes.
They hurry back, disconnecting the scent
10 of chamomile and water, they speed back into dust.
And here already the tumbler on broken paws,
stuck all over with foliage, sprinkles fear.
We, too, hurry. Where to? Still not washed away
from the walls of existence is the congealed blood.
15 We fall into the tumbler, into the glass trough,
and the age swallows us for glory and for love.

156 The Storm

Snorting and exulting, and ruffling the air,
the soul of a steed, like a spark, flew past,
as if in search of its lost body,
hurling itself like lightning at the salient of the hut.
5 There was a storm. And, sitting in the hut,
we saw that, radiant and lilac-colored,
the meadow rolled by the scruff of its neck,
like a distended horse's eye, and in our souls
we gave thanks to all the saints—three,
10 three times a pillar of fire seized our clothes,
repudiating into emptiness salvation and hope,
like a fatal shot, black on the inside.
The air was suffused with blood and banditry,
the steed's soul poured and drizzled,
15 some unknown force
dragged us into the fatherland of the crows.
Who drew his sword? Who straightened up the shot?
Whose battle is this? Who smoothed it out?
For this battle there are probably no rules—

20 мы в проигрыше все! Из наших жил
    натянута стрела, она гудит
    и мечется, как нитка болевая,
    и ржет, и топчется, и, полночь раздвигая,
    ослепшей молнией горит.
25 Гроза становится все яростней и злей,
    в соломе роются прозрачные копыта,
    и грива черная дождя насквозь прошита
    палящим запахом стеклянных тополей.
    Струится кривизна граненого стекла,
30 ребристое стекло хмелеющего шара—
    вот крона тополя. Над нами чья-то кара,
    пожара отблески на сумерках чела.
    Глядело то чело, уставясь на меня,
    и небо прошлого в его глазах дышало,
35 и форма каждого зрячка напоминала
    кровавый силуэт убитого коня.
    Его убили здесь когда-то. На лугу,
    на мартовском снегу, разбрасывая ноги,
    упал он в сумерках, в смятенье и тревоге
40 на радость человеку и врагу.
    Не надо домыслов, подробностей. Рассказ
    предельно краток: здесь коня убили.
    И можно справиться, пожалуй, без усилий
    со всем, что здесь преследовало нас.
45 Нам не вернуть языческих времен,
    спят идолы, измазанные кровью.
    И если бродят среди нас они с любовью,
    то эти идолы отечества ворон.

157 Пророк

    Если горы читаются слева направо
    или так же неспешно в обратном порядке,
    но не снизу—как днем, и не сверху—как ночью,
    это значит, что время устало воочью,
5   отказалось от возраста, и без оглядки
    изменилось его неподкупное право.

    И когда ты в угоду бессчетным затеям
    навязаться захочешь какой-нибудь цели,
    расплетая дорогу на тропы провидца
10 (словно подвиг Гераклу навязан Антеем

20 All of us lose! Out of our sinews
    an arrow has been stretched tight, it buzzes
    and lurches, like a painful thread,
    and neighs, and stamps, and, parting the midnight,
    burns like blinded lightning.
25 The storm gets more furious and malevolent,
    transparent hooves rummage in the straw,
    and the black mane of rain is stitched right through
    with the scorching smell of glass poplars.
    The curve of a thick glass tumbler streams,
30 the ribbed glass of an inebriating sphere—
    that's the crown of the poplar. Above us is someone's punishment,
    the reflection of a blaze on the twilight of a brow.
    That brow observed, gazing intently at me,
    and the sky of the past breathed in its eyes,
35 and the form of each pupil recalled
    the bloody silhouette of the murdered steed.
    It was murdered here at some time. In the meadow
    on the March snow, splaying its legs,
    it fell in the twilight, in confusion and alarm
40 to the joy of man and enemy.
    No need for conjectures, details. The story
    is brief in the extreme: here a steed was murdered.
    And one can probably come to terms without effort
    with everything that victimized us here.
45 We cannot bring back pagan times,
    The idols sleep, smeared with blood.
    And if they wander among us with love,
    then these idols are of the fatherland of the crows.

157 The Prophet

    If the mountains are read from left to right,
    or just as unhurriedly in the reverse order,
    but not from below, as in daytime, and not from above, as at night,
    this means that time has plainly grown tired,
 5 has renounced its age, and without looking back
    its incorruptible right has changed.

    And when you, to please countless undertakings,
    begin wanting to foist yourself upon any goal,
    unwinding the road to the paths of a seer
10 (as if his exploit was foisted onto Hercules by Anteus

для того, чтобы только в безумном веселье
от земли оторваться и ввысь устремиться)—

вот тогда ты увидишь впритык, изумленно
прозревая, что нет ни вблизи, ни в округе
15 ни тебя, ни того, что тебя возносило.
Ты поймешь, как ужасно зиянье канона.
Ты—аспект описанья, изъятый в испуге,
наводящая страх бесприютная сила.

Можно вынуть занозу из мака живого,
20 чтобы он перестал кровяниться в отваге,
можно вынуть историю из пешехода,
научить красотой изнуренное слово
воздвигать закрома из болящей бумаги,
чтобы в них пустовала иная природа.

25 Можно сделать парик из волос Артемиды,
после смерти отросших в эфесском пожаре,
чтобы им увенчать безголовное тело,
тиражировать шок, распечатать обиды
или лучше надежду представить в товаре,
30 но нельзя, потому что... и в этом все дело.

Ты увидишь, как горы уходят, и с каждой—
горизонт и возможность иного простора,
и умение помнить времен исчисленье.
Если только тобой управляет паденье
35 в неуемную жажду высот разговора—
все терзанья твои объясняются жаждой.

158

Памяти сестры

Область неразменного владенья:
облаков пернатая вода.
В тридевятом растворясь колене,
там сестра все так же молода.

5 Обрученная с невинным роком,
не по мужу верная жена,
всю любовь, отмеренную сроком,
отдарила вечности она.

in order that only in insane joy
he should tear himself away from the earth and soar upward)—

at that time you will see right up close, in astonishment
recovering your sight, that neither near at hand, nor in the neighborhood
15 there is neither you, nor the thing that raised you up.
You will understand how horrible is the gaping of the canyon,
you're an aspect of description, withdrawn in terror,
a shelterless force that inspires fear.

A splinter can be extracted from a living poppy,
20 so it stops valiantly pouring blood,
history can be extracted from a pedestrian,
to teach the word by which beauty is exhausted
to raise up granaries from hurting paper,
so that a different nature should be empty in them.

25 A wig can be made from the hair of Artemis,
that has grown out after death in the conflagration at Ephesus,
so as to crown the headless body,
to make copies of the shock, to unseal the offenses
or better to offer hope in its wares,
30 but it can't be done, because... And that's the whole point.

You will see that the mountains go away and with each of them
the horizon and the possibility of a different expanse
and the ability to remember the calculation of the times.
If it is only you that falling directs
35 into the incessant thirst for the heights of conversation—
all your torments are explained by thirst.

158

In memory of my sister

A region of unexchangeable possession:
the feathered water of clouds.
Dissolving in the thrice-ninth generation,*
there my sister is still just as young.

5 Betrothed to an innocent fate,
a wife faithful, but not to her husband,
all the love measured out by her allotted time
she has given away to eternity.

Как была учительницей в школе,
10 так с тех пор мелок в ее руке
троеперстием горит на воле,
что-то пишет на пустой доске.

То ли буквы непонятны, то ли
нестерпим для глаза их размах:
15 остается красный ветер в поле,
имя розы на его губах.

И в разломе символа-святыни
узнается зубчатый лесок:
то ли мел крошится, то ли иней,
20 то ли звезды падают в песок.

Ты из тех пока что незнакомок,
для которых я неразличим.
У меня в руке другой обломок—
мы при встрече их соединим.

159 Завоевание стихий, 4

Я был, как письма самому себе
из будущего моего, оттуда,
где возраст, предназначенный на вырост,
уже заполнен прошлым до предела,
5 к тому же не моим, я был орудьем
для приручения его, дорогой
и путником на ней, и даже целью,
хранилищем, проводником, который
не мог меняться, изменять себя
10 без опасенья изменить себе.
И все-таки душа припоминает
сама себя и что она не только
всего лишь место где-нибудь в груди,
а то, с чем может вдруг отождествиться
15 пространство—как забытое письмо,
оставленное для тебя на случай—
между рукой и будущим твоим.

As she was a teacher in a school,
10 so ever since the chalk in her hand
burns at liberty like a three-fingered sign,*
writing something on the empty board.

Either the letters are incomprehensible, or
their sweep is intolerable to the eye—
15 the red wind remains in the field,
the name of the rose on its lips.

And in the breakup of the sacred symbol
the jagged-toothed forest can be recognized:
either the chalk is crumbling, or hoarfrost,
20 or stars falling into the sand.

You are one of those as yet unknown women,
for whom I am indistinguishable.
In my hand there is a different fragment,
and when we meet, we'll join the two.

159 The Conquest of the Elements, 4

I came, like letters to myself
from my future, from a place
where age, destined to put out shoots,
is already filled with the past to the limit,
5 and also not my own, I was an instrument
for bringing it to heel, a road
and also a wayfarer on it, and even goal,
repository, guide, who
could not alter or change himself
10 without misgivings about betraying himself.
And all the same my soul remembers
by itself and that it is not only
no more than a place somewhere in one's breast,
but that with which space can suddenly
15 become identical—like a forgotten letter,
left for you just in case—
between a hand and your future.

Ольга Седакова

160 Неверная жена

—С того дня, как ты домой вернулся
и на меня не смотришь,
все во мне переменилось.

Как та вон больная собака
5 третий день лежит, издыхает,
так и душа моя ноет.

Грешному весь мир—заступник,
а невинному—только чудо.
Пусть мне чудо и будет свидетель.
10 Покажи ему, Боже, правду,
покажи мое оправданье!—

Тут собака, бедное созданье,
быстро головой тряхнула,
весело к ней подбежала,
15 ласково лизнула руку—
и упала мертвая на землю.

Знает Бог о человеке
чего человек не знает.

161 Старушки

Как старый терпеливый художник,
я люблю разглядывать лица
набожных и злых старушек:

Olga Sedakova

160 The Unfaithful Wife

"From the day when you came home
and stopped looking at me,
everything's changed in me.

Like that sick dog
5 that's been lying there two days dying,
so does my soul ache.

To the sinner the whole world is an intercessor,
but to the innocent it's only a miracle.
May miracle be my witness.
10 Show him, O God, the truth,
show him my justification!"

At this the dog, that poor creature,
rapidly shook its head,
merrily ran up to her,
15 tenderly licked her hand—
and fell dead on the ground.

God knows about man
what man does not know.

161 Old Women

Like an old patient artist,
I like to look long at the faces
of pious and nasty old women:

смертные их губы
5 и бессмертную силу,
которая им губы сжала,

(будто сидит там ангел,
столбцами складывает деньги:
пятаки и легкие копейки...
10 Кыш!—говорит он детям,
птицам и попрошайкам—
кыш, говорит, отойдите:
не видите, чем я занят?)—

гляжу—и в уме рисую:
15 как себя перед зеркалом темным.

162

Неужели, Мария, только рамы скрипят,
только стекла болят и трепещут?
Если это не сад—
разреши мне назад,
5 в тишину, где задуманы вещи.

Если это не сад, если рамы скрипят
оттого, что темней не бывает,
если это не тот заповеданный сад,
где голодные дети у яблонь сидят
10 и надкушенный плод забывают,

где не видно огней,
но дыханье темней
и надежней лекарство ночное...
Я не знаю, Мария, болезни моей.
15 Это сад мой стоит надо мною.

their mortal lips
5 and the immortal power
that has drawn those lips together,

(as if an angel were sitting there
and setting out money in piles,
five-kopek coins, lightweight one-kopeks...
10 "Shoo!" he says to children,
birds, and beggars,
"Shoo," he says, "Go away;
can't you see what I'm doing?")

I look, and sketch in my mind:
15 like, as it were, myself before a dark mirror.

162

Surely, Maria, it's not just the frames creaking,
not just the panes aching and trembling?
If this is not the garden,
allow me to go back,
5 into the silence where things are invented.

If this is not the garden, if the frames are creaking
because it never gets darker than this,
if this is not that foreordained garden,
where hungry children sit by the apple trees
10 and forget the fruit that's been bitten into,

where no lights can be seen,
but breathing is darker,
and the medicine of the night more safe...
I do not know, Maria, my sickness.
15 This is my garden that stands over me.

163 Кузнечик и сверчок

The poetry of Earth is never dead.
John Keats

Поэзия земли не умирает.
И здесь, на Севере, когда повалит снег,
кузнечик замолчит. А вьюга заиграет
и забренчит сверчок, ослепший человек.
5 Но ум его проворен, как рапира.
Всегда настроена его сухая лира,
натянут важный волосок.
Среди невидимого пира—
он тоже гость, он Демодок.
10 И словно целый луг забрался на шесток.

Поэзия земли не так богата:
ребенок малый да старик худой,
кузнечик и сверчок откуда-то куда-то
бредут по лестнице одной—
15 и путь огромен, как заплата
на всей прорехе слуховой.
Гремя сердечками пустыми,
там ножницами завитыми
все щелкают над гривами златыми
20 коней нездешних, молодых—
и в пустоту стучат сравненья их.
Но хватит и того, кто в трубах завывает,
кто бледные глаза из вьюги поднимает,
кто луг обходит на заре
            и серебро свое теряет—
25 и всё находит в их последнем серебре.

Поэзия земли не умирает,
но если знает, что умрет—
челнок надежный выбирает,
бросает весла и плывет—
30 и что бы дальше ни случилось,
надежда рухнула вполне
и потому не разучилась
летать по слуховой волне.
Скажи мне, что под небесами
35 любезнее любимым небесам,

163 The Grasshopper and the Cricket

> The poetry of Earth is never dead.[*]
> John Keats

The poetry of the earth does not die.
And here, in the North, when heavy snow comes,
the grasshopper falls silent. But the blizzard starts to play
and the cricket, the blind man, starts to twang.
5 But his mind is adroit like a rapier.
His dry lyre is always tuned,
the weighty hair is stretched tight.
Amidst the invisible feast
he too is a guest, he is Demodocus.[*]
10 And it's as if a whole meadow had climbed onto his perch.

The poetry of the earth is not so rich:
the small child and the thin old man,
the grasshopper and cricket from somewhere to somewhere
wander up the same stair—
15 and the way is enormous, like a patch
over the entire rent of hearing.
Rattling their empty little hearts
there like curved scissors
they clink above the golden manes
20 of unearthly steeds, young ones—
and their comparisons sound into emptiness.
But it is enough to have the one who roars in trumpets,
who lifts his pale eyes from the blizzard,
who goes round the meadow at dawn and loses his silver—
25 and finds everything in their last silver.

The poetry of the earth does not die,
but if it knows it is going to die—
it chooses a trusty little bark,
abandons the oars, and sails away—
30 and whatever happens after that,
hope has entirely come to ruin
and has therefore not forgotten how
to fly along the wave of hearing.
Tell me, what beneath the heavens
35 is more kind to the kind heavens,

чем плыть с открытыми глазами
на дне, как раненый Тристан?...

Поэзия земли—отважнейшая скука.
На наковаленках таинственного звука
40   кузнечик и сверчок сковали океан.

164

В пустыне жизни... Что я говорю,
в какой пустыне? В освещенном доме,
где сходятся друзья и говорят
о том, что следует сказать. Другое
5   и так звучит, и так само себе,
как дерево из-за стекла кивает.
В саду у дружелюбных, благотворных,
печальных роз: их легкая душа
цветет в Элизии, а здесь не знает,
10   как выглянуть из тесных лепестков,
как показать цветенье без причины
и музыку, разредившую звук,
как рассказать о том, что будет дальше,
что лучшее всего... В саду у роз,
15   в гостях у всех—и все-таки в пустыне,
в пустыне нашей жизни, в худобе
ее несчастной, никому не видно—
Вы были больше, чем я расскажу.

Ни разум мой и ни глухой язык,
20   я знаю, никогда не прикоснутся
к тому, чего хотят. Не в этом дело.
Мы все, мой друг, достойны состраданья
хотя бы за попытку. Кто нас создал,
тот скажет, почему мы таковы,
25   и сделает, какими пожелает.
А если бы не так... Найти места
неслышной музыки: ее созвездья, цепи,
горящие переплетенья счастья,
в которой *эта* музыка сошлась,
30   как в разрешенье—вся большая пьеса,
доигранная. Долгая педаль.
Глубокая, покойная рука
лежала б сильно, впитывая все

than to sail with open eyes
on the bottom, like the wounded Tristan?

The poetry of the earth is the most courageous boredom.
On the anvils of mysterious sound
40 the grasshopper and cricket have forged an ocean.

164

In the desert of life... What am I saying,
in what desert? In a well-lit house,
where friends come together and talk
about what ought to be said. Another thing
5 sounds out anyway, and does so of its own accord,
like the tree nodding from behind the pane.
In the garden with hospitable, salutary,
sad roses: their light soul
blooms in Elysium, but here does not know
10 how to look out from the furled petals.
How to show the flowering that has no reason
and the music that has made sound grow thin,
how to tell about what will happen later,
that's best of all... In the garden by the roses,
15 everybody's guest—and all the same in the desert,
in the desert of our life, in its unfortunate
thinness, nobody can see—
You were more than I can tell.

Neither my reason nor my obscure tongue,
20 I know, will ever touch
that which they want to. That's not the point.
We are all, my friend, worthy of compassion
if only for having tried. He who created us
will say why we are like this,
25 and will make us the way he wants us.
And if it's not so... To find the places
of the inaudible music: its constellations, chains,
the burning interweavings of happiness,
in which *this* music has come together,
30 as in a resolution—this whole great play,
which has been played through. A long pedal note.
A profound and restful hand
would lie there powerfully, drawing in everything

из клавышей... Да, это было б лучше,
35 чем жестяные жалобы разлуки
и совести больной... Я так боюсь.
Но правда ведь, какая-то неправда
в таких стенаньях? Следует конец
нести на свет руками утешенья
40 и, как в меха, в бесценное созданье
раскаянье закутать, чтоб оно
не коченело—бедное, чужое...
А шло себе и шло, как красота,
мелодия из милости и силы.
45 Вы видите, я повторяю Вас...

165 На смерть Леонида Губанова

До свиданья, друг мой, до свиданья.
С. Есенин

Или новость—смерть, и мы не скажем сами:
все другое *больше* не с руки?
Разве не конец, летящий с бубенцами,
составляет звук строки?

5 Самый неразумный вслушивался в это—
с колокольчиком вдали.
Потому что, Леня, дар поэта
так отраден для земли.

Кто среди сокровищ тяжких, страстных
10 ларчик восхищенья выбрал наугад?
Кто еще похвалит мир прекрасный,
где нас топят, как котят?

Как эквилибрист-лунатик, засыпая,
преступает через естество,
15 знаешь, через что я преступаю?
Чрез *ненужность ничего.*

До свиданья, Леня. Тройкой из романса
пусть хоть целый мир летит в распыл,
ничего не страшно. Нужно постараться.
20 Быть не может, чтобы Бог забыл.

from the piano keys... Yes, that would be better
35 than the tinny complaints of separation
and the guilty conscience... I'm so afraid.
But surely it's true that there is something untrue
in these moanings? One ought to bring
the end into the world with the hands of consolation
40 and as if in furs, in the priceless creation
wrap remorse, so that it
won't grow stiff—poor, alien thing...
But that it should go on and on, like beauty,
a melody made from kindness and power.
45 You see, I am repeating You...

165 On the Death of Leonid Gubanov[*]

> Au revoir, my friend, au revoir.[*]
> S. Esenin

Or death *is* something new, and we ourselves wouldn't say
that everything else is *more* inconvenient?
Surely it's the end, flying with harness bells,
that forms the sound of the line?

5 The most unwise man listened hard to this,
this thing with a bell far away.
Because, Lenya, the poet's gift
is so full of joy for the earth.

Who amidst the burdensome, passionate treasures
10 chose at random the little box of delight?
Who else will praise the beautiful world,
where we are drowned like kittens?

As a sleepwalking tightrope-walker, dozing off,
transgresses Nature,
15 do you know what I transgress?
The unnecessariness of nothing.

Au revoir, Lenya. Like the troika from the song
let even a whole world be rubbed out,
nothing's frightening. One must try.
20 It cannot be that God has forgotten.

166 Семь стихотворений, 2

Ни морем, ни древом, ни крепкой звездой,
ни ночью глубокой, ни днем превеликим—
ничем не утешится разум земной,
но только любовью отца и владыки.

5 Ты, слово мое, как сады в глубине,
ты, слава моя, как сады и ограды—
как может больной поклониться земле—
тому, чего нет, чего больше не надо.

167 Кода

Поэт есть тот, кто хочет то, что все
хотят хотеть. Как белка в колесе,
он крутит свой вообразимый рок.
Но слог его, высокий, как порог,
5 выводит с освещенного крыльца
в каком-то заполярье без конца,
где все стрекочет с острия копья
кузнечиком в траве небытия.

И если мы туда скосим глаза—
10 то самый звук случаен, как слеза.

166 Seven Poems, 2

Not by sea, nor by tree, nor by powerful star,
nor by depth of night, nor by greatest of day—
Not by anything will earthly reason be consoled,
but only by the love of the father and master.

5 You, my word, like gardens in the deep,
you, my fame, like gardens and fences—
as a sick man can bow to the earth—
to that which is not, which is no longer needed.

167 Coda

The poet is he who wants that which everyone
wants to want. Like a squirrel in a wheel,
he spins his imaginable destiny.
But his style, high as a threshold,
5 leads away from the illuminated porch
into some trans-polar region without end,
where he keeps chirring from a spear's point
like a grasshopper in the grass of non-existence.

And if we glance sideways in that direction,
10 the sound itself is arbitrary as a teardrop.

Бахыт Кенжеев

168

Прошло, померкло, отгорело,
нет ни позора, ни вины.
Все, подлежавшие расстрелу,
убиты и погребены.

5 И только ветер, сдвинув брови,
стучит в квартиры до утра,
где спят лакейских предисловий
испытанные мастера.

А мне-то, грешному, все яма
10 мерещится в гнилой тайге,
где тлеют кости Мандельштама
с фанерной биркой на ноге.

1974

169

Кун-цзы уверял, что музыку следует
Слушать на церемониях, и не слишком редко.
Счастлив, кто вовремя спит и обедает,
Чтит родителей, уважает предков.

5 А Лао-цзы в своих откровениях
Советовал жить одиноко и сухо,
Ибо пять цветов утомляют зрение,
Пять музыкальных звуков вредны для слуха.

Bakhyt Kenzheev

168

It's over, gone dark, burned out,
there's no shame and no blame.
Everyone due to be shot
has been killed and buried.

5 And only the wind, knitting its brows,
knocks at the apartments before morning,
where sleep the experienced masters
of servile prefaces.

But I, unworthy, keep having visions of
10 a pit in the rotted taiga
where the bones of Mandelstam lie moldering
with a cardboard name tag on the foot.

1974

169

Confucius argued that music should be
Listened to at ceremonies, and not too rarely.
Happy is he who sleeps and dines at the right time,
Esteems his parents, respects his forebears.

5 But Lao-Tse in his revelations
Advised us to live in isolation and restraint,
For five colors exhaust one's vision,
Five musical sounds are harmful to the ear.

О, как изящен узор на шкатулке лаковой,
10 Как хорошо состязаться в стрельбе из лука!
Не соглашаясь, оба Учителя одинаково
Любили осень в горах и цветы бамбука.

Играют литавры военной славы. Сто
Тысяч мужей державных проходят чужим проселком.
15 Никто не отстанет, не перевяжет никто
Обезьяну, раненую осколком...

1 марта 1979

170

в россии грустная погода
под вечер дождь наутро лед
потом предчувствие распада
и страха медленный полет
5 струится музыка некстати
стареют парки детвора
играет в прошлое в квадрате
полузабытого двора

а рядом взрослые большие
10 они стоят навеселе
они давно уже решили
истлеть в коричневой земле
несутся листья издалёка
им тоже страшно одиноко
15 кружить в сухую пустоту
неслышно
                тлея на лету

беги из пасмурного плена
светолюбивая сестра
беги не гибни постепенно
20 в дыму осеннего костра
давно ли было полнолуние
давно ль с ума сходили мы
в россии грустной накануне
прощальной тягостной зимы

O, how elegant is the pattern on the lacquered box,
10 How good to compete at archery!
Without consulting, both Teachers identically
Loved autumn in the mountains and bamboo flowers.

The kettledrums of military glory play. One hundred
Thousand mighty men pass through an alien settlement.
15 Nobody falls behind, nobody bandages
The monkey wounded by a shell splinter...

1 March 1979

170

in russia there's melancholy weather
toward evening rain by morning ice
then a presentiment of decline
and the slow flight of fear
5 music streams not to the point
parks grow old kids
play at the past in the square
of a half-forgotten courtyard

and next to them are big grown-ups
10 they stand feeling merry
they long ago decided
to rot away in the brown earth
leaves come rushing from far away
they too feel afraid and alone
15 as they swirl in the dry emptiness
inaudibly
           decaying in flight

flee from overcast captivity
light-loving sister
flee do not perish gradually
20 in the smoke of an autumn bonfire
was the full moon a long time ago
was it long ago that we went out of our minds
in sad russia on the eve of
the wearisome farewell winter

25 она любила нас когда-то
не размыкая снежных век
но если в чем и виновата
то не признается вовек
лишь наяву и в смертном поле
30 и бездны мрачной на краю
она играет поневоле
пустую песенку свою

1979

171

В Переделкине лес облетел,
над церквушкою туча нависла,
да и речка теперь не у дел—
знай, журчит без особого смысла.

5 Разъезжаются дачники, но
вечерами по-прежнему в клубе
развеселое крутят кино.
И писатель, талант свой голубя,

разгоняет осенний дурман
10 стопкой водки. И новый роман
(то-то будет отчизне подарок!)
замышляет из жизни свинарок.

На перроне частушки поют
про ворону, гнездо и могилу.
15 Ликвидирован дачный уют—
двух поездок с избытком хватило.

Жаль, что мне собираться в Москву,
что припаздывают электрички,
жаль, что бедно и глупо живу,
20 подымая глаза по привычке

к объявленьям—одни коротки,
а другие, напротив, пространны.
Снимем дом. Продаются щенки.
Предлагаю уроки баяна.

25 she loved us at one time
without parting her snowy eyelids
but if she's to blame for something
she won't confess ever
only in full sight and on the fatal field
30 and on the edge of the gloomy abyss
she plays willy-nilly
her empty song

1979

171

In Peredelkino* the forest has lost its leaves,
over the little church a cloud hangs,
and even the stream has stopped work—
looks as if it's gurgling without meaning anything special.

5 The dacha people are going their separate ways, but
in the evenings as before in the club
there's oh-such-a-happy movie.
And a writer, coddling his talent,

disperses the autumn blues
10 with a flask of vodka. And his new novel
(a real gift to the fatherland!)
he dreams up, taken from the life of swineherds.

On the station platform they're singing ditties
about the crow, the nest, and the grave.
15 The snug comfort of the dacha is liquidated,
two trips was more than enough.

Pity that I have to go back to Moscow,
that the electric trains are always a bit late,
pity I live poorly and stupidly,
20 raising my eyes in the accustomed way

to the small ads—some are short,
others, on the contrary, are extensive.
House to rent wanted. Puppies for sale.
I give accordion lessons.

25 Дурачье. Я и сам бы не прочь
поселиться в ноябрьском поселке,
чтобы вьюга шуршала всю ночь,
и бутылка стояла на полке.

Отхлебнешь—и ни капли тоски.
30 Соблазнительны, правда, щенки
(родословные в полном порядке)
да котенку придется несладко.

Снова будем с тобой зимовать
в тесном городе, друг мой Лаура,
35 и уроки гармонии брать
у бульваров, зияющих хмуро,

у дождей затяжных, у любви,
у дворов, где в безумии светлом
современники бродят мои,
40 словно листья, гонимые ветром.

1981

172

Все на свете выходит из моды, родная, и мы
превращаемся в анахронизм, в пережиток
отдаленной эпохи, когда накануне зимы
лед блистал, словно гвозди на конских копытах,

5 и падучие звезды не вскрикивали на лету,
не сжимали зубов, не роняли кровавую пену,
а летели безропотно в ласковую глухоту,
и шептали—до встречи, конечно, пиши непременно...

Неужели мы все-таки выжили? Я не могу,
10 не хватает зацепки, такой ерундовой...
а оставленный город алеет на свежем снегу,
и сияет крестами, и блазнится гладью ледовой...

1984

25 Foolishness. I myself wouldn't be against
settling down in a November village,
so the snowstorm could rustle all night,
and a bottle be standing on the shelf.

Take a sip—not a drop of anxiety left.
30 Tempting, true, are those puppies
(pedigrees in complete good order)
but it wouldn't be nice for our kitten.

Once more you and I will spend the winter
in the packed city, Laura my friend,
35 and take harmony lessons
from the boulevards that gape gloomily,

from the drawn-out rains, from love,
from the courtyards, where in unclouded madness
my contemporaries roam
40 like leaves being chased by the wind.

1981

172

Everything in the world goes out of fashion, my love, and we
are turning into an anachronism, a survival
of a distant epoch, when on the eve of winter
the ice shone like nails on horses' hooves,

5 and falling stars didn't cry out in their flight,
didn't clench their teeth, didn't drop bloody foam,
but flew uncomplainingly into caressing emptiness,
and whispered: "Until next time, of course, be sure and write..."

Have we really survived? I can't,
10 not enough grip, something that matters so little...
but the deserted city shows scarlet against the fresh snow,
its crosses shine, it seduces with its flat icy expanse...

1984

173

Пустые улицы, провалы подворотен.
Осенний мир прохладен и бесплотен.

Сорокалетний тополь надо мной
Еще шумит листвою жестяной.

5 Его хозяин к будущему лету
Должно быть, спилит—чтоб не застил света,

Чтоб не шумел, не пел над головой,
Корнями не корежил мостовой,

И не надышишься—а хочется—хотя бы
10 Сентябрьской горечью, последним солнцем слабым...

1984

174

Восторги, усы, полумаски. Галдит у подъезда толпа
с мешками, и страшно, как в сказке, и тыквенные черепа
таращат пустые глазницы с горящею свечкой внутри.
Зануде—томиться и злиться, а городу—жечь фонари,

5 раскрашивать плоские крыши, кубышки, наряды до пят.
До самого неба и выше багряные листья летят.
И будь я силен в этих играх, и сам увлекаться умей—
давно бы их вынес в эпиграф к испуганной жизни своей.

Пройдет. Поболит и привыкнет. И радостно вдруг в тишине
10 бродящий утопленник гикнет и гибелью встанет в окне.
Ах, черное наше веселье, проделки детей заводных.
Орехами ли, карамелью давай откупаться от них.

173

Empty streets, deep spaces under doors.
The autumn world is cool and fleshless.

The forty-year-old poplar over my head
Still makes noise with its tinfoil foliage.

5 Its owner by next summer,
Is bound to saw it down, so it doesn't block the light,

So it doesn't make noise, doesn't sing overhead,
Doesn't rumple the pavement with its roots,

And you can't breathe deep enough, though you want to, of even
10 The September bitterness, the final weak sun...

1984

174

Excitement, moustaches, half-masks. A crowd rowdy at the doorway
with sacks, and it's scary like in a fairy tale, and the pumpkin skulls
glare their empty eyesockets with a burning candle inside.
The grouch must suffer and be mad, the town must light its lanterns,

5 and decorate the flat roofs, money boxes, full-length costumes.
Right up to the sky and higher the crimson leaves fly.
And if I were good at these games, if I knew how to get involved—
I would long ago have made them an epigraph to my terrified life.

It'll pass. Hurt a bit, then be normal. And joyfully suddenly in the quietness
10 a wandering drowned man will whoop and rise up in the window like death.
Agh, our black joy, the pranks of clockwork children.
Let's buy our way out with some nuts or caramels.

И копотью пахнет, и смехом отхлынувший Хэллоуин.
Потянет по улочке эхом—и вновь остается один
15 писатель таинственной прозы. Скрипеть ему школьным пером,
глотая холодные слезы на темном ветру мировом.

2 ноября 1987

And it smells of soot and laughter, Halloween that's now swept on its way.
It'll stretch as an echo along the street—and once again will remain alone
15 the writer of mysterious prose. He must squeak with his school pen,
swallowing cold tears in the dark wind of the world.

2 November 1987

Александр Еременко

175 Переделкино

Гальванопластика лесов.
Размешан воздух на ионы.
И переделкинские склоны
смешны, как внутренность часов.

5 На даче спят. Гуляет горький
холодный ветер. Пять часов.
У переезда на пригорке
с усов слетела стая сов.

Поднялся вихорь, степь дрогнула.
10 Непринужденна и светла,
выходит осень из загула,
и сад встает из-за стола.

Она в полях и огородах
разруху чинит и разбой
15 и в облаках перед народом
идет-бредет сама собой.

Льет дождь. Цепных не слышно псов
на штаб-квартире патриарха,
где в центре англицкого парка
20 стоит Венера. Без трусов.

Рыбачка Соня как-то в мае,
причалив к берегу баркас,
сказала Косте:—Все вас знают,
а я так вижу в первый раз.

Aleksandr Eremenko

175 Peredelkino*

Galvanized plastic of the forests.
The air is kneaded with ions.
And the Peredelkino slopes
are funny, like the inside of a clock.

5 They're asleep in the dacha.* There roams a bitter
cold wind. Five o'clock.
At the crossing on the knoll
from its moustache a flock of owls has flown.

A whirlwind arises, the steppe shudders.
10 Relaxed and bright,
autumn emerges from its booze-up,
and the garden gets up from the table.

In fields and vegetable gardens
[autumn] causes destruction and pillage,
15 and in the clouds before the people*
it goes wandering of its own accord.

The rain pours down. Watchdogs can't be heard
at the HQ apartment of the patriarch,*
where in the center of an English park
20 stands Venus. With no underpants.

Fisherwoman Sonya* once in May,
mooring her skiff to the bank,
said to Kostya: "Everybody knows you,
but I'm seeing you for the first time!"

25 Льет дождь. На темный тес ворот
На сад, раздерганный и нервный,
На потемневшую фанерку
и надпись «Все ушли на фронт».

На даче сырость и бардак,
30 И сладкий запах керосина.
Льет дождь. На даче спят два сына,
допили водку и коньяк.

С крестов слетают кое-как
криволинейные вороны.
35 И днем, и ночью, как ученый,
по кругу ходит Пастернак.

Налево—белый лес, как бредень.
Направо—блок могильных плит.
И воет пес соседский, Федин,
40 и, бедный, на ветвях сидит.

И я там был, мед-пиво пил,
изображая смерть, не муку,
но кто-то камень положил
в мою протянутую руку.

45 Играет ветер, бьется ставень,
а мачта гнется и скрипит.
А по ночам гуляет Сталин.
Но вреден север для меня.

176 Памятник

Я добрый, красивый, хороший
и мудрый, как будто змея.
Я женщину в небо подбросил—
и женщина стала моя.

5 Когда я с бутылкой «массандры»
иду через весь ресторан,
весь пьян, как воздушный десантник,
и ловок, как горный баран,

25 The rain pours down. Onto the dark planks of the gates,
    onto the garden, dishevelled and nervous,
    on the darkened plywood
    and the notice "All have left for the front."

    In the dacha is dampness and a hell of a mess,
30 And the sweet smell of kerosene.
    The rain pours down. In the dacha sleep two sons,
    they've drunk up their vodka and cognac.

    From the crosses fly off any old how
    the curvilinear crows.
35 And day and night,* like a scholar,
    in a circle walks Pasternak.

    To the left is a white* wood like a drag-net.
    To the right a block of gravestones.
    And the neighbor's hound Fedin* howls
40 and, poor thing, sits on the branches.

    I was there too, I drank the honey brew,
    depicting death, not torture,
    but someone put a stone
    into my outstretched hand.

45 The wind plays, a shutter bangs,
    the mast bends and creaks...*
    And at night Stalin walks abroad.
    But the north is harmful for me.*

176 Monument

    I'm kind, and handsome, and good
    and wise as if I were a serpent.
    I threw a woman up into the sky—
    and that woman became mine.

5   When with a bottle of Massandra*
    I walk across an entire restaurant,
    pissed as a paratrooper,
    and nimble as a mountain ram,

Все пальцами тычут мне в спину
10 и шепот вдогонку летит:
«Он женщину в небо подкинул—
и женщина в небе висит...»

Мне в этом не стыдно признаться:
когда я вхожу—все встают
15 и лезут ко мне обниматься,
целуют и деньги дают.

Все сразу становятся рады
и словно немножко пьяны,
когда я читаю с эстрады
20 свои репортажи с войны,

И дело до драки доходит,
когда через несколько лет
меня вспоминают в народе
и спорят, как я был одет.

25 Отважный, красивый и быстрый,
собравший все нервы в комок,
я мог бы работать министром,
командовать крейсером мог!

Я вам называю примеры:
30 я делать умею аборт,
читаю на память Гомера
и дважды сажал самолет.

В одном я виновен, но сразу
открыто о том говорю:
35 я в космосе не был ни разу,
и то потому, что курю.

Конечно, хотел бы я вечно
работать, учиться и жить
во славу потомков беспечных
40 и в пику детекторам лжи,

чтоб каждый, восстав из рутины,
сумел бы сказать, как и я:
«Я женщину в небо подкинул—
и женщина стала моя»!

all fingers jab at my back
10 and a whisper flies after me:
"He tossed a woman up into the sky—
and that woman hangs in the sky."

I'm not ashamed to confess this:
that when I come in, everyone stands up
15 and tries to embrace me,
they kiss me and give me money.

Everyone gets happy right away
and as if slightly drunk,
when I declaim from the stage
20 my reports from the war,

And things lead to a fight
when several years later
I'm remembered among the people
and they argue about what I was wearing.

25 Bold, handsome, and adroit,
screwing all my nerves into a ball,
I could do a minister's job,
I could command a cruiser!

I give you some examples:
30 I know how to perform an abortion,
I can declaim Homer by heart
and I've twice landed an airplane.

There's one thing I'm guilty of, but immediately
I speak about it openly:
35 I was never once in space,
and that's because I smoke.

Of course, I would like forever
to work, labor and live
to the glory of carefree descendants
40 and to spite the lie detectors,

so that everyone, arising out of routine,
should be able to say, as I do:
"I tossed a woman into the sky—
and that woman became mine!"

177 Стихи о сухом законе, посвященные свердловскому рок-клубу

«Высоцкий разбудил рокеров, рокеры
предопредили решения XXVII съезда»
(А. Козлов. «Рок, как двигатель ускорения»)

Он голосует за сухой закон,
балдея на трибуне, как на троне.
Кто он? Издатель, критик, чемпион
зачатий пьяных в каждом регионе,
5 лауреат всех премий... вор в законе!
Он голосует за сухой закон.

Он раньше пил запоем, как закон,
по саунам, правительственным дачам,
как идиот, забором обнесен,
10 по кабакам, где счет всегда оплачен,
а если был особенно удачлив—
со Сталиным коньяк «Наполеон».

В 20-х жил (а ты читай—хлестал),
чтобы не спать, на спирте с кокаином
15 и вел дела по коридорам длинным,
уверенно идя к грузинским винам,
чтобы в конце прийти в Колонный зал
и кончить якобинской гильотиной...
Мне проще жить—я там стихи читал.

20 Он при Хрущеве квасил по штабам,
при Брежневе по банькам и блядям,
а при Андропове—закрывшись в кабинете.
Сейчас он пьет при выключенном свете,
придя домой, скрываясь в туалете...
25 Мне все равно—пусть захлебнется там!

А как он пил по разным лагерям
конвойным, «кумом», просто вертухаем,
когда, чтоб не сойти с ума, бухая
с утра до ночи, пил, не просыхая...
30 Сухой закон со спиртом пополам.

177 Lines on Prohibition, Dedicated to
the Sverdlovsk Rock Club*

"Vysotsky stirred up the rockers, and the rockers
determined the decisions of the XXVII Congress"
(A. Kozlov, "Rock as the Engine of Acceleration")

He votes for prohibition,
going crazy on the platform, like on a throne.
Who is he? Publisher, critic, champion
of drunken conceptions in every region,
5 laureate of all prizes... thief "in the law"!*
He votes for prohibition.

He used to go on binges without fail,
in saunas, government dachas,
like an idiot surrounded by a fence,
10 in pubs where the bill was always paid,
and if he was especially lucky—
Napoleon brandy with Stalin.

In the 20s he lived (for which read "guzzled")
to stay awake, on spirits with cocaine
15 and conducted business on long corridors,
confidently going to the Georgian wines,
so as in the end to come to the Hall of Columns*
and finish with the Jacobin guillotine...
Life's easier for me—I've read poetry there!

20 Under Khrushchev he downed it around the HQs,
under Brezhnev in bathhouses and around whores,
but under Andropov, locked up in his office.
Now he drinks with the light turned off,
when he gets home, hiding in the toilet...
25 I don't care, let him choke in there!

And how he used to drink round various camps
as transit guard, "godfather,"* just a "screw,"
when, so's not to go mad, raining blows
from morn till night he drank without drying out...
30 Prohibition mixed half and half with spirits.

Я тоже голосую за закон,
свободный от воров и беззаконий,
и пью спокойно свой одеколон
за то, что не участвовал в разгоне
35 толпы людей, глотающей озон,
сверкающий в гудящем микрофоне!

Я пью за волю, с другом, не один,
За выборы без дури и оглядки,
я пью за прохождение кабин
40 на пунктах в обязательном порядке,
пью за любовь и полную разрядку,
Еще—за наваждение причин.

Я голосую за свободы клок,
за долгий путь из вымершего леса,
45 за этот стих, простой, как без эфеса
куда хочу направленный клинок,
за безусловный двигатель прогресса,
за мир и дружбу—
за свердловский рок!

178 Добавление к сопромату

Чтобы одной пулей
погасить две свечи,
нужно последние расположить так,
чтобы прямая линия,
5 соединяющая мушку
с прорезью планки прицеливания
одновременно проходила бы
и через центры обеих мишеней.
В этом случае, произведя выстрел,
10 можно погасить обе свечи
при условии, что пуля
не расплющится о пламя первой.

I too vote for a law!
Free of thieves and lawlessness,
and I calmly drink my eau-de-cologne*
to not having taken part in the dispersal
35 of a crowd of people swallowing ozone
that glitters in a humming microphone!

I drink to freedom, with a friend, not alone.
To elections without bull and looking over your shoulder.
I drink to going through the booth
40 at voting stations in obligatory order,
I drink to love and to total disarmament,
and also to the delusion of reasons…

I vote for a wisp of freedom,
for the long journey out of the dead forest,
45 for this verse, simple as [a sword] without a guard
its blade pointed where I please,
for the unconditional engine of progress,
for peace and friendship—
and for Sverdlovsk rock!

178 An Addendum to *Sopromat**

In order with one bullet
to put out two candles,
one needs to arrange the latter in such a way
that a straight line
5 connecting the foresight
with the groove on the backsight
should simultaneously pass along
and through the centers of both targets.
In this case, by carrying out the shot
10 one can put out both candles
on condition that the bullet
isn't crushed on the flame of the first.

179

Да здравствует старая дева,
когда, победив свою грусть,
она теорему Виета
запомнила всю наизусть.

5 Всей русской душою проникла,
всем пламенем сердца вошла
и снова, как пена, возникла
за скобками быта и зла!

Она презирает субботу,
10 не ест и не пьет ничего.
Она мозговую работу
поставила выше всего.

Ее не касается трепет
могучих инстинктов ее.
15 Все вынесет, все перетерпит
суровое тело ее,

когда одиноко и прямо
она на кушетке сидит
и словно в помойную яму
20 в цветной телевизор глядит.

Она в этом кайфа не ловит,
но если страна позовет,
коня на скаку остановит,
в горящую избу войдет!

25 Малярит, латает, стирает,
за плугом идет в борозде,
и северный ветер играет
в косматой ее бороде!

Она ничего не кончала,
30 но мысли ее торжество,
минуя мужское начало,
уходит в начало—всего!

179

Long live the old maid,
when, overcoming her sadness,
she has learned Viète's* theorem
right through by heart.

5 With all her Russian soul she penetrated,
with all the flame of her heart she entered
and rose again, like foam,
outside the brackets of everyday life and evil!

She despises the Sabbath,
10 eats and drinks nothing.
Above all else
she has placed brainwork.

She is not touched by the tremor
of her mighty instincts.
15 It withstands everything, endures everything,
her severe body.

When isolated and straight
she sits on her couch
and as if at a cesspit
20 looks at her color TV.

She doesn't get a high from this,
but if the country should call,
she would stop a galloping horse,
or go into a burning wooden hut!

25 She housepaints, patches, launders,
walks the furrow behind the plow,
and the northern wind plays
in her matted beard!

She's graduated in nothing,
30 but the triumph of her thought,
bypassing the male principle,
goes back to the beginning—of everything!

Сидит она, как в назиданье,
и с кем-то выходит на связь,
35 как бы над домашним заданьем,
над всем мирозданьем склонясь.

She sits as if for edification
and goes out to meet someone,
35 as if over a piece of homework,
bending over the entire universe.

Алексей Парщиков

180

I

Улитка или шелкопряд,
по черной прихоти простуды,
я возвращался в детский сад
и видел смерть свою оттуда.

5 В сомнамбулической броне
наверняка к ядру земному
с повинной полз к родному дому,
а дом курился на спине.

Внизу картофельный шахтер
10 писклявым глазом шевелил,
и рвались угли на простор
от птеродактилевых крыл.

Я встретил залежи утрат
среди ракушечного грунта,
15 нательный крест Джордано Бруно
и гребни эллинских дриад.

II

Природа пеплами жива
да фотографиями в раме,
как перед новыми снегами
кто ходит в лес, кто по дрова.

Aleksei Parshchikov

180

I

Snail or silkworm,
by the black whim of a cold,
I was going back to nursery school
and saw my death from there.

5 In somnambulistic armorplate
for sure toward the earth's core
I crawled to confess toward my native home,
but the building was smoking on its back.

Underneath, a potato miner
10 shifted his squeaky eye,
and coals rushed to the expanse
from pterodactyl wings.

I encountered deposits of loss
among the cockleshell soil,
15 the pectoral cross of Giordano Bruno
and the combs of Hellenic dryads.

II

Nature is alive in ashes
and photographs in a frame,
as before the new snows
some go to the forest, others for firewood.

5 Дышать водой, губить медведя
и нацарапать на бревне—
когда я спал, приснилось мне...

181 Петр

Скажу, что между камнем и водой
червяк есть промежуток жути. Кроме—
червяк—отрезок времени и крови.
Не тонет нож, как тонет голос мой.

5 А вешний воздух скроен без гвоздя,
и, пыль скрутив в горящие девятки,
как честь чужую, бросит на лопатки,
прицельным духом своды обведя.

Мария! пятен нету на тебе.
10 Меня ж давно литая студит ересь,
и я на крест дареный не надеюсь,
а вознесусь, как копоть по трубе.

Крик петушиный виснет, как серьга
тяжелая, внезапная. Играют
15 костры на грубых лирах. Замолкают
кружки старух и воинов стога.

Что обсуждали пять минут назад?
Зачем случайной медью похвалялись,
зачем в медведей черных обращались,
20 и вверх чадящим зеркалом летят?

182 Автостоп в горах

Пока мы голосуем у окраин,
мой дух похож на краденый мешок:
снаружи—строг, а изнутри—случаен.

Пустых пород приподняты слои,
5 под фарами они скрипят, крошатся,
и камешек ползет, как мозг змеи.

5 To breathe water, destroy a bear
and scratch on a log—
while I was asleep, I saw in my dreams…

181 Peter

I'll say that between stone and water
a worm is an interval of terror. Besides
a worm is a section of time and blood.
A knife doesn't sink the way my voice sinks.

5 But the vernal air is patterned without nails,
and twirling up in the dust into burning figure 9s
like someone else's honor, it throws onto shovels
going round the vaults with an aimed spirit.

Mary! there is no spot on thee.
10 But ingot heresy has long been chilling me,
and I do not put my hope in a presented cross,
but will ascend like soot up the chimney.

The rooster's cry will hang like an earring,
heavy and sudden. Bonfires
15 play on coarse lyres. Circles
of old women fall silent, and the haystacks of warriors.

What were they discussing five minutes ago?
Why did they boast about random bronze,
why were they turning into black bears,
20 and flying up like a smoky-burning mirror?

182 Autostop in the Mountains

While we're trying to hitch a lift near the outskirts
my spirit's like a stolen sack:
from outside stern, but from inside arbitrary.

Strata of empty species are raised up,
5 beneath headlights they creak, crumble,
and a small stone slides like the brain of a snake.

Ремни геометрических сандалий
ослабив, ты хребтов заводишь гребни,
мизинцем растирая кровь на кремне.

10 Вовлечена в шоссейный оборот,
ты тянешь сны за волосы. Твой рот
самовлюбленней ртути на смоле.

И поголовья бабочек багровых
друг друга подымали на рога,
15 от белокровья крючась на дорогах.

И души асов, врезавшись, могли
из меди перепрыгнуть в алюминий
и вспыхнуть в километре от Земли.

И трасса поутру была рыжа,
20 и прожита в течение ножа.
Тень кипариса на угле. Жара.

183

Я выпустил тебя слепящим волком
с ажурным бегом, а теперь мне стыдно:
тебе ботинки расшнуровывает водка,
как ветер, что сквозит под пляжной ширмой.

5 Гляжу, как ты переставляешь ноги.
Как все. Как все, ты в этом безупречен.
Застенчивый на солнечной дороге,
раздавленный, как вырванная печень.

Собака-водка плавает в нигде,
10 И на тебя никто ее науськивает.
Ты вверх ногами ходишь по воде,
и волосах твоих гремят моллюски.

Having slackened the straps of geometrical sandals,
you wind up the crests of ridges,
with your little finger spreading like blood on the flint.

10 Inveigled into the main-road circulation,
you drag dreams by the hair. Your mouth
is more in love with itself than mercury on pitch.

And the livestock-counts of crimson butterflies
have lifted each other onto horns,
15 writhing with leukemia on the roads.

And the souls of aces, impacted, could
hop over from copper into aluminum
and burst into flame a kilometer from Earth.

And the roadway was red-haired in the morning,
20 and lived through in the course of a knife.
The shade of a cypress on coal. Stifling heat.

183

I released you like a blinding wolf
with openwork run, and now I'm ashamed:
vodka is taking the laces out of your shoes,
like the wind that comes through under a beach curtain.

5 I watch you putting one foot in front of the other.
Like everyone. Like everyone, you're irreproachable in this.
Bashful on the sunny road,
squashed like a ripped-out liver.

Dog-vodka floats in nowhere,
10 And nobody sicks it on you.
You walk on water upside down,
and in your hair the mollusks thunder.

184 Львы

М.б., ты и рисуешь что-то
серьезное, но не сейчас, увы.
Решетка
и за нею—львы.

5 Львы. Их жизнь—дипломата,
их лапы—левы, у них две головы,
со скоростью шахматного автомата
всеми клетками клетки овладевают львы.

Глядят—в упор, но никогда—с укором,
10 и растягиваются, словно капрон;
они привязаны к корму, но и колокольням
дальним, колеблющимся над Днепром,

Львы делают: ам!—озирая закаты.
Для них нету капусты или травы.
15 Вспененные ванны, где уснули Мараты—
о, львы!

Мы в городе спрячемся, словно в капусте,
в выпуклом зеркале он рос без углов,
и по Андреевскому спуску
20 мы улизнем от львов.

Львы нарисованные сельв и чащоб!
Их гривы можно грифелем заштриховать,
я же хочу с тобой пить, пить, а еще
я хочу с тобой спать, спать, спать.

185 Когда

Авианосцы туманные время накапливают, и мы их наблюдаем,
сложное время, как смятая простыня.
Америка ищет историю, жмя на педали в так далее...
А у тебя амнезия, чтобы не помнить меня.

184 Lions

P'haps, you really are sketching something
serious, but not now, alas.
Bars
and behind them, lions.

5 Lions. Their life is that of a diplomat,
their paws are on the left,* they have two heads,
at the speed of an automatic chess machine
lions take charge of all the cells of their cages.

Their gaze is steady, but never reproachful,
10 and they stretch out like kapron;*
they're hitched to their fodder, but also to belfries
far away, oscillating over the Dnepr.

Lions go "I'll eat you!" as they survey sunsets.
For them there's no cabbage or grass.
15 Foaming baths, where Marats have fallen asleep—
O, lions!

We will hide in the city as if in cabbage,
in a convex mirror it has grown without corners,
and along St. Andrew's Slope*
20 we'll slip away from the lions.

Lions, sketched of selva and thickets!
Their manes can be shaded in with a slate pencil,
I, though, want to drink, drink, with you, and also
I want to sleep, sleep, sleep with you.

185 When

Misty aircraft carriers accumulate time, and we observe them,
complex time, like a rumpled sheet.
America searches for a history, squeezing the pedal into the and so forth…
But you have amnesia, so as not to remember me.

5 Язык мой подробно смакует краба,
этот узел эволюции, что сложнее рельефа Скалистих гор,
Рабы бара, исключая одного араба,
глядят на меня в упор,

когда я слышу жилистый гудок здешнего тепловоза,
10 а владыки авиакомпаний и короли агробизнеса сидят,
умирая от демократизма, когда настольная роза,
умирая от деспотизма, экономит свой аромат.

186

О сад моих друзей, где я торчу с трещоткой
и для отвода глаз свищу по сторонам,
посеребрим кишки крутой крещенской водкой,
да здраствует нутро, мерцающее нам!

5 Ведь наши имена не множимы, но кратны
распахнутой земле, чей треугольный ум,
чья лисья хитреца потребует обратно
безмолвие и шум, безмолвие и шум.

5 My tongue relishes in detail a crab,
this node of evolution more complex than a relief of the Rocky Mountains.
The slaves of the bar, excepting a single Arab,
gaze fixedly at me,

when I hear the sinewy siren of a local diesel locomotive,
10 but the sovereigns of the airline companies and the kings of agribusiness sit
    there,
dying of democratism, when a rose on the table,
dying of despotism, is being sparing with its fragrance.

186

O garden of my friends, where I hang about with my rattle
and to create a diversion whistle to one side,
let's silver our intestines with harsh twelfth-night* vodka,
long live the insides that glimmer for us!

5 After all, our names are not multipliable, but divisible
by the ploughed-up earth, whose triangular mind
and whose foxy cunning demand in return
silence and sound, silence and sound.

NOTES ON THE POETS

AND THE POEMS

Boris Slutsky (1919-1986)

Boris Abramovich Slutsky was born in the Don Basin and brought up in Kharkov. He came to Moscow in 1937 to train as a lawyer, and from 1939 simultaneously studied at the Gorky Institute of Literature. He served through the Great Patriotic War as a political officer, joining the Communist Party in 1943. Slutsky then settled in Moscow; his wounds were severe enough to entitle him to a disability pension. Although he had published one poem before the war, his first collection came out only in the year he joined the Union of Writers, 1957; he was soon recognized as an eminent war poet. His philosophical lyrics added to his reputation in the 1960s, but he was never near the top of the official canon. Further collections appeared regularly, but by the time of his death, less than half of Slutsky's work had been published. Beginning in the late 1950s, some of this suppressed work had appeared abroad after circulating in *samizdat*, but never with the poet's permission. After the death of his wife in 1977, Slutsky suffered a mental breakdown and stopped writing. The first reasonably full collections began to be published in the USSR in 1990.

4   *FORGIVENESS*
Slutsky was one of the members of the Union of Writers who spoke in favor of and voted for the expulsion of Boris Pasternak in 1958; this act left him with a festering sense of guilt. Lev Loseff has written a poem about this incident, *31 oktyabrya 1958 goda*, coupling Slutsky's name with that of Leonid Martynov, another poet who voted against Pasternak, concluding with the lines "If anyone knows any real prayers,/ pray for them."

7   "HUSBANDS WITH THEIR DOINGS AND NERVES"
Slutsky's wife, Tatyana Borisovna Dashkovskaya, died at the age of 47 in February 1977. The poem makes a poignant contrast with a well-known earlier poem by Slutsky about the women left isolated by the slaughter of the male population in World War II, "Old Women without their Men" (1961).

Boris Chichibabin (b. 1923)

Boris Alekseevich Polushin, who uses the pen name Chichibabin, was born in Kremenchug and brought up in various Ukrainian towns. He entered the literary faculty of Kharkov University in 1940, and then served in the armed forces from 1942 to 1945, when he went back to the university. He was arrested in June 1946 for "anti-Soviet agitation" and was in the Gulag until 1951; he was rehabilitated in 1955. He returned to Kharkov and eventually found work as an accounts clerk at a tram depot; he was still holding this job in 1990. Chichibabin published four books of enthusiastically orthodox poetry in the 1960s; he became a member of the Union of Writers in 1966. From 1964 until he was sacked in 1968 for organizing a session celebrating Pasternak, he led a literary workshop in Kharkov. He was expelled from the Union of Writers in 1973 for writing politically unacceptable poetry. His work began to appear outside the USSR in the late 1970s, and inside from 1987. Chichibabin was readmitted into the Union of Writers, and awarded a State Prize for literature in 1990.

9   *CONFESSION*
3   Sholom Aleikhem: the founder of modern Yiddish literature (1859-1916), who was born and lived in Russia and had extensive contacts with Russian writers; he left for the USA after the Kiev pogroms of 1905, settled in Geneva in 1907, returned to Russia briefly in 1908, and was last in Russia in the spring of 1914, after which he left again for New York, where he died.

12   "TO THEE, MY RUSSIA, NOT TO GOD..."
4   Razin: the Cossack Stepan Razin, executed in 1671 after the suppression of the peasant revolt he led; see also Kublanovsky below.
14   Levitan: Isaak Ilich Levitan (1860-1900), the landscape painter.
18   *oprichniki*: Ivan the Terrible's personal intelligence and enforcement apparatus (1565-1572), sometimes regarded as a precursor of the secret police.
29   Herzen: Alexander Herzen (1812-1870), the Russian political exile, who lived outside Russia from 1847, mainly in London.
30   Avvakum: (1620?-1682), the Old Believer Archpriest, well known for his unprecedented autobiography telling the story of his persecution at the hands of the civil and ecclesiastical authorities.

15   "FLOWERS LAY ON THE SNOW"
7   the grave of Pasternak: Pasternak is buried in Peredelkino (see also Akhmadulina, Kenzheev, and Eremenko, below); the "three pine trees" (line 19) stand over his grave.
17   Mayakovsky at the Taganka: the play *Listen Here!* (premiered in 1967), one of the greatest early successes of Yurii Lyubimov's Taganka Theater in Moscow; based on Mayakovsky's poetry, with the poet played by five different actors simultaneously.

Bulat Okudzhava (b. 1924)

Bulat Shalvovich Okudzhava was born in Moscow; his parents, both Party officials, were arrested in 1937, his father being shot and his mother imprisoned until 1954. He volunteered for the army in 1942. After the war he became a teacher; he joined the Party in 1955, moved to Moscow, and began a full-time career as a writer in 1956. He started writing and performing songs in the late 1950s and attained wide and lasting popularity through their circulation on clandestine tape recordings. He stopped writing songs for a while in the 1970s and produced a series of historical novels. In the late 1970s he turned to poetry again. A good deal of previously suppressed poetry has appeared since 1985, and Okudzhava became one of the leading voices in literary glasnost.

17   "NO MATTER HOW THEY INSULTED OUR COURTYARD..."
3   Volodya: Vladimir Vysotsky (1938-1980), the poet, singer, and actor with the Taganka Theater.
9   who then stole the wagon: Okudzhava explains this phrase by reference to the alleged theft of the truck carrying the freshly printed copies of the first volume of Vysotsky's poems to be published in the USSR, *Nerv* (Moscow: Sovremennik, 1982).
19   Taganka: Taganka Square in central Moscow, the site of the Taganka Theater (see Chichibabin, above); Fili: a western Moscow suburb. The sense of the line is "all across the city."

18   "THE ROMAN EMPIRE IN ITS PERIOD OF DECLINE"
21   *rassol:* brine, the liquid left over after pickling vegetables, commonly resorted to by Russian men as "the hair of the dog."

19   "THE POET HAS NO RIVALS"
11   The field's been crossed: refers to the Russian proverb "To live one's life is not like crossing a field," which Pasternak used as the last line of his poem "Hamlet" in *Doctor Zhivago.*

21   *THE OMEN*
Dedication: Anatolii Vladimirovich Zhigulin (b. 1930), the Soviet poet. Arrested in 1949 as a member of an anti-Stalinist organization based in Voronezh, he spent several years in the Gulag and has written a book of memoirs about this experience, *The Black Stones.*

23   "WHEN A SPEECH BEGINS..."
Dedication: Academician Andrei Dmitrievich Sakharov (1921-1989), the nuclear physicist, "father of the Soviet H-bomb," who became an eminent dissident and received the Nobel Peace Prize in 1975; he was in internal exile from 1980 to 1987, after which he took part in public political life.

Vladimir Kornilov (b. 1929)

Vladimir Kornilov was born in the Ukrainian city of Dnepropetrovsk, a port at the mouth of the Dnepr, in 1929 (1928, according to some sources). He moved to Moscow after World War II and graduated from the Gorky Literary Institute in 1950 (see the poem *Forty Years On*, below). He made his debut as a poet in 1953 and published his first book of poetry in 1964. His work appeared widely in the 1960s. Kornilov began writing major prose in the 1960s, but it was found unsuitable for publication in Soviet journals; it circulated in *samizdat* and was published abroad. His poetry began to appear abroad in 1975. He was expelled from the Union of Writers in 1977 and reinstated under Gorbachev; his work began to be published again in the USSR in 1986.

25 *MUSIC FOR ONESELF*
The poem echoes a lyric by Boris Slutsky, "Muzyka na vokzale,/ Igrayushchaya dlya vsekh…," published in 1969.
17-18   Whoever…fate: a reference to Pasternak's late lyric "O, had I known…," with the lines "And here art ends,/ and soil and fate breathe."

26   *FORTY YEARS ON*
4   Literary Institute: the Gorky Literary Institute in Moscow, founded in 1932 and run by the Union of Writers to train budding Soviet writers. According to a recent Soviet critic, the Institute "was for a long time…a refuge for laggards and literary bureaucrats"; it was radically reformed in 1986. See also Slutsky, above, and Akhmadulina, Morits, and Parshchikov, below.
36   Andrei Platonov: the Soviet prose writer (1899-1951), who had difficulty publishing after 1929 and was finally drummed out of Soviet literature in 1946. He contracted tuberculosis from his son, who had been sentenced to internal exile and died in 1940. During the Gorbachev period Platonov became one of the most vaunted modern Russian writers in the USSR. There are many legends about Platonov's last years: he did not actually work as a yardman, but lived in the writer's building near the Literary Institute and was frequently to be seen hanging about the area.

27   *A RUSSIAN PARADISE*
1   Yaroslavl' region: a region in northern Russia on the Volga; the city of Yaroslavl' is first recorded in the eleventh century and was the center of an independent princedom from 1218 until its absorption into Muscovy in 1463. Many churches and monasteries, the most important of them architecturally dating from the seventeenth century, survive there in ruinous condition.
20   the Horde: the army and state of the Mongols, who maintained supremacy over Russia from the early thirteenth century until the early sixteenth and caused considerable damage to Russian civilization—or, according to another interpretation, shielded it from the menace of Catholicism and supplied models for some of the major institutions of the Russian state.

29   *FREEDOM*
17   poke into other people's: the Russian phrase has the metaphorical meaning "to worm oneself into someone's confidence."

30 *YOUNG POETRY*
For a writer of Kornilov's generation, the idea of "young poetry" would include the work of Zhdanov, Parshchikov, and Eremenko of the poets included in this anthology.

31 *RHYME*
12 white foam: in Russian the adjective meaning "blank" of verse is *belyi,* "white."
25 wear the cross: Russian Orthodox believers wear a cross on a chain round their neck.

German Plisetsky (b. 1931)

German Plisetsky was born in Moscow; he was educated at Moscow University, where he graduated from the Faculty of Philology, and then moved to Leningrad to do postgraduate work at the Institute of Theater, Music, and Cinema. His original poetry began to appear in the West in the early 1960s, but in the USSR he published very little of it, and became known as a translator; his versions of Omar Khayyam and Hafiz are very highly esteemed. His first collection was published in 1990.

42 *STILL LIFE*
16 omul: a fish of the salmon family, once plentiful in Lake Baikal, now becoming rare and degenerate because of pollution.
21-22 with my own hand...gone by: Plisetsky cites the last two lines (in reverse order) of Blok's well-known lyric "Virtue, valor, fame," in which the poet removes a portrait of his lover from his table.

43 "TO STAND IN LINE FROM EARLY MORNING..."
1 *Ogonek:* the Soviet illustrated weekly, which after 1986 became one of the foremost standard-bearers of glasnost, with a circulation that peaked in December 1990 at over four and one-half million.
9 times that were: Plisetsky uses the adjective from the title of the early twelfth-century *Primary Chronicle.*
10 "Be Prepared": the watchword of the Soviet organization for children aged between 10 and 16, the Pioneers, borrowed from the Boy Scouts; the reply to the challenge is "Always Prepared!"

44 *SONNET*
Dedication: the dedicatee is Boris Slutsky (see above), and the first line of the poem slightly adapts that of a famous underground lyric by him, "When Russian prose went off into the camps"; it was first published in *Sovetskaya potaennaya muza,* ed. Boris Filippov (Munich, 1961), p. 127.

Evgenii Rein (b. 1935)

Evgenii Rein was born in Leningrad; he was evacuated during World War II, during which his father was killed. Rein was a prominent and influential figure in literary circles as a young man; he was one of the poets close to Akhmatova. He graduated from the Leningrad

Technological Institute as an engineer, then moved to Moscow in the early 1960s and retrained as a journalist and film scenarist. He became a member of the Union of Writers in the mid-1960s. He published several books for children during the 1970s, but very little of his most important poetry. His first collection did not appear until 1984. It had first been submitted for publication twenty years before but was delayed by its nonconformist style and unacceptable subject matter, and then again when Rein became one of the contributors to the dissident literary almanac *Metropol* in the late 1970s (see also Akhmadulina and Kublanovsky below). Since 1985, Rein's work has been appearing regularly in Russia.

45   *THE MONASTERY*
31   Goslit: short for Goslitizdat, an acronym meaning "State Publishing House for Artistic Literature."
35   Yurii Olesha: the Soviet writer (1899-1960), author of the important novel *Envy* (1927), after which he was mainly silent, remaining a somewhat dissident presence on the Moscow literary scene until the end of his life.

46   *MY NEIGHBOR GRIGORIEV*
27   From his coffin rises the emperor: Rein paraphrases a famous line from Lermontov's "The Aerial Ship," a ballad based on two poems by Zedlitz, and referring to Napoleon.

48   *IN THE MARGINS OF A BOOK BY V. KHODASEVICH*
Khodasevich: the Russian poet Vladislav Khodasevich (1886-1939), who emigrated in 1922 and died in Paris. The epigraph cites a well-known lyric, "The Automobile" (1921), containing a nightmare vision of "another car" stimulated by seeing a car at night in revolutionary Petrograd.

50   *"THE NIGHT WATCH"*
1   "The Night Watch": the painting by Rembrandt (Rein's namesake) in the Rejksmuseum, Amsterdam.
9   Dzerzhinsky: Feliks Edmundovich Dzerzhinsky (1877-1926), organizer and head of the Soviet internal security organs, the VChK or CheKa (All-Russian Extraordinary Commission for Fighting Counter-Revolution and Sabotage, ancestor of the OGPU, NKVD, MGB, KGB).
10   Yagoda: Genrikh Grigor'evich Yagoda (1891-1938), who headed the NKVD from 1934 to 1936; he was arrested in 1937 and subsequently executed.
13   Yezhov: Nikolai Ivanovich Yezhov (1894-1939), the most notorious head of the NKVD, succeeded Yagoda, and was in charge during the Great Purge of 1937, which is colloquially called after him *Yezhovshchina*; he was replaced by Beria in 1938 (see Chukhontsev, below) and soon after arrested and executed.
14   Blyumkin: a CheKa operative, the assassin of the German ambassador to Moscow in 1918; he was a flamboyant and sinister figure in the 1920s, and is particularly remembered for one incident in which the poet Mandelstam seized a list of intended victims from him and tore it up, after which Blyumkin regularly menaced Mandelstam in public.
24   VChK: see Dzerzhinsky, above.

51   *BENEATH THE COATS OF ARMS*
15   Dima, Tolya, Osya: Rein mentions the three other "Akhmatova orphans," young Leningrad poets who were close to Anna Akhmatova in the last years of her life; besides

himself, they were Dmitrii Bobyshev (Dima), Iosif Brodsky (Osya) (both of whom see elsewhere in this anthology), and Anatolii Naiman (Tolya).

52   *JUST BEFORE EASTER*
7   dead duck: the Russian equivalent of English "red herring."
28   Gennesaret: one of the names in the New Testament for the Sea of Galilee.

Dmitri Bobyshev (b. 1936)

Dmitri Bobyshev was born in Mariupol (later Zhdanov, now again Mariupol), but grew up in Leningrad. He lost his father in the blockade. He came into contact with literature in the late 1950s as a student at the Leningrad Technological Institute, where he met Evgenii Rein and Anatolii Naiman. With Rein, Naiman, and Joseph Brodsky he was one of the young poets who were close to Anna Akhmatova and became known as her "orphans" after she died in 1966. His work appeared in the Moscow *samizdat* journal *Syntax* in 1960, but he published hardly anything officially in the USSR. He worked as an engineer during the 1960s and 1970s. In March 1972 he underwent a profound mystical experience and was subsequently received into the Orthodox Church by Father Dmitrii Dudko. He emigrated in 1979, settling first in Milwaukee, then moved to the University of Illinois at Urbana-Champaign. His work up to the time of his emigration is collected in *Ziyaniya (Gapings)* (Paris: YMCA, 1979). Bobyshev publishes widely in the journals of the emigration, and he is beginning to be translated into English; in his turn he has translated several American poets into Russian. His work began to appear in the USSR in 1990 (see *Znamya*, 10, pp. 65-69).

53   "MOMMY, THIS IS YOUR SON WRITING TO YOU"
This is the first section of Bobyshev's long composite work *Zvezdy i polosy* (Stars and Stripes), his first poetic reaction to life in America.

57   *URBANA LIFE, 3*
This is the third section of Bobyshev's four-part poem on life in Urbana-Champaign, Illinois. It is modeled on Derzhavin's *To Evgenii. Life at Zvanka* (1805), one of the most famous celebrations of bucolic life in Russian poetry.
41   "the amusing style": a well-known phrase of Derzhavin, referring to the originality of his poetic language.

Natalya Gorbanevskaya (b. 1936)

Natalya Gorbanevskaya was born and educated in Moscow. She took a prominent part in the civil rights movement in the 1960s, helping to found and edit the *samizdat* journal *Chronicle of Current Events*. Gorbanevskaya was one of the seven people who demonstrated against the Soviet invasion of Czechoslovakia on Red Square, 25 August 1968. For this action she was confined in a psychiatric hospital and then prison. She emigrated in late 1975 and has lived since then in Paris, working as Deputy Editor of the principal journal of the Third Wave, *Kontinent*, and as a member of the editorial board of the principal émigré newspaper, *Russkaya mysl'*. She has published seven collections of original poetry and has translated many East European poets, particularly Polish. Her poetry began to be published in the USSR in 1990 (see *Oktyabr'*, 7(1990), pp. 102-108).

61 "NOT TO SING OUT—TO LISP OUT..."
4-5 Gorbanevskaya plays with the Russian expression *ne vsyako lyko v stroku*, literally "not every [piece of] bark [fits] into the line," the equivalent of "one must make allowances."

62 "...WHERE RIVERS FLOW PURER THAN SILVER"
3-4 "bright/ is the Admiralty spire": a quotation from the introduction to Pushkin's *Bronze Horseman:* it refers to the spire on the Admiralty building at the top of the Nevskii Prospekt in St. Petersburg.

63 "IT WAS THE YEAR OF EVIL PREDICTIONS"
10 Presnya district: a west-central working-class district of Moscow; its official name since 1918 has been "Red Presnya," in memory of the skirmishes that took place there during the Revolution.
11-12 "cockroaches/ as big as plums": an echo of a phrase in chapter 1 of Gogol's *Dead Souls*.
17 the Okhta: a small tributary of the Neva that has given its name to an east-central residential district of St. Petersburg.

Aleksandr Kushner (b. 1936)

Aleksandr Semenovich Kushner was born in Leningrad, the son of an army officer, and has lived there all his life, with the exception of a period during the blockade of the city in World War II, when he was evacuated. He trained as a teacher and worked for several years in schools after qualifying but has been a full-time writer since the late 1960s. He published his first collection in 1962 and soon became a member of the Union of Writers; further collections have appeared regularly since that time.

68 *MEMORIES*
3 S.R.: Socialist Revolutionary, a member of the political party suppressed by the Bolsheviks in 1922.
8 Taganrog: a town in southern Russia, on the Sea of Azov, occupied by the Germans in 1918, the Whites in 1919, and the Reds in 1920.
11 Ciniselli Circus: the earliest permanent commercial circus in St. Petersburg, founded in 1877.
12 Trotskyite: Trotsky was expelled from the USSR in 1929; the trumped-up accusation of conspiratorial adherence to his views was commonly used under Stalin as a motive for administrative repression.
15 Crimea: the bitter final battles of the Civil War were fought in the Crimea in 1920-1921.
24 blockade: the 900-day siege of Leningrad by Hitler's army during World War II.

69 "HISTORY TEACHES US NOTHING"
14 average grades: the Soviet education system uses a five-point scale of assessment. The grade mentioned in the original of Kushner's poem is 3; "bottom of the class" gets 2.

70 "IF I'D BEEN BORN ABOUT SEVEN YEARS EARLIER..."
4-8 the anger of the state: in particular, the purge of the intelligentsia, and particularly its Jewish members, in the last years of Stalin (1948-1953). Linguistics was the subject of a famous pronouncement by Stalin personally in 1950 (see also Chukhontsev's "The Double," below).

72 "IN VERSE, MEANING SPARKLES..."
10 two other pelts...in other people's poems: a reference to Mandelstam's lyric "Tristia" (1918): "Like a squirrel's stretched pelt,/ Leaning over the wax, a young woman watches," which is itself an echo of the second line of Anna Akhmatova's "High in the sky a cloud showed gray" (1911): "Like the spread-out pelt of a squirrel." Cf. also Elena Shvarts's "The Invisible Hunter," below.
19-20 the break...is healed: a reference to Mandelstam's famous lyric "The Age" (1922), which includes the lines "But your spine is broken,/ My beautiful, pitiful age."

74 "WE USED TO WRITE HAPPY POEMS"
13 "There Once Was a Songthrush": a film (1971) by the Georgian director Otar Ioseliani, about a carefree young musician.

75 "LIGHT FLOWS. WATER WANDERS IN THE DARKNESS"
2 star talks with star: Kushner quotes the fourth line of Lermontov's classic lyric "Alone I Go Out onto the Road."

76 "NOTHING BRINGS US CLOSER TO DEATH"
2 a wish come true: Kushner was able to travel abroad for the first time in his life in 1989.
15 Baratynsky: See Loseff, *One Day in the Life...*, below.

Bella Akhmadulina (b. 1937)

Bella Akhmadulina was born in Moscow and graduated from the Gorky Literary Institute there in 1960. She published her first collection of lyrics in 1962, and five more have followed at differing intervals. Akhmadulina is well known as a translator, especially of Georgian poetry. She was involved in the *Metropol* scandal of 1979-1980 (see also Rein and Kublanovsky elsewhere). Akhmadulina has been a visiting writer in residence at the University of California, Los Angeles.

77 "I FIND ENVIABLE THE AGE-OLD HABIT"
15 white crow (*belaya vorona*): a Russian expression referring to someone out of the ordinary, a "rara avis."

78 *THE NIGHT OF FALLING APPLES*
Dedication: Semen Lipkin (b. 1911), a poet who made his name as a translator and was not known to be a major original poet until the 1960s.

80 *PASHKA*
15 "The storm with gloom...[is covering the sky]": the first words of a famous lyric by Pushkin.

30-31 (also 38)   Belka... animal that shares my name: the diminutive of Akhmadulina's first name is identical to the common noun meaning "squirrel".

82   *DRESSING THE CHILD*
26   zurna: the folk oboe of the Caucasus.

Yunna Morits (b. 1937)

Yunna Petrovna Morits was born in Kiev. Her first book of poems came out in 1957; she graduated from the Gorky Institute of Literature in 1961. She continued to publish original poetry extensively through the 1960s and 1970s; a selected volume came out in 1982. She has also published many translations, especially from Hungarian, verse for children, and some powerful and original short stories. A good deal of her previously suppressed work has appeared since 1985.

84   *BETWEEN SCYLLA AND CHARYBDIS*
Epigraph: *akhmatsvet*, an imaginary unit of measure derived from the surnames of the poets Anna Akhmatova (1889-1966) and Marina Tsvetaeva (1892-1941).
3   Kushka: a town in Turkmenia, the southernmost point of the territory of the former USSR.
15   Hafiz: the Persian poet, c. 1325-1390.
19   Zhenya: the Soviet poet Evgenii Evtushenko (b. 1933); Andrei: the Soviet poet Andrei Voznesensky (b. 1933).
20   Bella: Bella Akhmadulina (see elsewhere in this anthology); Novella: the Soviet poet Novella Matveeva (b. 1934).

89   "POETRY IS ALIVE THROUGH FREEDOM AND LOVE"
10   AAD: Anti-Aircraft Defense *(Protivovozdushnaya oborona).*
11   Ruslan: "the dog in G. Vladimov's story *Faithful Ruslan*" (author's note), a guard dog in a labor camp; Mandelstam's madness: the poet died insane in a transit camp near Vladivostok in December 1938. See also Kenzheev's poem, below.
18   the bloody anthrophobe: Joseph Stalin.

90   "...AND YOUNG SAVAGES WILL COME..."
18   profoundly degraded: Morits plays with the phrase *gluboko uvazhaemyi*, "profoundly esteemed," used in formal address.

91 "STUFFY AVENUES COVERED IN DUST"
4   smalt: deep-blue glass colored with cobalt.

92   "WHEN ALL OF OURS SLAUGHTER ALL OF THEIRS"
3 (also 4)   those...not-those: the original has also the sense of "the right ones" versus "the wrong ones."

Lev Loseff (b. 1937)

Lev Loseff was born in Leningrad, the son of a well-known children's poet, Vladimir Lifshits. He lived there until his emigration to the USA in 1976, working as a children's writer and journalist. He began writing "serious" poetry only about the time of his emigration. He is Professor of Russian at Dartmouth College, Hanover, New Hampshire, and has published widely on Russian literature in the scholarly press and in the journals of the Third Wave. His poetry has been published in the major literary journals of the USSR since 1989.

94 "'I UNDERSTAND—YOKE, STARVATION'"
1 yoke: the "Tartar yoke," a phrase often used in Russian to refer to the period of Mongol domination over medieval Russia. See also Kornilov's poem *A Russian Paradise*, above.
12 dostoevsky: the name of the novelist is used as an adjective.
17 bards: the Russian "guitar poets" of the 1960s and 1970s, principally Bulat Okudzhava, Aleksandr Galich, and Vladimir Vysotsky. See Okudzhava's poem on Vysotsky above.
25 land of nogoodniks: from the title *(Strana negodyaev)* of a drama in verse by Sergei Esenin.
27 Chaadaev: the Russian thinker Petr Yakovlevich Chaadaev (1794-1856), who was declared insane by Tsar Nicholas I after the publication of his first "Philosophical Letter" in 1836.

95 "...I USED TO WORK ON *THE CAMPFIRE*..."
1 *The Campfire (Koster)*: a prestigious Leningrad-published monthly magazine for children, founded in 1936; because of its reputation for harboring dissident writers, publication was suspended from 1947 to 1956.
10 Lotman: Yurii Mikhailovich Lotman (b. 1922), the Soviet literary historian and semiotician, Professor of Russian Literature at the University of Tartu (Estonia), and author of a famous textbook on the theory of poetry.
17 Tauride Garden: a formal garden in central St. Petersburg adjoining the late eighteenth-century Tauride Palace.
20 Morozov: Pavlik Morozov, a Russian peasant boy from Sverdlovsk province who denounced his own father for corruption and was lynched in 1932 at the age of 13. Under Stalin he was made the subject of a cult as the principal ethical and ideological model for the Soviet youth movement, the Pioneers. Since 1987 the case has been reexamined by journalists, and allegations made that the local NKVD carried out the murder of Pavlik as a provocation.

99 *ONE DAY IN THE LIFE OF LEV VLADIMIROVICH*
1-2 Northern...Palmyra: a conventional poetic name for St. Petersburg; New...Holland: a district of St. Petersburg.
16 Baratynsky: the Russian poet Evgenii Abramovich Baratynsky (b. 1800), who in 1843 made an extended trip to Western Europe and died suddenly in Naples in 1844; see also Kushner "Nothing Brings Us Closer to Death," above.
45 weaving words: a reference to the medieval literary technique known as *pletenie slovés*, "word-weaving."

52   Banner headline on Sen'ka: a play on words; the phrase is a proverb meaning "serve someone right."

100   "THE POET IS HUMUS, WITHIN HIM DEAD WORDS"
10   ways of the grain: a reference to John 12:24; the passage is used as the epigraph to Dostoevsky's *The Brothers Karamazov* and is also the title of a collection of poetry by Vladislav Khodasevich (1886-1939).

102   *THE TWELVE COLLEGES. AN ELEGY IN THREE PARTS*
The Twelve Colleges: the former Leningrad University, now again the University of St. Petersburg, occupies the premises originally built by Peter the Great to house the twelve colleges (later ministries) of the government.
2   ...groans the gray-blue dove: an echo of the first line of a song by the eighteenth-century Russian poet Dmitriev which is now often thought to be folklore.
18   "I lie": the Russian initials of Leningrad State University, *LGU*, spell the first person singular of the verb *lgat'*, "to tell a lie."
19-20   stood on the banks...looked afar: Loseff cites the opening of Pushkin's *Bronze Horseman*, in which Peter the Great stands on the bank of the Neva, where St. Petersburg is to be built, and looks into the distance.
20   "victories": the "Pobeda" ("Victory"), a small Soviet car of the 1940s and 1950s, built with Opel machinery that had been requisitioned after the defeat of Germany.
23   future Aesop scholars: i.e., experts in Aesopian language; Loseff himself is the author of a scholarly book on this subject, *On the Beneficence of Censorship: Aesopian Language in Russian Literature* (Munich, 1984).
24   potato picking duty: Soviet students were until the late 1980s compelled to go to the countryside and assist with the harvest.
29   go out on recce: a common Soviet saying dating from World War II; the sense is "to trust someone."
35   Propp: Vladimir Yakovlevich Propp (1895-1970), the great Soviet folklorist, who taught at Leningrad University.
39   the hut showed me its backside: a magic formula used in Russian fairy tales.

Oleg Chukhontsev (b. 1938)

Oleg Chukhontsev was born in the textile town of Petrovskii Posad, not far east of Moscow. He moved to Moscow in the late 1950s and has remained there. His poetry began to appear in the Soviet periodical press in the late 1950s, but his first book was not published until 1984; it was followed by two more substantial volumes in 1989.

104   *THE DOUBLE*
5   "Herzegovina Flor": a brand of *papirosa*, no longer made, but well remembered as Stalin's favorite; he would break open the *papirosy* and use the tobacco to fill his pipe; "Pamir": a low-grade Soviet brand of *papirosa*.
21   sink barges: during the Civil War, at Tsaritsyn, Stalin ordered a barge full of captured White Officers to be sunk; this is sometimes considered to be the first manifestation of his evil cruelty.
24   *khashi*: offal soup or stew with garlic and aromatics.

26 *tsitsmati*: an herb resembling cress; *lavash*: thin, white, oval-shaped Georgian wheat flatbread, resembling pita.

30 *chacha*: very strong Georgian grape vodka; *tarkhun:* tarragon-steeped spirits.

31 sell Venus Before the Looking-Glass: the reference is to the numerous sales abroad of important works of art by Stalin's government in the 1930s.

40 Lavrentii: Lavrentii Pavlovich Beria (1899-1953), Stalin's Minister of the Interior from 1938 to 1945, overlord of the security services.

41 Marr: academician Nikolai Yakovlevich Marr (1864-1934); his controversial "Japhetic theory" of linguistic evolution became official dogma under Stalin and was then denounced by Stalin himself in his *Marxism and Problems of Linguistics* (1950). (See also Kushner's "Had I been born five years earlier," above).

43 *khachapuri:* Georgian bread, made as large loaves or individual portions, filled with salt sheep's milk cheese.

45 Trotskyites: see above, Kushner, "Memories," line 12; Weissmanites: August Weissman (1842-1914), the eminent German naturalist, author of a post-Darwinian theory of evolution; Morganists: Thomas Hunt Morgan (1866-1945), the American geneticist whose work in heredity was anathematized under Stalin in favor of the theories of Trofim Lysenko (1898-1976).

49 clean clean clean: the Russian verb is also the normal word for "to purge" in the political sense.

105 *ABOUT THAT LAND*

The poem concerns the flooding of a large territory on the northern Volga to form the Rybinsk Reservoir in the 1930s, part of the Volga-Baltic Waterway, one of the most gigantic civil engineering projects undertaken under Stalin; Chukhontsev's forebears came from this area.

32 Monastery of the Don: an ancient monastery in central south Moscow.

87 Jan Sapega (1569-1611): a Polish noble active as a military commander with interventionist forces in Russia during the Time of Troubles in the early seventeenth century.

99 Kitezh: according to legend, the town of Kitezh sank into the earth when faced by attack from the Tartar army of Khan Batu; a lake formed over the site, and the church bells can sometimes be heard from beneath the waters.

107, 108 Perebory...Poshekhone: small towns on the Rybinsk Reservoir.

Joseph Brodsky (b. 1940)

Joseph Brodsky was born and brought up in Leningrad. He has described his early life in the autobiographical essays included in his *Less Than One* (New York: Farrar, Straus and Giroux, 1986). He left school at age 15 and worked at various manual jobs. In 1964 he was arrested as a "parasite" and sentenced to administrative exile. He returned to Leningrad in 1965. He was close to Anna Akhmatova in her last years (see Rein and Bobyshev, above). Brodsky was able to publish very little poetry in the USSR but was recognized and published in the West from the mid-1960s. In 1972 he emigrated and settled in the USA, since when he has taught at various universities; he became an American citizen in 1977. His eminence has been recognized through the award of numerous distinctions and honors, culminating in the Nobel Prize for Literature in 1987 and the Poet Laureateship of the USA in 1991. In December 1987 his poetry began to be published in the USSR, and it has continued to appear regularly since; two collections came out in 1990. Brodsky has been translated widely into Western languages, and he has also written original prose and poetry in English.

108   *FIFTH ANNIVERSARY (4 JUNE 1977)*
The "fifth anniversary" is that of Brodsky's emigration from the USSR.
12   the enchained oak: a reference to the opening of Pushkin's *Ruslan and Lyudmila* (see also Eremenko, below).
60   Aivazovsky: Ivan Konstantinovich Aivazovsky (1817-1900), the Russian painter renowned for his seascapes.

109   *YORK*
Dedication: W. H. A., the British/American poet W. H. Auden (1907-1973), who was born in York; on Brodsky and Auden, see Brodsky's essay "To Please a Shadow" in his *Less Than One* (New York: Farrar, Straus and Giroux, 1986).
6   three great poets: Brecht, Frost, and Yeats (see "To Please a Shadow").
12   Chester: Auden's close friend Chester Kallman (1921-1975).

110   *"YOU, GUITAR-SHAPED THING..."*
3   à la Kazimir: the reference is to the famous picture "White on White" by the Russian artist Kazimir Malevich (1878-1935).
12   Kovalevskaya: Sofia Kovalevskaya (1850-1891), the Russian mathematician, whose professional career was made in Sweden.

114   *TO URANIA*
Brodsky has explained that Urania is the muse of astronomy and of poetry.
19   Przeval-horses: the only surviving species of wild horse, discovered in Mongolia by the Russian explorer Nikolai Mikhailovich Przevalsky (1839-1888) in the 1870s.

Dmitrii Prigov (b. 1940)

Dmitrii Aleksandrovich Prigov was born in Moscow. He studied to become a sculptor and is a member of the Union of Artists. He has also worked as an architect and at several other trades. Between 1970 and 1980 he wrote 42 manuscript books of lyrics and also a dozen long poems, plays, and five "text cycles." He was a member of the *Katalog* group that came together in Moscow in the spring of 1980. His poetry has been published outside the USSR since the late 1970s, and in Soviet periodicals since January, 1988. Prigov's first book to be published in Russia appeared in 1990; it contains only a tiny selection from his complete work in verse.

119   "WHEN HERE ON DUTY STANDS A PLICEMAN"
2   Vnukovo: the site, southwest of the city, of Moscow's international airport.

120   "IN THE BUFFET OF THE HOUSE OF WRITERS"
1   House of Writers: the club belonging to the Union of Writers in the center of Moscow.

124   "WHEN I ONCE HAPPENED TO BE IN KALUGA"
The poem parodies Pushkin's famous lyric *The Black Shawl.*

128   *A BANAL DISQUISITION...*
"To be famous isn't beautiful" is the first line of a famous late lyric by Pasternak; the second adjective is used in the sense of "well-mannered, the done thing."
9   "beauty will save [the world]": an aphorism of Dóstoevsky.

Yurii Kublanovsky (b. 1948)

Kublanovsky was born in Rybinsk. He moved to Moscow, graduated from the Art History Department of Moscow University, and participated in the underground literary scene in the 1960s and 1970s. A *samizdat* article on Solzhenitsyn brought him to the attention of the KGB. Kublanovsky's poetry was included in the *Metropol* anthology of writing, edited by Vasilii Aksenov and others, that had been refused publication in the USSR, but was eventually published in the USA in 1980 (see also under Rein and Akhmadulina, above). In 1982, under threat of arrest and internal exile, he was forced to emigrate, since which time he has lived in Germany. He is a prolific author of reviews and literary essays in the émigré press, and he has published four collections of lyrics. Kublanovsky's work began to appear in the USSR in 1988 (*Znamya*, 11(1988), pp. 106-111). In 1989 he revisited Moscow, and his work is now frequently published there.

132   *STUDY*
The poem is concerned with the famous equestrian statue of Peter the Great in St. Petersburg, the "Bronze Horseman."

134   "DON'T RUSH TO ABDICATE—WE'LL BE CONSOLED"
19   European night: the title of a group of poems written in emigration in the early 1920s by Vladislav Khodasevich (1886-1939); see also Rein, above.

135   "THE FATE OF VERSE IS WORLD-SOVEREIGN"
16   Elizaveta Petrovna: Empress Elizabeth (1709-1762), the daughter of Peter the Great, who seized the throne by a bloodless coup d'etat in 1741.

136   "UNDER WAN, MEAGER SNOW"
2   capital city: Moscow is sometimes referred to as "the first capital city" as opposed to St. Petersburg, which was the capital of the Russian empire during the eighteenth and nineteenth centuries.

137   "BEFORE WHAT IVANS, BIRONS,/ AND STENKAS..."
1-2   Ivans, Birons, and Stenkas: refers to Ivan the Terrible; Ernst Johann Biron (1690-1771), favorite of Empress Anne, who conducted a reign of terror in the 1730s, known as the *bironovshchina*; Stenka Razin (see under Kornilov, above).

Aleksei Tsvetkov (b. 1948)

Aleksei Tsvetkov was born in Zaporozh'e, in western Ukraine, but grew up and studied in Moscow, attending the faculties of History and Journalism at Moscow University. He then had a variety of jobs: translator, proofreader, reporter, and at the last, night watchman. Three of his poems were published in the USSR before he emigrated to the USA in 1975; he was a leading light in the unofficial "Moscow Time" group of poets (see also Kenzheev below). Tsvetkov wrote a doctoral dissertation at the University of Michigan, then taught Russian literature at Dickenson College in Carlisle, Pennsylvania. From 1984 to 1990 he worked for the Voice of America in Washington, D.C., and he then moved to Radio Liberty in Munich. His poems began to be published in the USSR in 1989 (see *Znamya*, 6(1989), pp. 167-171).

138 "ON A BENCH BY THE EDGE OF THE PARK"
12 *arshin:* an obsolete Russian measure of length, equal to 28 inches (71 cm.).

143 "THE CHIMES AT THE ZENITH WERE FORGING THE AGES"
3 DK: *Dom kul'tury,* "House of Culture," a club building and its attendant organizations that used to form the focus of official cultural life at the local level in the USSR.
10 *veche*: the medieval citizens' assembly of Novgorod.
15 leeuwenhoek: Antony van Leeuwenhoek (1632-1723), the Dutch inventor of the microscope.

144 "HERE'S THE OLD FELLOW ADVOCATE OF THE MUSSELS"
7 minos: Minos, king and lawgiver of Crete, who after his death was supposed to have become supreme judge of the underworld.

145 "DOWN IN A GULCH A WHISTLE-STOP..."
8 przevalsky's bison: see above, Brodsky, *To Urania*. Because of their physical resemblance, there is a legend that Przevalsky was Stalin's father, and "bison" here refers to Stalin.
9 thou tsar live on thy own; a reference to a famous Pushkin lyric, "To a Poet."
11 surgut: Surgut, a small town in Tyumen *oblast* on the river Ob in western Siberia; Turgai: Turgai, a small town and also a river in Kazakhstan.
17, 23-24 no all i will not die...; for the nonce savage...: Tsvetkov parodies Pushkin's lyric "Exegi Monumentum."

Elena Shvarts (b. 1948)

Elena Shvarts was born in Leningrad and has remained there. She made no serious attempt to take part in official literature and published practically nothing in the USSR until a small and unrepresentative selection of her work appeared in the Leningrad almanac *Krug* in 1985 along with that of several other nonconformist Leningrad writers of her generation. Her work was also slow to be recognized abroad. Her first collection in the USSR, *Storony sveta,* appeared in Leningrad in 1989. In the spring of 1989 she was the single Soviet poet invited to the "Child of Europe" festival in London.

149 "ONCE AGAIN FATHER INTERFERED, EXHORTING"
This poem forms one segment of the cycle of poems put into the mouth of Kinfiya (Cynthia), an aristocratic woman of ancient Rome.

150 AND 151   *CIRCUMCISION OF THE HEART* AND *THE RAVEN*
Two of the constituent poems of the long sequence "The Works and Days of Lavinia, Nun of the Order of the Circumcision of the Heart."

Ivan Zhdanov (b. 1948)

Ivan Zhdanov was born in the Altai region. He worked at various manual jobs and as a journalist, then graduated from Barnaul Pedagogical Institute in Siberia. He began publishing poetry in various Soviet journals and almanacs in the late 1970s, and his first collection, *Portret (Portrait)* caused a furor in literary circles when it was published in Moscow in 1982. Zhdanov's poetry has been published in the émigré Russian press, in France and Scandinavia, and translated into several foreign languages.

158   "A REGION OF UNEXCHANGEABLE POSSESSION"
3   thrice-ninth generation: in Russian folklore, the adjective "thrice-ninth" *(tridevyatyi)*, meaning "three times nine," is usually applied to the word "land" and means "far, far away."
11   three-fingered sign: in the Russian Orthodox Church, the sign of benediction is made with three fingers raised.

Olga Sedakova (b. 1949)

Olga Sedakova was born in Moscow and educated at Moscow University. She wrote her dissertation on the burial rites of the Eastern Slavs at the Institute of Slavonic Studies in Moscow, and she has written several academic articles on problems of cultural anthropology. Sedakova has published many more translations in the USSR than she has original poetry, which only began to appear there, in small selections, in 1988; they had been preceded by a book published in Paris in 1986.

163   *THE GRASSHOPPER AND THE CRICKET*
Epigraph: the first line of Keats's sonnet with the same title (1816).
9   Demodocus: the minstrel at the feast of King Alkinoos in book VIII of the *Odyssey;* after his song about Troy, Odysseus, who has been incognito, is betrayed by his tears and admits his identity.

165   *ON THE DEATH OF LEONID GUBANOV*
Leonid Gubanov (1947-1983) was a pioneering poet of the Moscow underground in the early 1960s; in 1965 he was arrested for demonstrating against the trial of Sinyavsky and Daniel and spent some time in a mental hospital. His poetry has been widely published outside the USSR, but inside only since 1989. Sedakova is the author of an article on Gubanov which is mainly a personal *profession de foi:* "O pogibshem literaturnom pokolenii—Pamyati Leni Gubanova," *Volga,* 6(1990), pp. 135-146; the article was written in 1984.
Epigraph: the first line of Esenin's renowned suicide poem (1925), which concludes: "In this life it's nothing new to die,/ But to live, of course, is nothing newer."

Bakhyt Kenzheev (b. 1950)

Bakhyt Kenzheev was born in Moscow. He graduated from Moscow University and worked as a technical translator. He published hardly any poetry in the USSR, preferring to remain a member of the underground, taking part in the "Moscow Time" group (see also Tsvetkov, above), which began in 1974. Kenzheev emigrated in 1980 and settled in Canada. He brought out a selected works in 1985, and he publishes prolifically in the émigré press. His work began to appear in the USSR in the late 1980s (see *Znamya*, 10[1989], pp. 72-82).

171   "IN PEREDELKINO THE FOREST HAS LOST ITS LEAVES"
1   Peredelkino: burial place of Pasternak (see also Chichibabin and Akhmadulina, above, and Eremenko, below).

Aleksandr Eremenko (b. 1950)

Aleksandr Eremenko studied at the Institute of World Literature in Moscow. His poetry has been known in Soviet literary circles since the late 1970s and published in anthologies and almanacs, but he has not yet published a collection.

175   *PEREDELKINO*
On Peredelkino, see Chichibabin, Akhmadulina, and Kenzheev, above.
5   They're asleep in the dacha: a quotation from Pasternak's "Second Ballade" (1930).
15   in the clouds before the people: from Pushkin's *Ruslan and Ludmila*, a reference picked up again in line 31.
18   the patriarch: the country house of the Patriarch of the Russian Orthodox Church is in Peredelkino.
21   Fisherwoman Sonya: Eremenko refers to the heroine of a famous song from the wartime movie *Two Soldiers*, sung by Mark Bernes; initially she does not recognize the hero, but eventually marries him.
31   And day and night: Eremenko begins here an extended parody of the first part of Pushkin's *Ruslan and Ludmila*.
35   Fedin: the dog is named after Konstantin Fedin (1892-1977), the famous Soviet novelist and high literary official under Stalin, Chairman of the Union of Soviet Writers from 1959 to 1971, chief persecutor of Pasternak and Solzhenitsyn.
37   white: the adjective is the pseudonymous surname of the poet Andrei Bely (1880-1934); in the following line appears his friend and rival Aleksandr Blok (1880-1921).
42   the mast...: a line from Lermontov's lyric "The Sail."
44   But the north...: a line from Pushkin's *Eugene Onegin*.

176   *MONUMENT*
5   Massandra: wine from the Crimean town of that name, location of one of the largest wine-producing enterprises of the former USSR.

177 *LINES ON PROHIBITION, DEDICATED TO THE SVERDLOVSK ROCK CLUB*
Prohibition, literally "the Dry Law": the law limiting sales of alcohol. A law of this kind was one of the first measures promulgated by the incoming Gorbachev regime in 1985, leading to great resentment among the male population, a tremendous increase in illegal distilling, and a catastrophic loss of tax revenue to the state.
5   thief "in the law": a criminal who faithfully observes the customs of the underworld.
17   Hall of Columns: an elaborate room in the Trade Union House (formerly the Moscow Club of the Nobility), used for Soviet ceremonial occasions such as lyings-in-state.
27   "godfather" *(kum)*: Soviet criminal slang for the commandant of a labor camp.
33   eau-de-cologne: used as a substitute for alcohol by hardened and impoverished Russian drinkers.

178 *AN ADDENDUM TO* SOPROMAT
Sopromat: Soviet student slang for the academic subject of the science of the strength of materials, a truncation of *soprotivlenie materialov*.

179 "LONG LIVE THE OLD MAID"
The poem parodies one of the most renowned paeans of praise to Russian womanhood, the section "There are women in Russian settlements" from *The Red-Nosed Frost* by Nikolai Nekrasov (1821-1878).
3   Viète: the French mathematician François Viète (1540-1603).

Aleksei Parshchikov (b. 1954)

Aleksei Parshchikov was born near Vladivostok (or in Moscow, according to some sources); brought up in the Ukraine, he moved to Moscow to study at the Gorky Literary Institute. His poetry started appearing in the Soviet periodical press in the late 1970s; his first book was published in 1986, and a second, *Figury intuitsii (Figures of Intuition)*, in 1989. In 1990 he became a graduate student and instructor at Stanford University.

184 *LIONS*
6   on the left: this may also be read as "levs," i.e., the Bulgarian coin that bears a lion with upraised paw.
10   kapron: Soviet synthetic polymer used to make plastic raincoats.
19   St. Andrew's Slope: a famous precipitous street in Kiev.

186 "O GARDEN OF MY FRIENDS, WHERE I HANG ABOUT..."
3   twelfth-night: in early January, when the frost is particularly biting.

SOURCES OF THE TEXTS

Boris Slutsky

All selections from *Stikhotvoreniya* (Moscow: Khudozhestvennaya literatura, 1989).

Boris Chichibabin

Priznanie from *Novyi mir*, 7(1989), pp. 83-84; "Ne veryu ya, chto rusy" from *22*, 9(1979), p. 43, reprinted in *The Blue Lagoon Anthology of Modern Russian Poetry*, ed. Konstantin Kuzminsky and Grigorii Kovalev, vol. 3A (Newtonville, Mass.: Oriental Research Partners, 1986), p. 84; "Snimi s menya ustalost', mater' Smert'" from *Kontinent*, 35(1983), pp. 70-71, also *Glagol*, 1 (Ann Arbor: Ardis, 1977), p. 132, also in Boris Chichibabin, *Kolokol* (Moscow: Izvestiya, 1989); "Tebe, moya Rus', ne bogu, ne zveryu" from ibid.; "Dai vam Bog s kornei do kron" from ibid.; *Bitva* from *Glagol*, 1 (Ann Arbor: Ardis, 1977), p. 118; "Tsvety lezhali na snegu" from *Ogonek*, 24(1989), p. 21, also in *Kolokol*, p. 52.

Bulat Okudzhava

"Vse glushe muzyka dushi," "Davaite pridumaem despota," "Rimskaya imperiya vremeni upadka," "Kak nash dvor ni obizhali...," *Primeta*, *Pis'mo k mame*, "U poeta sopernikov netu" from Bulat Okudzhava, *Posvyashchaetsya vam. Stikhi* (Moscow: Sovetskii pisatel', 1988); "Rimskaya imperiya..." also in *Pesni*, t. II (Ann Arbor: Ardis, 1986); "Davaite pridumaem despota," *Pis'mo k mame* also in *Rekviem. Stikhi russkikh sovetskikh poetov* (Moscow: Sovremennik, 1989), pp. 279, 285; *Pamyati A. D. Sakharova* from *Yunost'*, 4(1990), pp. 2-3; "Chto-to synochek moi..." from *Yunost'*, 8(1991), pp. 10-11.

Vladimir Kornilov

Muzyka dlya sebya from *Znamya*, 11(1986), p. 157; also in *Moskovskii komsomolets*, June 1990, unpaginated insert; *Sorok let spustya* from *Novyi mir*, 4(1987), pp. 117-118, also in

Rekviem. Stikhi russkikh sovetskikh poetov (Moscow: Sovremennik, 1989), p. 306; *Russkii rai* from *Moskovskii komsomolets*, June 1990; *Bezbozhie* from *Znamya*, 10(1987), pp. 96-97; *Svoboda* from ibid., p. 95, also *Moskovskii komsomolets*, June 1990; *Molodaya poeziya* from ibid.; *Rifma* from *Novyi mir*, 4(1987), p. 120; *Dva zhanra* from *Znamya*, 8(1988), p. 95; *Spor*, "Ottogo, chto dela nikakogo" from *Moskovskii komsomolets*, June 1990; all poems also in Vladimir Kornilov, *Izbrannoe. Stikhotvoreniya i poemy* (Moscow: Sovetskii pistatel', 1991).

German Plisetsky

Kustari from *Kontinent*, 26(1980), p. 96, collected in German Plisetsky, *Prigorod. Stikhi* (Moscow: Pravda, 1990); "Prisnilsya mne gorod, otkrytyi vesne" from ibid.; *Filarmoniya* from *Kontinent*, 24(1980), pp. 54-55, collected in German Plisetsky, *Prigorod. Stikhi* (Moscow: Pravda, 1990); *Mertvyi chas*, "Ty ne revnui menya k slovam," "Usnuli my, obnyav drug druga" from ibid.; "Razbudil menya grokhot na kryshe" from *Kontinent*, 24(1980), p. 53, collected in *Prigorod. Stikhi* (Moscow: Pravda, 1990); *Natyurmort* from *Kontinent*, 60(1989), p. 103; "Stoyat' s utra v khvoste za *Ogon'kom*" from ibid., p. 106; *Sonet* from ibid., p. 108.

Evgenii Rein

Monastyr' from *Metropol'. Literaturnyi al'manakh* (Moscow, 1979; facsimile edition, Ann Arbor: Ardis, 1979), pp. 14-15, also in *The Blue Lagoon Anthology of Modern Russian Poetry*, ed. Konstantin Kuzminsky and Grigorii Kovalev, vol. 2B (Newtonville, Mass.: Oriental Research Partners, 1986), pp. 227-228, also in *Ogonek*, 13(1989), p. 9; *Sosed Grigor'ev* from *Novyi mir*, 2(1988), p. 93, also in Evgenii Rein, *Temnota zerkal* (Moscow: Sovetskii pisatel', 1990); *Kot na prichale gavani v Leningrade* from *Poeziya* 51(1988) (Moscow, 1989), p. 34; *Na polyakh knigi V. Khodasevicha* from *Poeziya* 51(1988) (Moscow, 1989), p. 32; *Posvyashchaetsya stantsiyam metro Kirovskaya-Radial'naya i Park kul'tury-Kol'tsevaya* from *Chast' rechi. Al'manakh literatury i iskusstva*, 1 (New York: Serebryanyi vek, 1980), p. 88; "U 'Nochnogo dozora' ya stoyal tri minuty" from *Novyi mir*, 1(1990), pp. 95-96; *Pod gerbami* from *Ogonek*, 20(1990), p. 9; *Pered Paskhoi* from *Druzhba narodov*, 6(1991), p. 132.

Dmitrii Bobyshev

"Mama, pishet tebe tvoi syn" from *Vremya i my*, 56(1980), p. 156; *Polnota vsego* from *Kontinent*, 36(1983), pp. 48-49; "Nado zhe, est' takie mesta" from *Tret'ya volna*, 15(1983), p. 3; *Pominki po zhivm, 1* from *22*, 32(1983), pp. 83-84; *Zhizn' Urbanskaya, 3* from *Kontinent*, 52(1987), pp. 99-101; *Zveri sv. Antoniya. Bestiarii. 17. Sobstvennoe telo* from *Strelets*, 1(61)(1989), p. 36.

Nataliya Gorbanevskaya

"Vot ona, *la vie quotidienne*" from Nataliya Gorbanevskaya, *Pereletaya snezhnuyu granitsu* (Paris: YMCA, 1979); "O bednaya, dryakhlaya, vpavshaya v detstvo" from ibid.; "Ne propet'—proshepelyavit'..." from *Kontinent*, 26(1980), p. 139; "gde reki l'yutsya chishche serebra" from *Russkie poety na zapade* (Paris-New York: Tret'ya volna, 1986); "Shel god nedobrykh predskazanii" from ibid.; "Proiznoshu zauchennyi refren" from *Kontinent*, 50(1986), p. 146; "Eto peto na zare" from ibid., p. 148; *K diskussii o statistike* from ibid., p. 151, also in *Oktyabr'*, 7(1990), p. 106; "I, etu melodiyu zapev" from *Kontinent*, 61(1989), p. 62, also in *Oktyabr'*, 7(1990), p. 107.

Aleksandr Kushner

Vospominaniya, "Istoriya ne uchit nichemu," "Let na sem' ran'she ya rodis'—i zhizn' inache," "Vek, mozhet byt', i atomnyi, no deti," "V stikhakh sverkaet smysl, kak budto pere-strelka" from Aleksandr Kushner, *Zhivaya izgorod'. Kniga stikhov* (Leningrad: Sovetskii pisatel', 1988); *Vospominaniya* also in *Oktyabr'*, 8(1987), p. 68-69; "V stikhakh blestit" in *Neva*, 7(1986), p. 90; "Kak raskapriznichavshiisya rebenok" from Aleksandr Kushner, *Nochnaya muzyka* (Leningrad: Lenizdat, 1991), p. 77; "Schastlivye stikhi pisali my" from *Oktyabr'*, 1(1990), p. 136, collected in *Nochnaya muzyka* (Leningrad: Lenizdat, 1991), p. 26, with dedication to Bulat Okudzhava; "L'etsya svet. Voda bredet vo mrake" from *Zvezda*, 3(1990), p. 52, collected in *Nochnaya muzyka* (Leningrad: Lenizdat, 1991), p. 40; "Nichto tak k smerti nas ne priblizhaet" from *Nochnaya muzyka* (Leningrad: Lenizdat, 1991), pp. 93-94.

Bella Akhmadulina

"Zavidna mne izvechnaya privychka," *Noch' upadan'ya yablok*, *Babochka*, *Pashka*, "Voskresen'e nastalo. Mne ne bylo grustno nicut'" from Bella Akhmadulina, *Izbrannoe. Stikhi* (Moscow: Sovetskii pisatel', 1988); *Noch' upadan'ya yablok* also in *Dvoynaya raduga/A Double Rainbow* (Moscow: Molodaya gvardiya, 1988), p. 184, with translation into English; *Pashka* from *Grani*, 133(1984), pp. 186-87, also in *Oktyabr'*, 3(1987), pp. 111-112; *Odevanie rebenka* from *Literaturnaya gazeta*, 24(5298), 13 June 1990, p. 5.

Yunna Morits

"Vechno zhdat' krovavykh novostei" from *Oktyabr'*, 6(1990), p. 7; *Mezhdu Stsilloi i Kharibdoi*, "Ya s geniyami vodku ne pila," "Iyul' vos'midesyatogo. V Moskve," *Na grani vydokha i vdokha* from Yunna Morits, *Na etom beregu vysokom* (Moscow: Sovremennik, 1987); *Nad telom smertnym* from Yunna Morits, *V logove golosa* (Moscow: Moskovskii rabochii, 1990), pp. 383-384; "Poeziya zhiva svobodoi i lyubov'yu" from *Oktyabr'*, 1(1989), p. 127; "...i pridut dikari molodye..." from ibid., 6(1990), pp.12-13; "Allei dushnye v pyli" from ibid., p. 5; "Kogda vse nashi vsekh ne nashikh pereb'yut" from ibid., p. 11; "Plavuchaya toska predzhiznennykh temnot" from ibid., p. 8; all selections also in Yunna Morits, *V logove golosa* (Moscow: Moskovskii rabochii, 1990).

Lev Loseff

"Ponimayu,—yarmo, golodukha," "V *Kostre* rabotal...," *Puteshestvie. 4. U zhenevskogo chasovshchika, Stansy,* "Grammatika est' Bog uma," *Odin den' L'va Vladimirovicha* from *Chudesnyi desant* (Tenafly, N.J.: Ermitazh, 1985); "Ponimayu...," "V *Kostre*...," *Odin den'*... also in *Znamya*, 11(1989), pp. 172-181; "Poet est' peregnoi, v nem mertvye slova" from *Tainyi sovetnik* (Tenafly, N.J.: Ermitazh, 1987); *Samodeyatel'nost'* from *Kontinent*, 59(1989), p. 195; *Dvenadtsat' kollegii. Elegiya v trekh chastyakh* from *Grani*, 139(1986), pp. 89-91.

Oleg Chukhontsev

"Etot gorod derevyannyi na reke" from *Kontinent*, 17(1976), p. 323; *Dvoinik, O toy zemle,* "Vot derevushka na krayu ovraga," "Po giblomu nastu, po taloi zvezde" from Oleg Chukhontsev, *Vetrom i peplom* (Moscow, 1989); all selections also in Oleg Chukhontsev, *Stikhotvoreniya* (Moscow: Khudozhestvennaya literatura, 1990).

Joseph Brodsky

Pyataya godovshchina from *Kontinent*, 36(1983), pp. 7-10, also in *Osenniy krik yastreba. Stikhotvoreniya 1962-1985 godov* (Leningrad, 1990); "Kak davno ya topchu...," "Ty, gitaroobraznaya veshch'...," "Ya byl tol'ko tem, chego...," *Iork, K Uranii,* "Ya vkhodil vmesto dikogo zverya v kletku..." from Iosif Brodsky, *Uraniya* (Ann Arbor: Ardis, 1987); "Kak davno ya topchu..." reprinted in *Literaturnaya gazeta*, 17(5291), 25 April 1990, p. 6; "Konchitsya leto. Nachinaet sentyabr'. Razreshat otstrel," "Tol'ko pepel znaet, chto znachit sgoret' dotla" reprinted in *Literaturnaya gazeta*, 17(5291), 25 April 1990, p. 6, also collected in Joseph Brodsky, *Primechaniya paporotnika* (Bromma: Hylaea, 1990); *K Uranii* also collected in *Osennii krik yastreba*, also in *Dvoinaya raduga/A Double Rainbow* (Moscow: Molodaya gvardiya, 1988), p. 226, with translation into English; "Dorogaya, ya vyshel segodnya iz domu pozdno vecherom" from *Kontinent*, 61(1989), pp. 8-9, also *Ogonek*, 44(1989), p. 23, also collected in *Primechaniya paporotnika* and *Osennii krik yastreba*; *Pyataya godovshchina*, "Kak davno ya topchu...," "Ty, gitaroobraznaya veshch'...," "Ya byl tol'ko tem, chego...," *K Uranii,* "Ya vkhodil vmesto dikogo zverya v kletku...," "Konchitsya leto. Nachinaet sentyabr'. Rasreshat otstrel," "Tol'ko pepel znaet, chto znachit sgoret' dotla," "Dorogaya, ya vyshel segodnya iz domu pozdno vecherom" also in Iosif Brodsky, *Nazidanie* (Leningrad: SP "Smart," 1990); all selections also in Joseph Brodsky, *Chast' rechi. Izbrannye stikhi 1962-1989* (Moscow: Khudozhestvennaya literatura, 1990).

Dmitrii Prigov

"Ya ustal uzhe na pervoi strochke" from D. Prigov, *Slezy geral'dicheskoi dushi* (Moscow: Moskovskii rabochii, 1990), reprinted in *Ogonek*, 43(1991), p. 25; "Kogda zdes' na postu stoit Militsaner" from *Katalog* (Ann Arbor: Ardis, 1982), p. 207, also in *Neue russische Literatur. Almanach 2-3*, 1979-80, p. 54, also in *Kulturpalast. Neue Moskauer Poesie & Aktionskunst*, ed. Gunter Hirt & Sascha Wonders (Wuppertal: S-Press, 1984), p. 94, also in *Zerkala. Al'manakh 1989. Vypusk 1* (Moscow: Moskovskii rabochii, 1989), p. 218; "V bufete Doma literatorov" from *Den' poezii 1988* (Moscow, 1989), p. 165; "Narod on ved' ne tol'ko p'et" from *Katalog* (Ann Arbor: Ardis, 1982), p. 209, also in *Neue russische Literatur. Almanach 2-3*, 1979-80, p. 47; "Orel nad zemlei proletaet" from *Katalog* (Ann Arbor: Ardis, 1982), p. 214; "Izvestno, chto mozhno zhit' so mnogimi zhenshchinami" from ibid., pp. 220-221; "Kogda ya v Kaluge po sluchayu byl" from *A-Ya. Revue d'art russe non-officiel*, 1(1985), p. 86; "Vot ya, predpolozhim, obychnyi poet" from ibid., p. 87; "Kogda ya razmyshlyayu o poezii..." from *Al'manakh Poeziya*, 32 (Moscow: Molodaya gvardiya, 1989), p. 91; "Premudrost' Bozhiya pred Bozhiim litsom" from *A-Ya. Revue d'art russe non-officiel*, 1(1985), p. 88; *Banal'noe rassuzhdenie na temu: byt' znamenitym nekrasivo* from *Kulturpalast. Neue Moskauer Poesie & Aktionskunst*, ed. Gunter Hirt & Sascha Wonders (Wuppertal: S-Press, 1984), p. 104; "A vot Moskva epokhi moei zhizni" from ibid., p. 108; "Zhenshchina v metro menya lyagnula" from *Zerkala. Al'manakh 1989. Vypusk 1* (Moscow: Moskovskii rabochii, 1989), p. 231; "Izvestno nam ot davnikh dnei" from ibid., p. 233; "Visit na nebe voron-ptitsa" from ibid., p. 235.

Yurii Kublanovsky

Etyud from Yurii Kublanovsky, *S poslednim solntsem* (Paris: La Presse Libre, 1983); "Rostovshchich'i klenovye grabki," "Ne speshi otreshat'sya—uteshimsya" from Yurii Kublanovsky, *Ottisk* (Paris: YMCA Press, 1985); "Rostovshchich'i klenovye grabki" also in *Ogonek*, 6(1989), p. 9; "Sud'ba stikha—miroderzhavnaya" from Yurii Kublanovsky, *Zatmenie* (Paris: YMCA Press, 1989); "Pod snegom tusklym" from *Znamya* 9(1990), p. 122, also *Grani*, 158(1990), pp. 53-54; "Kakim Ioannam, Bironam" from *Znamya*, 10(1991), pp. 41-42.

Aleksei Tsvetkov

"na lavochke u parkovoi opushki," "Sud'ba igraet chelovekom" from *Sbornik p'es dlya zhizni solo* (Ann Arbor: Ardis, 1978); "otverni gidrant i voda tverda," "(ne prityazaya na glubinu uma...)" "predmet nablyuden'ya priroda" from *Sostoyanie sna* (Ann Arbor: Ardis, 1981); "kuranty v zenite kovali veka" from *Edem* (Ann Arbor: Ardis, 1985); "vot dedushka storonnik midii" from *Kontinent*, 49(1986), p. 81; "V lozhbine stantsiya..." from *Edem* (Ann Arbor: Ardis, 1985), p. 55; "(ne prityazaya na glubinu uma...)" also in *Znamya*, 2(1992), p. 64.

Elena Shvarts

Nevidimyi okhotnik, Vospominanie o strannom ugoshchenii, "Ya by vynula rebro svoe tonkoe," "Snova sunulsya otets s pouchen'em" from *Tantsuyushchii David. Stikhi raznykh let* (New York: Russica, 1985); "Snova sunulsya otets..." also in Elena Shvarts, *Storony sveta* (Leningrad: Sovetskii pisatel', 1989); *Obrezanie serdtsa, Voron* from *Trudy i dni Lavinii, monakhini iz ordena obrezaniya serdtsa* (Ann Arbor: Ardis, 1987); "Mne snilos'—my plyvem po risovym polyam," "Kogda za mnoyu demony golodnye pomchalis'" from *Stikhi* (London-Paris-Munich: Beseda, 1987); "Mne snilos'—my plyvem po risovym polyam" also in *Molodoi Leningrad. Sbornik molodykh poetov* (Leningrad: Sovetskii pisatel', 1989), pp. 122-123; "Kogda za mnoyu demony golodnye pomchalis'" also in *Rodnik*, 5(17)(1988), p. 11. "Nevidimyi okhotnik," "Vospominanie o strannom ugoshchenii," and "Kogda za mnoi demony golodnye pomchalis'" also in Elena Shvarts, *Stikhi* (Leningrad: Assotsiatsiya "Novaya literatura," 1990).

Ivan Zhdanov

Portret ottsa from *Poeziya*, 25 (Moscow, 1979), pp. 126-127, collected in Ivan Zhdanov, *Mesto zemli* (Moscow: Molodaya gvardiya, 1991), p. 6; *Stikhi na peske, 2* from *Vremya i my*, 81(1984), p. 79; "Khrapya i raduyas', i vozdukh vorosha" from *Vremya i my*, 93(1986), pp. 92-93, collected as *Groza* in *Mesto zemli*, pp. 12-13; *Prorok* from *Poeziya*, 46 (Moscow, 1986), p. 36, also *Poryv. Sbornik stikhov. Novye imena* (Moscow: Sovetskii pisatel', 1989), pp. 122-123, also (entitled *Proroki. Sovremennyi [Antiprorok]*) in Ivan Zhdanov, *Nerazmennoe nebo* (Moscow: "Sovremennik," 1990), collected in *Mesto zemli*, pp. 86-87; "Oblast' nerazmennogo vladen'ya..." from *Ogonek*, 24(1989), p. 11, also in *Nerazmennoe nebo* (Moscow: "Sovremennik," 1990), collected in *Mesto zemli*, p. 104; *Zavoevanie stikhii, 6* from *Al'manakh poeziya*, 55 (Moscow: Molodaya gvardiya, 1990), p. 59, also in *Nerazmennoe nebo* (Moscow: "Sovremennik," 1990).

Olga Sedakova

Nevernaya zhena, Starushki, "Neuzheli, Mariya...," *Kuznechik i sverchok,* "V pustyne zhizni... Chto ya govoryu," *Na smert' Leonida Gubanova, Sem' stikhotvorenii, 2, Koda* from Olga Sedakova, *Vrata, okna, arki* (Paris: YMCA Press, 1986); *Nevernaya zhena* and *Starushki* also in *Laterna Magica. Literaturno-khudozhestvennyi, istoriko-kul'turnyi al'manakh* (Moscow: Izdatel'stvo "Prometei" MGPI im. V. I. Lenina, 1990), also in Olga Sedakova, *Kitaiskoe puteshestvie. Stely i nadpisi. Starye pesni* (Moscow: "Carte Blanche," 1990); "Neuzheli, Mariya...," *Kuznechik i sverchok,* "V pustyne zhizni... Chto ya govoryu," *Na smert' Leonida Gubanova* also in *Druzhba narodov*, 9(1988), pp. 122-124.

Bakhyt Kenzheev

"Proshlo, pomerklo, otgorelo," "Kun-tszy uveryal, cho muzyku sleduet," "v rossii grustnaya pogoda," "V Peredelkine les obletel" from *Izbrannaya lirika 1970-1981* (Ann Arbor: Ardis, 1984); "Vse na svete vykhodit iz mody, lyubimaya," "Pustye ulitsy, provaly podvoroten" from *Kontinent*, 46(1985), pp. 63-64, 66; "Vostorgi, usy, polumaski. Galdit u pod"ezda tolpa" from *Kontinent*, 56(1988), pp. 78-79.

Aleksandr Eremenko

Peredelkino, Pamyatnik, from *Poryv. Sbornik stikhov. Novye imena* (Moscow: Sovetskii pisatel', 1989), pp. 99-100, 101-102; *Stikhi o sukhom zakone, posvyashchennye sverdlovskomu rok-klubu* from *Poryv. Sbornik stikhov. Novye imena* (Moscow: Sovetskii pisatel', 1989), pp. 102-103, with variants in *Ogonek*, 24(1989) p. 11, also in *Den' poezii 1989* (Moscow: Sovetskii pisatel', 1989), pp. 131-132; *Dobavlenie k sopromatu* from *Ogonek*, 24(1989), p. 11: "Da zdravstvuet staraya deva" from *Poryv. Sbornik stikhov. Novye imena* (Moscow: Sovetskii pisatel', 1989), p. 105, also in *Dvoynaya raduga/A Double Rainbow* (Moscow: Molodaya gvardiya, 1988), p. 207, with translation into English; all selections also in Aleksandr Eremenko, *Dobavlenie k sopromatu* (Moscow: Pravda, 1990).

Aleksei Parshchikov

"Ulitka ili shelkopryad, I-II," *Petr, Avtostop v gorakh*, "Ya vypustil tebya slepyashchim volkom" from *Zerkala. Al'manakh 1989. Vypusk I* (Moscow: Moskovskii rabochii, 1989), pp. 163-164, 166, 168, 176; *Petr* (untitled, and with three additional stanzas) in *Vremya i my*, 81(1984), p. 91; *Kogda* from *Druzhba narodov*, 2(1992), p. 93; "O sad moikh druzei, gde ya torchu s treshchotkoi" from *Poryv. Sbornik stikhov. Novye imena* (Moscow: Sovetskii pisatel', 1989), p. 316.

SUGGESTIONS FOR

FURTHER READING

General

Aizenberg, Mikhail, "Nekotorye drugie...," *Teatr* 4 (1991), pp. 98-118. A supremely well-informed and judicious survey of poetry suppressed in the USSR from about 1970.

Betaki, Vasilii, *Russkaya poeziya za 30 let, 1956-1986* (Orange, Conn.: Antiquary, 1987). Brief characterizations of the work of more than 80 poets.

The Blue Lagoon Anthology of Russian Poetry, ed. Konstantin Kuzminsky and Grigorii Kovalev (Newtonville, Mass.: Oriental Research Partners, 1980-). Contains a large number of texts and uninhibited discussion of underground poetry in the USSR during the period since 1956; includes discussion of Chichibabin, Rein, Bobyshev, Kushner, Loseff, Brodsky, Kublanovsky, Shvarts.

Brown, Deming, "The Younger Generation of Poets," in his *Soviet Literature since Stalin* (Cambridge, London, New York, Melbourne: Cambridge University Press, 1978), pp. 106-144. The most useful survey in English of the period immediately preceding that of the present anthology; includes discussion of Slutsky, Okudzhava, Gorbanevskaya, Kushner, Akhmadulina, Brodsky.

Epshtein, Mikhail, "Metamorfoza," in his *Paradoksy novizny* (Moscow: Sovetskii pisatel', 1988), pp. 139-176. A pioneering discussion of conceptualism and metarealism in indigenous Russian poetry, referring among others to Prigov, Zhdanov, Sedakova, Eremenko, and Parshchikov.

Gasparov, M. L., *Ocherk istorii russkogo stikha* (Moscow: Nauka, 1984). A brilliant, concise account of the history of Russian versification.

A Handbook of Russian Literature, ed. Victor Terras (New Haven and London: Yale University Press, 1985). Contains entries on Slutsky, Okudzhava, Bobyshev, Gorbanevskaya, Kushner, Akhmadulina, Morits, Brodsky, Tsvetkov.

Kasack, Wolfgang, *A Dictionary of Russian Literature since 1917* (New York: Columbia University Press, 1988). Includes articles on Slutsky, Okudzhava, Kornilov, Bobyshev, Gorbanevskaya, Kushner, Akhmadulina, Morits, Chukhontsev, Brodsky, Kublanovsky, Tsvetkov, Shvarts.

Lowe, David, "Poetry," in his *Russian Writing since 1953: A Critical Survey* (New York: Ungar, 1987), pp. 125-158. The most recent general treatment of the subject.

The Poetry of Perestroika, ed. Peter Mortimer and S. J. Litherland, trans. Carol Rumens and Richard McKane (Cullercoats: Iron Press, 1991). Poetic translations of and information about 35 recent Russian poets; includes Akhmadulina, Brodsky, Chukhontsev, Morits, Okudzhava, Prigov, Sedakova, Shvarts, Slutsky.

Polukhina, Valentina, *Brodsky through the Eyes of His Contemporaries* (London: St. Martin's Press, 1992). A gold mine for students of recent Russian poetry; includes interviews with Rein, Gorbanevskaya, Kushner, Loseff, Kublanovsky, Shvarts, Sedakova, and Parshchikov.

Russian Poetry: The Modern Period, ed. John Glad and Daniel Weissbort (Iowa City: University of Iowa Press, 1978). An anthology in English from 1917 until the mid-1970s; includes Slutsky, Okudzhava, Gorbanevskaya, Brodsky.

Scherr, Barry, *Russian Poetry: Meter, Rhythm, and Rhyme* (Berkeley, Los Angeles, London: University of California Press, 1986). The most authoritative account of Russian versification in English.

Shaitanov, Igor, "Posle poeticheskogo buma: Novoe v poezii: semidesyatye—vos'midesyatye," in *Russkaya Literatura XX veka,* ed. F. Kuznetsov (Moscow: Prosveshchenie, 1991), pp. 263-281. An expert survey of developments in poetry published in Russia since 1970.

Smith, G. S., "Russian Poetry outside Russia since 1970: A Survey," in *Aspects of Modern Russian and Czech Literature,* ed. Arnold McMillin (Columbus: Slavica, 1989), pp. 179-187. The poetry of the Third Wave up to 1986.

Stevanovic, Bosiljka, and Vladimir Wertsman, *Free Voices in Russian Literature, 1950s-1980s: A Bio-Bibliographical Guide,* ed. A. Sumerkin (New York: Russica, 1987). Includes information on Slutsky, Chichibabin, Okudzhava, Kornilov, Plisetsky, Rein, Gorbanevskaya, Akhmadulina, Loseff, Chukhontsev, Brodsky, Prigov, Kublanovsky, Tsvetkov, Shvarts, Zhdanov, Sedakova, Kenzheev, Eremenko, Parshchikov.

Third Wave: The New Russian Poetry, ed. Kent Johnston and Stephen M. Ashby, introduction by Alexei Parshchikov and Andrew Wachtel, afterword by Mikhail Epstein (Ann Arbor: University of Michigan Press, 1992). Translations from 21 poets, with important commentaries; includes Parshchikov, Prigov, Sedakova, Zhdanov, Shvarts, Eremenko.

Individual Poets

Slutsky: Yurii Boldyrev, introduction to Boris Slutsky, "Iz neopublikovannogo," *Kontinent*, 65(1990), pp. 7-8; Il'ya Serman, "Mera vremeni," *Novoe russkoe slovo*, 30 November 1990; Vladimir Solovev, "Posmertnaya sud'ba Borisa Slutskogo," *Oktyabr'*, 2(1991), pp. 200-203; Yurii Boldyrev, "Vydayu sebya za samogo sebya...," in Boris Slutsky, *Sobranie sochinenii v trekh tomakh*, vol. 1 (Moscow: Khudozhestvennaya literatura, 1991), pp. 5-22; G. S. Smith, "Epitaph for the Soviet Experience," *Times Literary Supplement,* 19 June 1992, p. 22; David Samoilov, "Drug i sopernik," *Oktybr',* 9(1992), pp. 178-190.

Chichibabin: Yurii Miloslavsky, untitled introductory article, *22*, 9(1979), pp. 32-34; Vernik, "Boris A. Chichibabin," and Yurii Miloslavsky, "Boris Chichibabin," in *The Blue Lagoon Anthology of Modern Russian Poetry*, ed. Konstantin Kuzminsky and Grigorii Kovalev, vol. 3A (Newtonville, Mass.: Oriental Research Partners, 1986), pp. 40-46, 50-55; Boris Chichibabin, "Vybral sam," in his *Moi shestidesyatye* (Kiev: Dnipro, 1990), pp. 5-12; id., "I Chose My Own Fate," *Soviet Literature*, 7(1990), pp. 126-131; A. Pikach, "Chichibabin: ochishchenie svobodoi," *Oktyabr'*, 12(1990), pp. 199-202.

Okudzhava: 65 Songs (Ann Arbor: Ardis, 1980); and *Songs, Volume II* (Ann Arbor: Ardis, 1986), ed. Vladimir Frumkin. *Sovetskaya bibliografiya*, 1(239)(1990), pp. 58-75 gives a complete bibliography of Okudzhava's publications in the USSR. Gerald S. Smith, *Songs to Seven Strings* (Bloomington: Indiana University Press, 1984); id., "Okudzhava Marches On," *Slavonic and East European Review*, 66, 4(1988), pp. 553-563; "Uprazdnennyi teatr. S Bulatom Okudzhavoi beseduet zhurnalist Il'ya Mil'shtein," *Ogonek*, 19(1991), pp. 4-6; "'Byloe nel'zya vorotit', i pechalit'sya ne o chem...' Bulat Okudzhava v besede s Irinoi Ryshinoi," *Literaturnaya gazeta*, 6(5383), 5 February 1992, p. 3.

Kornilov: see Lev Anninsky, in his *Lokti i kryl'ya* (Moscow: Sovetskii pisatel', 1989); all poems also in Vladimir Kornilov, *Izbrannoe. Stikhotvoreniya i poemy* (Moscow: Sovetskii pisatel', 1991).

Rein: Dmitrii Bobyshev, review of *Imena mostov*, *Kontinent*, 44(1985), pp. 325-332; Aleksandr Mezhirov, "Nepopravimyi den'...," *Literaturnaya gazeta*, 43(5317), 24 October 1990, p. 5; Joseph Brodsky, "Tragicheskii elegik," *Znamya*, 7(1991), pp. 180-184.

Bobyshev: Barbara Heldt, "The Other Worlds of Dmitry Bobyshev," *World Literature Today* (Winter 1984), pp. 27-30.

Gorbanevskaya: Christine Rydel, "The Early Poetry of Natalya Gorbanevskaya," *Russian Language Journal*, 123/124(1982), pp. 236-252.

Kushner: "Chelovechnost'—vot chto neobkhodimo segodnya miru," *Kontinent*, 66(1991), pp. 361-372. A bibliography of Kushner's publications in the USSR is included in *Russkie sovetskie pisateli. Poety*, vol. 12 (Moscow: Knizhnaya palata, 1989), pp. 4-34. *Apollo in the Snow*, trans. Paul Graves and Carol Ueland (New York: Harvill, 1992).

Akhmadulina: see Elaine Feinstein, *Three Russian Poets* (Manchester: Carcanet, 1979); Yu. Kublanovsky, "'Taina' Belly Akhmadulinoi," *Grani*, 131(1984), pp. 291-293; S. Lubenskaya, "Poeticheskii yazyk Belly Ahmadulinoi," *Russian Literature*, 17(1985), pp. 157-182. *The Garden: New and Selected Poetry and Prose*, ed., trans., and intro. F. D. Reeve (London: Marion Boyars, 1991).

Morits: see Elaine Feinstein, *Three Russian Poets* (Manchester: Carcanet, 1979);

Loseff: G. S. Smith, "Flight of the Angels: The Poetry of Lev Loseff," *Slavic Review*, 47, 1(1988), pp. 76-88; Boris Paramonov, "Skromnoe obayanie Loseva," *Literaturnaya gazeta*, 6(5383), 5 February 1992, p. 5.

Chukhontsev: Naum Korzhavin, "Dobro ne mozhet byt' staro," *Kontinent*, 17(1978), pp. 315-330; G. S. Smith, "Sharing the Damage," *Times Literary Supplement*, 20-26 April 1990, p. 429.

Brodsky: Valentina Polukhina, *Joseph Brodsky: A Poet for Our Times* (Cambridge: Cambridge University Press, 1989); articles in *Literaturnaya gazeta*, 20(5234), 16 May 1990, p. 6; *Brodsky's Poetics and Aesthetics*, ed. Lev Loseff and Valentina Polukhina (London: Macmillan, 1990); Petr Vail and Aleksandr Genis, "V okrestnostyakh Brodskogo," *Literaturnoe obozrenie*, 8(1990), pp. 23-29; Anatolii Naiman, "Prostranstvo Uranii," *Oktyabr'*, 12(1990), pp. 193-198; "Iosif Brodskii. Evropeiskii vozdukh nad Rossiei," *Strannik*, 1(1990), pp. 35-42; Yurii Kublanovsky, "Poeziya novogo izmereniya," *Novyi mir*, 2(1991), pp. 242-246.

Kublanovsky: Semen Lipkin, "Sud'ba stikha—miroderzhavnaya", *Znamya*, 10(1991), pp. 43-45.

Tsvetkov: G. S. Smith, "Aleksej Cvetkov's Lost Paradise," *Slavic and East European Journal*, 30, 4(1986), pp. 541-552; Vadim Kreid, "*Edem* Alekseya Tsvetkova," *Literaturnyi kur'er*, 12(1986-1987), pp. 79-81.

Shvarts: Barbara Heldt, "The Poetry of Elena Shvartz," *World Literature Today* (Summer 1989), pp. 381-383; Olga Nikolaeva, "'...bez bytiya'," *Novyi mir*, 10(1991), pp. 244-248.

See also translations by Michael Molnar in *Child of Europe. A New Anthology of East European Poetry*, ed. Michael March (New York: Viking Penguin, 1990).

Sedakova: A. K. Shevchenko, "Pis'mo o smerti, lyubvi i kotenke," *Filosoficheskaya i sotsiologicheskaya mysl'*, 9(1989), pp. 110-120; "Vverkh idti trudnee. Okno dlya upavshikh s Luny," *Nezavisimaya gazeta*, 5 February 1992, p. 7.

Parshchikov: see translations by Michael Molnar in *Child of Europe. A New Anthology of East European Poetry*, ed. Michael March (New York: Viking Penguin, 1990).

INDEX OF RUSSIAN TITLES
AND FIRST LINES

(Numbers refer to the serial number of the poems.)

INDEX OF ENGLISH TITLES
AND FIRST LINES

(Numbers refer to the serial number of the poems.)

GERALD S. SMITH is Professor of Russian at the University of Oxford and Fellow of New College, Oxford. He taught previously at the universities of Nottingham, Birmingham, Liverpool, Indiana, and California (Berkeley). Smith is author of *Songs to Seven Strings: Russian Guitar Poetry and Soviet "Mass Song,"* coeditor (with A. G. Cross) of *Russian Literature in the Eighteenth Century,* and translator of Alexander Galich, *Songs and Poems.*